Handbook of Business Ethics

Handbook of Business Ethics

Ethics in the New Economy

Edited by Laszlo Zsolnai

PETER LANG

Oxford · Bern · Berlin · Bruxelles · Frankfurt am Main · New York · Wien

Bibliographic information published by Die Deutsche Nationalbibliothek.
Die Deutsche Nationalbibliothek lists this publication in the Deutsche National-
bibliografie; detailed bibliographic data is available on the Internet
at http://dnb.d-nb.de.

A catalogue record for this book is available from The British Library.

Library of Congress Control Number: 2012952072

ISBN 978-3-0343-0914-1

© Peter Lang AG, International Academic Publishers, Bern 2013
Hochfeldstrasse 32, CH-3012 Bern, Switzerland
info@peterlang.com, www.peterlang.com, www.peterlang.net

All rights reserved.
All parts of this publication are protected by copyright.
Any utilisation outside the strict limits of the copyright law, without the
permission of the publisher, is forbidden and liable to prosecution.
This applies in particular to reproductions, translations, microfilming,
and storage and processing in electronic retrieval systems.

Printed in Germany

Contents

Preface	vii
Acknowledgement	xi
List of Figures, Tables and Boxes	xiii

LASZLO ZSOLNAI
1 New Agenda for Business Ethics — 1

PETER ULRICH
2 Ethics and Economics — 7

LASZLO ZSOLNAI
3 The Moral Economic Man — 35

ALOY SOPPE
4 Ethics and the Theory of the Firm — 55

THOMAS BESCHORNER AND CHRISTOPH SCHANK
5 The Citizenship and Responsibility of Corporations — 85

JOSEP M. LOZANO
6 Organizational Ethics — 103

KNUT J. IMS AND LARS JACOB PEDERSEN
7 Personal Responsibility and Ethical Action — 127

DOIREAN WILSON AND LASZLO ZSOLNAI
8   Gender Issues in Business   151

ZSOLT BODA
9   International Ethics and Globalization   167

ANTONIO TENCATI
10 The Sustainability-Oriented Company   197

KNUT J. IMS
11 From Welfare to Well-Being and Happiness   217

LASZLO ZSOLNAI
12 Future of Capitalism   249

Notes on Contributors   265

Index   269

Preface

This volume is the revised edition of our book *Ethics in the Economy: Handbook of Business Ethics* originally published in 2002. Since the publication of the first edition a lot of things changed in business and economics in Europe and beyond. The present financial and economic crisis gives new light in the prevailing management model of mainstream business. The Occupy Wall Street and other anti-business movements, the widespread distrust in corporations, and the questionable behavior of many business leaders indicate the crisis of the materialistic management paradigm.

Materialistic management is based on the belief that the sole motivation for business is money-making, and that success should be measured solely by the generated profit. Psychologists have discovered serious side-effects of materialistic value orientation. A lot of studies demonstrate that the more people prioritize materialistic goals, the lower their personal well-being and the more likely they will engage in manipulative, competitive, and ecologically degrading behaviors.

Materialistic management aims at optimal economic performance that mandates attention to the welfare of the organization's shareholders. In *post-materialistic management* the "why" of organizational existence is the fulfillment of all those affected by the organization, and the maintenance and development of the organization's capacity to function. The new values of the post-materialistic management are frugality, deep ecology, trust, reciprocity, responsibility for future generations, and authenticity. Within this framework profit and growth are no longer ultimate aims but elements in a wider set of values. In a similar way, cost–benefit calculations are no longer the essence of management but are part of a broader concept of wisdom in leadership. Post-materialistic management requires intrinsic motivation for serving the common good and using holistic evaluation schemes for measuring success.

This book is a product of the *Business Ethics Faculty Group* of *CEMS – The Global Alliance in Management Education*. CEMS is a strategic alliance of leading business schools and multinational companies. Founded in 1988 in Europe, the network has grown steadily, largely due to the success and popularity of the CEMS Master in International Management program. Today, CEMS is the global league of leaders on the pre-experience Master's market and it cannot be equaled in terms of the reputation of its members: twenty-six world-class academic institutions collaborate together with more than seventy corporate partners and three NGOs to offer international, postgraduate students a unique blend of high-quality education and professional experience (http://www.cems.org).

The flagship program of CEMS is the Master in International Management (MIM), which is a pre-career graduate program in general management. It provides a select group of the best international students with the know-how and expertise needed to succeed in the new international business environment. Designed by both academic and business leaders, the CEMS MIM program bridges university education and business expertise, thus offering keen insights into management best practices. The program acquired a high international reputation. The *Financial Times* ranked it the best in the world in 2009 and first in the 2011 three-year ranking.

The authors of this book represent six CEMS universities. They include *Thomas Beschorner* (University of St. Gallen, Switzerland), *Zsolt Boda* (Corvinus University of Budapest, Hungary), *Knut J. Ims* (Norwegian School of Economics, Bergen, Norway), *Josep Lozano* (ESADE Business School, Barcelona, Spain), *Lars Jacob Pedersen* (Norwegian School of Economics, Bergen, Norway), *Christoph Schank* (University of St. Gallen, Switzerland), *Aloy Soppe* (Erasmus University Rotterdam, The Netherlands), *Antonio Tencati* (Bocconi University Milan, Italy), *Peter Ulrich* (University of St. Gallen, Switzerland), and *Laszlo Zsolnai* (Corvinus University of Budapest, Hungary). *Doirean Wilson* (Middlesex University, London, UK) served as co-author with Laszlo Zsolnai in contributing a paper on gender issues in business.

We excluded several chapters from the first editions and included five completely new chapters in the second edition. The remaining chapters

Preface

have been considerably revised and updated. Chapters in the book follow the same structure. Each chapter begins with a *short summary* of the topic and a *glossary* of the most important terms. Part 1 describes the *central issue*. Part 2 gives a *state of the art* of current theories and practices. Part 3 introduces *new approaches* and *solutions*. Part 4 analyzes *real-world examples*. Part 5 provides *conclusions*. To get closer to real life a variety of *cases* and other *empirical materials* are included in the text. Numerous *figures* and *tables* make the ideas presented more comprehensible.

The book presents a *European perspective* without falling prey to Eurocentrism. For us the European approach is about considering both the *material* and *non-materials aspects* of *human existence* and a dialogical attitude toward *non-European values* and *cultures*. In this spirit we would like to invite everyone interested in and dedicated to developing ethics in the economy to an *open dialogue* of equal parties. Ethics is one of the oldest projects of humanity and there can be no end to *rethinking ethics* in our economic affairs.

25 June 2012

— LASZLO ZSOLNAI
Chairman, Business Ethics Faculty Group
CEMS – The Global Alliance in Management Educations

Acknowledgement

The editorial work on the book was completed while I was Visiting Fellow at the *Smith School of Enterprise and the Environment, University of Oxford* in April–June 2012. The chapters "The Moral Economic Man," "International Ethics and Globalization," and "Future of Capitalism" were developed as part of a research project at the *Corvinus University of Budapest* called the "Társadalmi Megújulás Operatív Program" TÁMOP-4-2.1.B-09/1/KMR-2010-0005.

26 June 2012

—LASZLO ZSOLNAI

List of Figures, Tables and Boxes

Figures

Figure 2.1	The Two-dimensional Concept of Socio-economic Rationality	16
Figure 2.2	Three Approaches to Business Ethics	17
Figure 2.3	Two-level Conception of Corporate Ethics	29
Figure 3.1	Etzioni's Socio-economic Model	49
Figure 3.2	Determinants of the Ethicality of Behavior	50
Figure 4.1	Companies' Responsibilities	64
Figure 4.2	A Holistic View of Wealth Creation	65
Figure 4.3	The Firm as a Nexus of Stakeholders	76
Figure 6.1	The Levels of Culture and their Interaction	109
Figure 6.2	The Development of Corporate Values	114
Figure 6.3	Approaches to Organizational Ethics	116
Figure 6.4	Organizational Learning	118
Figure 6.5	How to Situate the Organization in the Social Context	124
Figure 7.1	The Triangle of Responsibility	136
Figure 7.2	The Triangle of Professional Ethics	138
Figure 11.1	Average Income and Happiness in the United States 1957–2002	221

Tables

Table 2.1	Ethical Reason versus Economic Rationality	19
Table 2.2	The Two-level Conception of the Politico-economic Order	28
Table 3.1	Corruption Indices of Selected Countries in 2011	50–51
Table 4.1	Summary of the Ethical Framework	71
Table 8.1	Gender Inequality Index and Related Indicators	154–155
Table 8.2	Male versus Female Morality	160
Table 10.1	Examples of Accounting and Reporting/Accountability Tools	204–207
Table 10.2	Examples of Market-based Instruments	208
Table 10.3	Examples of Certification Schemes	209–210
Table 10.4	Important Sustainability Initiatives Fostered by Coop	211–212
Table 11.1	Different Qualities of Life	224
Table 11.2	Value Scores Pertaining to Happiness	241
Table 12.1	Competitiveness versus Collaboration	255
Table 12.2	World Religions and the Economic Problematic	262

Boxes

4.1	Example of Aggressive Takeover and Unsustainable Behavior	61
4.2	Changing Moral Opinions	75
5.1	Apple and its Withdrawal from the US Chamber of Commerce	97
8.1	Minorities in the UK and the Need for Respect	157
8.2	Lynx Deodorant	159

List of Figures, Tables and Boxes

9.1	The Case of Climate Policies	173
9.2	The Case of Corruption	174
9.3	Selected Countries' Annual GDP and Company Revenues in 2010	175
9.4	Codes of Conduct for Multinationals	177
9.5	The Multilateral Agreement on Investment (MAI)	178
11.1	Happiness in the History of Ancient and Medieval Thought	226–229
11.2	The Happiness Hypothesis	234–235

LASZLO ZSOLNAI
(CORVINUS UNIVERSITY OF BUDAPEST)

1 New Agenda for Business Ethics

This handbook does not intend to be just another book in the field of business ethics. It is *against* the mainstream conception that ethics is only an *instrument* for improving business functioning. The authors of the book do not believe that ethics is something that should be introduced as a value added in business. We look at ethics as being fundamental to economic activities. For us ethics is a relevant aspect at all levels of economic activity from individual and organizational to societal and global.

In the world the ethicality of economic actions is often highly questionable and in many respects unacceptable. The ethicality of the economy should be considerably improved but there is a paradox here. If we want to develop the ethicality of our economic affairs only as a means to achieving higher efficiency, in the last result we will fail. We have a chance to improve the ethical quality of our economic activities only if our motivation is *genuinely ethical*; that is, only if we want to realize ethical conduct for its own sake.

The approach advanced in this book is *contextual* and *agent-centered*. In our view economic actions are jointly determined by the agents and the context in which they are functioning. Agents and context evolve together, so if we want to change the ethicality of economic actions, we should target both the ethical make-up of the agents and the rules and regularities of the context in which they play.

This introductory chapter presents the most important propositions that the authors developed throughout the book. The reader should realize that the propositions listed below form an integrated whole and ultimately provide a new agenda for academic research, corporate action and public policy, with the aim of improving *ethics* in the *new economic reality* of the twenty-first century.

(1) Business ethics is more than "applied ethics." The primary task of an "integrative" business ethics is to reflect on the form of economic reasoning – it is the critique of economic reason. The history of economic thought reveals the "emancipation" of economic rationality from moral philosophy, a process that mirrors the historical process of the "great transformation" described by Karl Polanyi, through which the economy has become disembedded from its social, environmental, and cultural context. Today, the problematic consequences of the disembedded and unencumbered economic rationality represent a growing, real-life experience. In this situation, business ethics may fill the gap left open since the classical political economy was reduced to "pure" economics.

(2) The task of business ethics is to ask for a new ethical foundation for economic reason itself. Business ethics may provide a powerful critique of "economism" including economic determinism (which argues for the "force of circumstances" against ethical claims) and economic reductionism (which argues that the "morality of the market" is a sufficient guarantor of ethical reason). Rethinking basic ethical aspects of economic reason includes questioning the meaning of economic "rationalization" with regard to the good human life and criticizing the politico-economic order with regard to the development of a just and well-ordered society of free and equal citizens.

(3) The Homo Oeconomicus model states that agents are rational, self-interest-maximizing beings. Overwhelming empirical evidence suggests that people do not just care about their own material payoffs but also consider the interests of others. They are willing to sacrifice their own material well-being to help those who are kind to them and to punish those who are unkind to them. They take into account the well-being of strangers whose interests are at stake. They are also interested in their reputations and care about their self-conceptions. Economic behavior is co-determined by utility calculations and moral considerations. Two major factors can explain the ethicality of economic behavior, namely the moral character of the agents and the relative cost of ethical behavior. Economic agents are essentially moral beings, but it depends on the context as to which face of the Moral Economic Man becomes effective.

(4) The shareholder paradigm is no longer a suitable concept in the modern stage of market capitalism. The traditional theory of the firm is too restrictive to incorporate ethical values into the financial framework. In the property rights model, it is the shareholder that holds the residual risk and therefore the residual profit. The company is considered a set of direct investment projects that converts inputs into outputs. From this materialistic viewpoint, a company is not a system of cooperating persons but a contracting institution that produces cash flow. From this perspective no social responsibility is involved. This approach is justified by selecting the shareholders as the optimal stakeholders in order to reduce the agency cost. This line of argument denies any explicit relationship between social cohesion and operational efficiency.

(5) In the "ethical finance" approach, the neoclassical paradigm is replaced by a broader view. In addition to the necessity of competition and profitability, it includes care for the environment, the social and physical health of employees, and a moral responsibility for the risk run by creditors and other stakeholders. Unbridled competition encourages operational efficiency, but at the same time it is too limited to serve as a balanced allocation mechanism. Sustainable behavior often requires an increase in governance costs (e.g., due to the virtue of prudence) and therefore probably higher agency costs. On the other hand, in a safer and more stable environment, contracting costs may fall and create additional wealth for society overall.

(6) The relationship between business and society and the responsibilities of business towards society have been discussed under the umbrella terms "corporate social responsibility" (CSR) and "corporate citizenship" (CC). Claims that analyze and emphasize the specific role of private corporations as "citizens" have recently gained increasing momentum. The citizenship role of corporations can be perceived as an ideal of the integral role of business in society that enables responsible business conduct.

(7) Both the liberal and the republican traditions provide an understanding of the nature of citizenship. While in the liberal tradition the good citizen respects the regulatory framework and protects his or her chartered rights against third parties, other citizens, or the state, the good citizen in the republican tradition takes a more proactive stance and becomes a

political actor. While liberalism emphasizes individual rights, republicanism emphasizes duties in and towards society. The corporate "citoyen" reflects the republican tradition, acting as an impartible citizen among citizens who is not torn between his or her economic interests and civic duties. Rather, he or she combines them in his or her modus operandi. From this republican perspective, corporate citizenship goes beyond corporate philanthropy and implies responsibility for a company's core business activities along its entire supply chain.

(8) Organizational ethics refers to the set of values that identifies an organization either as it is perceived by those working in the organization or by those who have dealings with the organization. Organizational ethics provides organizations with opportunities for learning and innovation. It is more than a process of awareness that allows organizations to reflect on themselves and renew their identities – it is a project. We can consider organizational citizenship as a new public manifestation of an advanced and reflective organizational ethics. Organizational citizenship implies a broader vision of organizations as actors operating in a social context, and it highlights the role of organizations as social contributors and innovators.

(9) There is a close connection between responsibility and ethicality. Personal responsibility has a crucial role to play in promoting ethical action in business organizations. From an action-oriented perspective the importance of deep emotions like empathy and a sense of justice should be emphasized. Personal responsibility can be contrasted to role-mediated behavior and common morality. In many cases the personally responsible action involves conflicting loyalties in organizations. "Exit," "voice," and "loyalty" described by Hirschman represent alternative strategies for personally responsible action in organizational life.

(10) Despite the universal agreement on gender equality, women are still in a disadvantageous position in contemporary society. The gender gap between men and women can be seen across many fields of life including business. Mainstream economics is male-biased as it presupposes an androcentric conception of the human person. With its exclusive focus on productivity today's businesses tend to undervalue female characteristics such as care and compassion. However, they like to use women as sex objects in marketing and advertising.

(11) Based on the moral experience of women, Carol Gilligan describes feminist ethics as an ethics of care. For women the self is constructed through relationships, and their typical problem-solving strategy is communication. Insights from feminist ethics induce a new model of corporate governance where the key issue is to maintain and manage the firm's relationships in a mutually satisfying way. The post-industrial economy is more congenial to women than to men. Today's companies require a more-feminine management style. Gender equality and feminist ethics are not only important for their own sake – they may increase the performance of businesses and economies while contributing to the quality of life for men and women alike.

(12) To overcome anarchy in the international economic system some global governance is needed. This means developing efficient international institutions, utilizing the pressure of global civil society, and reinforcing the self-regulation of business. Multinational companies have the duty of cooperating in governance systems. They also have the duty of reconciling universalism and cultural relativism in their daily activities; i.e., of applying universally valid ethical principles and respecting authentic local moral norms. Multinationals must be guided by their enhanced responsibility both at home and abroad.

(13) Globalizing efforts are important in overcoming international anarchy and protecting global commons; however, globalization in its present form is not sustainable. Globalizing tendencies have long been accompanied by political, cultural, and religious fragmentation. And the functioning of the globalized economy contradicts the goal of sustainable development, because it leads to ecological homogenization, causes the overuse of resources, and renders impossible the application of the precautionary principle. Some form of localization of the economy is certainly needed. The challenge is to find a way towards more global governance with less economic globalization.

(14) An ethical company has to pursue the overall objective of sustainability. At the corporate level, sustainability means the capacity of an organization to continue its activities over time, taking into consideration their impact on the natural, social, and human capitals. Sustainable development is a fundamental goal that requires dealing with the different

stakeholder groups in mutually reinforcing ways. In order to pursue sustainability, companies have to adopt advanced and innovative policies and tools.

(15) A tragic fallacy in the Western world is the belief that higher income leads to greater happiness. Empirical evidence shows that it is not money but people which make people happy. The more-the-better strategy is a destructive track. Happiness is activity-based and strongly related to self-realization and other-orientation. The Buddhist Kingdom of Bhutan demonstrates a comprehensive approach to human well-being by employing the measure of Gross National Happiness. In contrast Norway is a rich country which faces the problems of a welfare disease called "affluenza."

(16) The GDP-based welfare approach is a materialistic description of human wellness. There is a need to complement this approach with "well-being" as a holistic, multidimensional description of human wellness. Happiness research and positive psychology may contribute to a development of more fruitful measurements. Deep ecology assumes that self-realization for humans cannot be obtained unless they take into consideration the self-realization of other natural beings.

(17) The moral foundation of capitalism should be reconsidered. Modern capitalism is disembedded from the social and cultural norms of society. The market fundamentalism – the belief that all kinds of values can be reduced to market values, and that the free market is the only efficient mechanism which can provide a rational allocation of resources – should be abandoned. We should find substantive value-backgrounds to develop alternative views on economic activities. For example, the economic teachings of world religions have a great relevance to the renewal of economies. Among other world religions Judaism, Christianity, Buddhism, and Taoism proclaim life-serving modes of economizing which can ensure the livelihood of human communities and the permanence of natural ecosystems.

(18) Economic activities should pass the test of ecology, future generations, and society to get legitimacy in today's society. This implies that: (i) economic activities should not harm nature or allow others to come to harm; (ii) economic activities must respect the freedom of future generations; and (iii) economic activities must serve the well-being of society. Ecology, respect for future generations, and serving the well-being of society, calls for a radical transformation of business. The future of capitalism is highly dependent on its ability to adapt to the new reality of the twenty-first century.

PETER ULRICH
(UNIVERSITY OF ST. GALLEN)

2 Ethics and Economics

2.1 Business Ethics is More Than "Applied Ethics"

2.2 A Brief Historical Survey and Current Approaches
    2.2.1 Pure Economics and the "Disembedding" of the Economy
    2.2.2 Steps toward the Demystification of Market Metaphysics

2.3 Integrative Economic Ethics
    2.3.1. The Critique of Economic Reason and Economism
    2.3.2. The Ethical Aspects of a Socio-economic Rationality

2.4 The Loci of Socio-economic Responsibility
    2.4.1 Civic Ethics for Economic Players
    2.4.2 Politico-economic Ethics
    2.4.3 Corporate Ethics

2.5 Conclusion

Abstract

Business ethics is more than just "applied ethics." There is no domain which is "free" from normative presuppositions, and mainstream economics is nothing more than a strongly normative "ideal theory" of rational action. The primary task of "integrative business ethics" is therefore to reflect on the form of economic reasoning, the critique of economic reason.

This chapter provides a specific perspective on the "emancipation" of economic rationality from moral philosophy; a process mirroring the disembedding of the economy from society in what Karl Polanyi called the "great transformation." Today, there is a growing real-life experience of the problematic consequences of this disembedded, "ethics-free" economic rationality. In this situation, integrative economic ethics asks for a new ethical foundation for economic reason itself.

The fundamental tasks of integrative economic ethics are to critique "economism," including economic determinism and economic reductionism, as well as to rethink basic ethical aspects of economic reason. Pertinent issues include the meaning of economic 'rationalization' with regard to the good human life and the legitimacy of the politico-economic order with regard to a just and well-ordered society of free and equal citizens. The fundamental difference between "market freedom" and "citizens' freedom" has to be pointed out, which amounts to the difference between economic and republican liberalism.

In integrative economic ethics three loci of socio-economic responsibility are distinguished: the citizens in their different roles (citizens' ethics), the companies (corporate ethics), and the state in its function of defining the juridical and institutional framework of economic activities (regulatory ethics).

Keywords: economism, ethical reason vs. economic rationality; integrative business ethics; socio-economic rationality

2.1 Business Ethics is More Than "Applied Ethics"

The development of practical problems does not generally take the established boundaries between the various academic disciplines into consideration. This is particularly true of those disciplines which, while concerned with human action, have become reduced to theoretical concepts free of value judgments, a process which has taken place under the influence of twentieth-century positivism. The social sciences, thus attenuated, are at a loss to meet the growing human need for ethical orientation. On the other hand, academic philosophy sees its respective role in the domain of "applied ethics," i.e., of putting its practical relevance and currency to the test. There is no lack of interest on the part of society: These days, in nearly all areas of life in which – due to the insufficiency of traditional orientations for action – the existing circumstances have become the subject of public debate, the call for a field-specific "applied" ethics is heard.

In principle, the same also applies in the case of business. An ever greater number of people are posing questions regarding the practical sense and value of the economization process, which appears to many to be willful and governed by inherent constraints. And these questions are gaining in urgency, particularly in view of the daunting increase in questionable consequences to the natural, social, and cultural environments and the corresponding side effects. The call for business ethics thus does not simply fall from the sky as a manifestation of some naïve idealism but is an expression of the rising awareness of the problems of very real socio-economic development trends.

And yet the preconception of business ethics as an "application" of general ethics to the "area" of the economy does not suffice, for two reasons. Firstly, this area is to some extent already occupied by another discipline of normative content, a discipline which refers to itself traditionally – and not inappropriately – as Political Economy. The first and foremost task of economic ethics is therefore to concern itself critically with the normative foundations of supposedly value-free, "pure" economic thought. Secondly, present-day "pure" economics (Schumpeter 1908) of neoclassical mintage no longer defines itself in an area-related manner – as a theory of the area of society designated "economy" – but rather in an aspect-related manner as a general theory of human behavior and the development of societal institutions (Becker 1976). It is precisely in this sense that upholders of this approach attach a new positive association to the originally critical term "economic imperialism" (Boulding 1969) and view it as a methodological research program (Kirchgässner 1988; Homann & Suchanek 2000). The point of view from which they investigate societal phenomena is strictly economic rationality (efficiency).

Due to the fact that "rationality" is invariably a regulative idea involving how one should act and organize institutions rationally, pure economics – thus understood – implies not merely an explanatory (theoretical) purpose, but an action-oriented (practical) one. The strict economic rationality perspective thus represents the identity-forming principle of a normative discipline, namely an ideal theory of rational action in a world of scarce resources. At its core, pure economics is normative economics! And that means that there is no economic theory which is untouched by normative points of view and could simply be supplemented by business ethics without further ado. The seat which might be occupied by business ethics as "applied ethics" is virtually already taken.

The common two-world conception of "ethic-free" economic theory on the one hand and "extra-economic" business ethics on the other eludes these basic circumstances, which are characterized by two competing rationality perspectives. Contrary to popular belief, there is not a value-free economic logic specifically inherent to the market on one side of the coin and 'ethical reasoning' on the other; rather, both sides can be described as patterns of normative reasoning. Naturally, this claim as such can only be contemplated and substantiated in ethical categories, whereas in economics it is simply axiomatically introduced with the aid of the rationality model designated "Homo Oeconomicus." Normative economics thus represents a reductionist "ethics without morals" (Cortina 1992), and in this way – from the very outset – it evades the methodological claim of modern rational ethics to carry out its substantiations and criticisms from a moral point of view.

A principally critical conception of economic and business ethics accordingly suggests itself: Wherever universalistically conceived economic rationality claims to have a normative function, the very first concern of economic ethics is to shed light upon the implicit normative content of these claims. Thus an economic ethics that stays abreast of the real events of the present-day world cannot intellectually confine itself to an applied ethics for the area of business only. If today's mainstream economics serves as the leading scientific approach to promoting the aspect of "pure" economic rationality in nearly all areas of life, the systematic response is to be seen in a likewise aspect-related conception of economic ethics. Its primary task is to carry out ethical-critical reflection on the form of economic reasoning. In Kantian terms, a business ethics which takes this approach is concerned primarily with the ethical-rational orientation of political-economic thought; i.e., with the ethical substantiation and/or criticism of all claims advanced in the name of economic rationality. As an integrative economic ethics (Ulrich 2008) it thus explores the normative aspect within the economic thought pattern in order to be able to critically reflect upon the true meaning of the latter when it is applied to one practical context or another. To drive the point home, it could be said that the idea is to bring economic rationality – wherever its normative intention is emphasized – "to reason."

2.2 A Brief Historical Survey and Current Approaches

The call for an ethically integrated manner of economic reasoning may appear to "pure" economists as a provocation. However during the span of more than 2,000 years, from the Ancient Greeks to classical Political Economy, economic activity was always considered from ethical-practical points of view. The concern was with the instrumental role of the economy for a good life and the just coexistence of human beings. Conceptually, the economy remained embedded in superordinate models of the well-ordered society and derived its normative orientation from these models. An example is Aristotle's well-known triad of ethics, politics, and economics – lexically arranged in this sequence. The *Nicomachean Ethics* (Aristotle 2000) thus leads in the end to *The Politics* (Aristotle 1984), in which economic theory is found embedded. It is no coincidence that the founders of modern economic science – specifically Adam Smith – were also, and primarily, moral philosophers. Smith's liberal economic theory (Smith

1776/1976) still utilized a political economy with a moral-philosophical intention (Meyer-Faje & Ulrich 1991; Bürgin 1996, p. 366 ff.). The same is true for John Stuart Mill's (1836/1967) sophisticated approach to political economy as a methodically specialized branch of a more comprehensive social economy and political philosophy (Ulrich 2006).

From about 1870, the age of the neoclassical revolution, everything changed. Most economists no longer wanted to be moral philosophers or carry on with political economy, but instead wanted to have a theory following the example of the natural sciences at their disposal: value-free, objective, and as formalizable as possible. Present-day mainstream economics, which still bears the neoclassical stamp, conceives of itself as an autonomous, "value-free" science, i.e. as "pure economics." Myrdal (1932/1953) and Albert (1972) already pointed out the impossibility of an economics that was independent with regard to the issue of ethics. And even though this criticism remained uncontested, it has been largely ignored by the mainstream of the field to the very present. Thus the current necessity of a special economic and business ethics is not as pressing an issue as the counter-question: how an economics that conceived of itself as "ethic-free" and unpolitical could ever have developed. Only on that basis can the core problem of the systematic reconnection of ethics and economics be comprehended.

2.2.1 Pure Economics and the "Disembedding" of the Economy

The development of economic theory – from the pre-classical and liberal classical period to neoclassical and pure economics – can be understood as a theoretical reflection of what has actually been occurring in society for over 200 years (Ulrich 1993, p. 347 ff.), namely a progressive, institutionally "unleashed" and normatively "disinhibited" economization of all areas of life and even of thought (economic imperialism) throughout the world ("globalization," "deregulation"). According to Karl Polanyi (1944, p. 56 ff.), at the end of this development society is nothing more than an "appendage to the market": The economy is no longer embedded in social interrelationships but society is embedded in business relations. Specifically, that means that, according to the model of the "free" market, the societal context will be increasingly subject to the logic of exchange between human beings who are "mutually unconcerned" for one another (Gauthier 1986, p. 87 ff.), each of whom is pursuing his own advantage. Economic rationality thus "emancipates" itself from nearly all traditional normative constraints and becomes the dominant societal norm.

The "great transformation" from an embedded economy to a "disembedded" economy (Polanyi 1944) is academically reflected in the emancipation of economics from its mother discipline – moral philosophy – i.e. in the gradual replacement of classical political economy with the self-contained neoclassical approach. The concern with ethical issues was accordingly dropped to an ever-increasing extent from the curricula of economics and business administration departments. Since that time, ethics and economics have been cultivated in separate departments and have had little to say to one another. The occasional musings of high-ranking economists regarding the difficult relationship between the two disciplines have done little to change this circumstance. Even the cautious proposals by Sen (1987) and Hausman and McPherson (1996) to recognize an "ethics approach" alongside the dominant "engineering approach" and to relate the two perspectives to one another received practically no attention from mainstream economics.

Due to the fact that, in the age of positivism and scientism, philosophical ethics had difficulties of its own, even retreating for a time into the haven of meta-ethics, for a long time economic-ethical considerations were left to authors of theological provenance or ecclesiastical communiqués (the papal encyclicals of the Roman Catholic Church and the memoranda of the Reformed). And even theologians tended to view business ethics more as a form of "applied" (social) ethics than as a fundamental ethical-critical reflection of economic reason. This would appear almost paradoxical inasmuch as the unleashing of economic rationalism and its process of gaining independence was itself originally borne to a decisive extent by fundamentally Christian-oriented convictions. In the final analysis, the entire neoclassical endeavor to reduce ethics to normative economics is founded on a Christian, natural law oriented market metaphysics, according to which the market gives economic subjects "signs" pointing them toward actions that please God: "For if that God, whose hand the Puritan sees in all the occurrences of life, shows one of His elect a chance of profit, he must do it with a purpose. Hence the faithful Christian must follow the call by taking advantage of the opportunity" (Weber 1930, p. 162).

Within the framework of his famous studies of the economic ethics of the world religions, specifically "The Protestant Ethic and the Spirit of Capitalism," Max Weber defines this deeper inner relationship between the "modern economic ethos" and the Occidental modernization and rationalization process. He recognized the true nature of "economic rationalism" as the incarnation of that religious ethos. The emancipation of the early modern economy was made possible by the fact that – and this is the irony of history – the Protestant religion over-elevated the market to a sphere of higher morals.

2.2.2 Steps toward the Demystification of Market Metaphysics

The tradition of honoring the law of nature still exerts a considerable influence on present-day business ethics in the form of an underlying tendency to exaggerate the normative qualities of economic logic. The consequence is a strange construct that might be describable as a kind of internal justice to the concerns of the discipline – apparently not ascribable to justice between persons but based on an impersonal, inherent market morality. Koslowski (1998, p. 14 ff.), for example, still expressly refers to an "economic law of nature," arguing "that the moral obligation emerges from the nature of things [...]. Morality is fundamentally synonymous with doing justice to the nature of things and cannot consist in the abstract contrast between moral obligation and objective economic argumentation."

But what is the "nature" of the economic concern? It is the "willful" functional logic of the market economy. If this is the answer, however, the ethical-critical questioning of the market economy – and with it the question as to whether the societal interests it serves can be legitimized – never even enters the scene! What remains is an analysis of the function of human morality for a market system that works "well" according to its own inherent laws; i.e., one that functions efficiently. But efficient for whom and with regard to what? Questions such as these remain concealed behind a market-metaphysical fiction of common weal, a subject to which we will return in section 2.3. The danger that, in the final analysis, this type of functionalist economic ethics – as championed most strongly by the moral economist Karl Homann of Munich – merely serves the ideological apologetics of powerful economic interests can hardly be brushed aside.

There is another, more popular approach: that of corrective business ethics. At first glance it appears diametrically opposed to functional business ethics because it regards "ethics as corrective for economic failure" (Koslowski 2001, p. 26 ff.). Now ethics functions as an "antidote" against too much economic rationality, whereas in the functional approach it is regarded a "lubricant" for more economic rationality or efficiency. A corrective, however, presupposes that the aspect which it merely sets out to keep within bounds is – once within its bounds – a normatively valid coordination principle! In other words it is assumed that the market principle of the mutually beneficial exchange between players each acting in his own interest will function ethically well within certain normative bounds. The normative content of the market economy's "inherent logic" and of the orientations for action which dominate it – particularly the entrepreneurial profit maximization principle – thus go for the most part unchallenged by corrective business ethics.

It was not until a decisive reorganization of the problematic relationship between economic and ethical rationalization approaches became necessary on the practical level that a renaissance of interest in these fundamental questions of economic and business ethics got underway in the 1980s – to a smaller extent in the Anglo-Saxon countries than in those of continental Europe. This new orientation conceives of economic and business ethics not merely as a symptom-correcting "repair ethics" (Mittelstrass 1990, p. 36), but as a philosophically founded ethics of economic reasoning.

An integrative business ethics which takes this approach does not merely present arguments – from the external perspective of applied ethics – in favor of ethical correctives against economic rationality, but instead does it – from the internal perspective of a self-reflective way of economic thinking – in favor of a well-understood economic reason, for which ethical reason serves as a sound basis. Here the idea of economic reason is a regulative one, an ethically integrated socio-economic rationality. It does not simply comprise the technically rational (efficient) manner of coping with the scarcity of resources and goods, but also – and with precedence – the ethically rational manner of coping with the multifarious social (value and interest) conflicts over the fair distribution of the (internal and external) costs and benefits of the economization process (Figure 2.1).

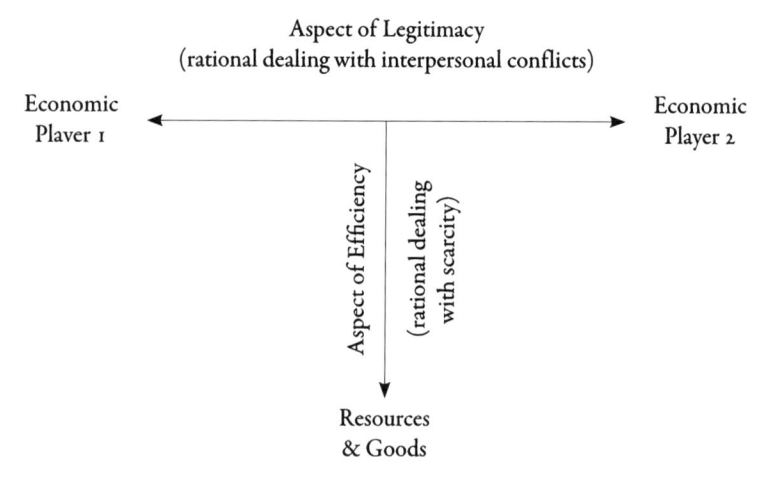

Figure 2.1 *The Two-dimensional Concept of Socio-economic Rationality*

The concept of socio-economic rationality can be defined as follows: Any action or institution is rational in a socio-economic sense if free and mature citizens could have consensually justified it as a legitimate way of creating value in a rational process of deliberation. Pure economics cannot achieve this integration under its own steam, for categorically it is one-dimensional. The necessary deontological categories of an ethically rational manner of coping with socio-economic issues (moral rights and duties, justice) cannot be reduced to the teleological categories of cost and benefit and are therefore axiomatically entirely alien to "pure" economics.

Integrative economic ethics systematically fills the gap left by classical Political Economy still rooted in moral philosophy and its neoclassical reduction to "pure" economics. From the point of view of the history of thought, modern business ethics thus has its place in the best of traditions. Today, however, it is concerned to a lesser extent than Smith's Political Economy of yore with justifying a disembedded market economy, and much more with the theoretical and practical re-embedding of the latter into the overall ethical and political context of a well-ordered society of free and equal citizens. In view of the increasingly questionable effects of

Ethics and Economics

the unleashed economic rationalization process on our life-world, it is precisely this characteristic which constitutes the current relevance of the new economic and business ethics.

Figure 2.2 shows the aforementioned three possible approaches to business ethics, namely functional business ethics, corrective business ethics, and integrative business ethics.

```
                    Ethics  ⇄?  Economics
           ┌───────────────┼───────────────┐
           ▼               ▼               ▼
    Business Ethics   Business Ethics   Business Ethics
         =                =                =
     Normative         Applied         Critique of
     Economics          Ethics      Economic Reason
           │               │               │
           ▼               ▼               ▼
    Presupposition   Presupposition   Presupposition
     of the morality  of given       of ethical
     of the market    circumstances   reasoning
     itself
           │               │               │
           ▼               ▼               ▼
     Ethics as a     Ethics as an      Ethics as a
     'lubricant'     'antidote'       'sound base'
     for more        against too much  for a different
     economic        economic          socio-economic
     rationality     rationality       rationality
           │               │               │
           ▼               ▼               ▼
      Functional       Corrective       Integrative
     Business Ethics  Business Ethics  Business Ethics
```

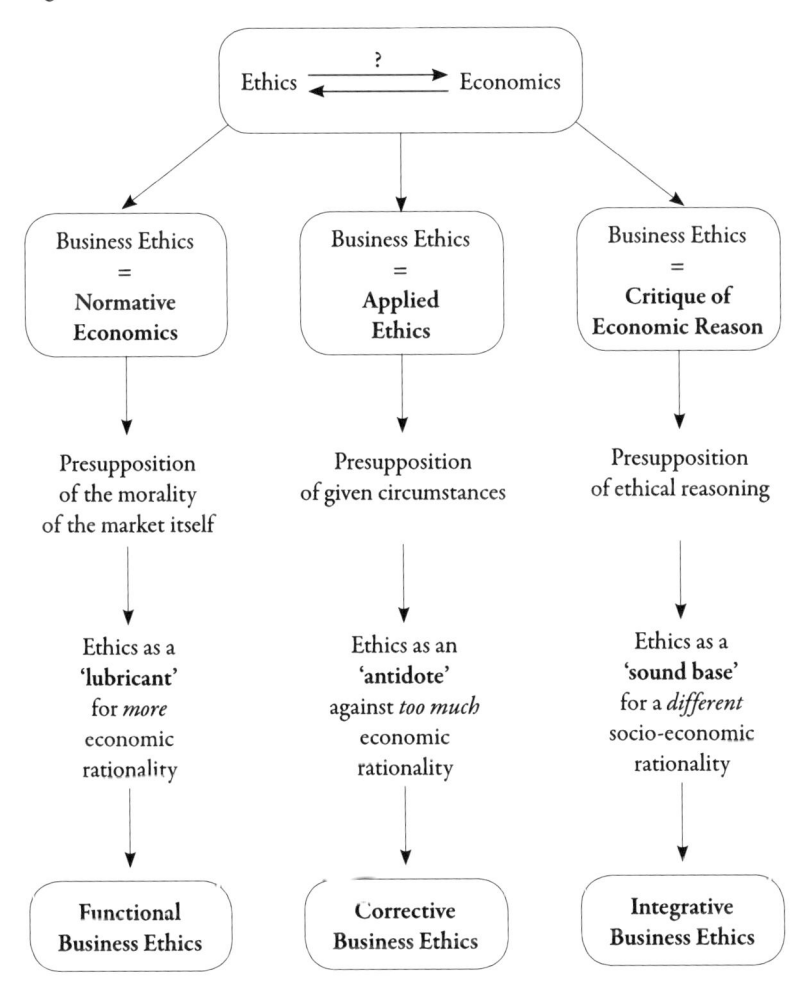

Figure 2.2 *Three Approaches to Business Ethics*

2.3 Integrative Economic Ethics

Once the question of the moral point of view of integrative economic and business ethics as a modern rational ethics has been fundamentally settled, the integrative approach differentiates between two systematic tasks: the critique of "pure" economic reason and of the over-expansion of its normative function as economism; and the clarification of the ethical aspects of an economy that is rational in a socio-economic, life-serving sense. A further task is to determine the "loci" of socio-economic responsibility. We will return to this in section 2.4.

2.3.1. The Critique of Economic Reason and Economism

One core element of the neoclassical conception of economic rationality is that economic agents are concerned strictly with maximizing their own advantage and are indifferent to one another, so that no moral obligation influences their interactions. The clever, but one-sided, homunculus who corresponds to this assumption of rationality is called Homo Oeconomicus (see Chapter 3 for further discussion). With perfect consistency, pure economics develops the general logic of the success-oriented rational action of individuals strictly concerned with their own interests. This logic – which springs from the market model – is generalized far beyond the sphere of the market: Every form of human interaction and cooperation is now interpreted as a variation of the exchange and mutual advantage. It is for this reason that pure economics can conceive of itself as a systematic rationalization perspective for all areas of life and action (economic imperialism).

In a similar manner, modern philosophical ethics develops its specific idea of reason – namely the universal "normative logic of interpersonal relations" (Ulrich 2008, p. 13 ff.); or, to phrase it differently: the grammar of inter-subjectivity. In contrast to the economic perspective of exclusively (benefit-oriented) conditional interaction and cooperation between players, deontological ethics, or moral philosophy is concerned precisely with the substantiation of inter-subjective obligations associated with the unconditional mutual recognition of persons as beings of equal dignity and the resulting reciprocal moral rights and duties. This inter-subjective demand structure is constitutive for all human morality and thus for the moral point of view (Tugendhat 1994).

The difference between economic rationality and the ethical idea of reason is considerable (Table 2.1). In the first case, the "given" interests of the individuals already form what is regarded to be a sufficient proviso for a rational "balancing of interests" among the participants. In the second case, however, those interests are merely the object of ethical-critical examination from the point of view of their legitimacy under the terms of the moral rights of all affected and the protection of those rights. In short: economic rationality is power-based while ethical reason is justice-based. The market principle of mutual advantage can thus in no way be equated with the moral principle (Thielemann 1996). This results in the fundamental economic-ethical realization of the primacy of (political) ethics over the logic of the market.

Table 2.1 *Ethical Reason versus Economic Rationality*

Economic rationality: *normative logic of* *mutual advantage*	*Ethical reason:* *normative logic of* *interpersonal relations*
power-based (what can be asserted is what counts)	justice-based (what is legitimate is what counts)
interest in maximization of private success	inter-subjective obligations
benefit-oriented *conditional* cooperation between self-interested, mutually unconcerned individuals	*unconditional* reciprocal respect and recognition of persons as beings of equal dignity
market principle	moral principle

The relationship between ethical and economic rationality is ignored by all who assert that the "morality of the market" is an ethically adequate social organization principle. This approach amounts to a normative superelevation of the logic of the market, which – whether intentionally or unintentionally – works in favor of the ideology of a total market society. With the aid of Weisser (1934, p. 49 ff.; 1954/1978, p. 574), one can speak in this context of *economism*. This phenomenon occurs in two elementary forms: (i) as an assertion of factual constraints ("The market forces us...") and (ii) as a market-metaphysical common weal fiction ("...but in the end it serves the general well-being"). In the first, empiricist version, the consideration of ethical principles is labeled "impossible" under the conditions of market competition (economic determinism); in the second, normativist version, they are rejected as "unnecessary" (economic reductionism).

(i) *Economic determinism* rejects ethical claims on economic agents, arguing that it is entirely "impossible" to take such claims into account under the conditions of market competition. These days this "factual-constraint" argument is particularly popular in the form of reference to global competition. To a certain extent, of course, the world market is a compulsory element for business – but only to the extent to which the market participants want to be successful as competitors. Only under the norm of strict profit maximization is it entirely "impossible" for the economic players to take into consideration other valuation criteria. It is not difficult to discern here the "bourgeois" image of mankind and society elucidated by Macpherson (1962) in his famous study on the political theory of possessive individualism.

The economic "factual-constraint" mentality is thus based on an interruption of the reflection process in the face of normative goal determination by the economic players. "Not wanting to" is ideologically reinterpreted as "not being able to." Whenever market participants are willing to waive their claim to the maximization of their profit, they emancipate themselves to some extent from the inherent constraints. But should they waive their claim? Or more precisely: To what extent can it be legitimately expected of an economic player to renounce his own claim to individual success in order to be able to take the claims of others into account? A substantial answer must take the legitimate claims (i.e., moral rights) of all persons involved into consideration: On the one hand, the economic player's action should be responsible with regard to the legitimate claims of the persons involved; but on the other hand, the claims of the persons involved on the economic player should also be reasonable. For the player also has certain legitimate claims to self-assertion in the market; to expect him to abandon them completely would be asking too much. The principle should therefore be a fair symmetry of reciprocal consideration.

The extent to which the ethically justified self-limitation in striving for economic advantage can be reasonably expected of the market participants depends on the quality of the political framework of the market. These market regulations determine which aspects enjoy legal precedence over the striving for success, and a good market framework thus, at the very least, relieves the economic subjects of extreme moral dilemmas. For that reason, economic-ethically enlightened persons of good will welcome the role of a good regulatory framework as a normative basis for fair competition.

(ii) *Economic reductionism* declares the inherent "morality of the market" ethically adequate. The "market principle" itself is said to be the impersonal guarantor of the general welfare. As mentioned above, this idea has its roots in the Christian and natural law belief in the "invisible hand" of God, which is given full play to do its salutary work in free market competition. In neoclassical Welfare Economics this market-metaphysical conviction was rationalized with the aid of utilitarian ethics (Bohnen 1964). It thus adopted the calculative form of the utilitarian concept of social benefit on which the belief in economic growth as a patent recipe for the solution of nearly all socio-economic problems still feeds to the present day.

Once Myrdal (1932/1953) and Rawls (1971) had proven that this was an untenable "communist fiction" which ignored the liberal principle of inviolable individual rights, however, the younger generation of neo-classicists reoriented itself towards the axiomatic basis of methodological individualism. Here social circumstances based on the individual consent of all involved are considered to be "tolerable to the public weal." Every change that improves the position of at least one individual without worsening the life conditions of another is thus considered an improvement in the well-being of the society. This normative criterion is known as the Pareto efficiency. It is Buchanan (1975) who developed what is probably the most consistent and differentiated version of this contractualist concept of economic rationality.

This individualist refinement of neoclassical economics does nothing, however, to change the fact that every concept of rational action essentially possesses normative significance. Buchanan expressly regards himself as a political philosopher with economic means and emphasizes that "the Pareto rule is itself an ethical proposition" (Buchanan 1987, p. 4). Methodological individualism thus functions as normative individualism. Arrow (1994, p. 1) knew very well what he was talking about when he conceded that "this distinction is not easy to keep clear, and the temptation to join methodology and ideology is strong."

But what, precisely, is the "ideological temptation" of methodological and normative individualism? Economics neglects the fundamental difference between efficiency and justice. Because methodological individualism recognizes the empirically expressed preferences of individuals as the final normative instance, it first negates the ethical necessity of everybody's moral self-limitation to pursuing only those personal interests which could be generally pursued (principle of universalization). Second, it disregards the social circumstances and with them the balance of power under which the contract partners encounter one another. The "pure" economists thus routinely overlook the structural partiality of the market for the powerful capitalist interests in profitable investments and the antipathy against all claims opposing these interests, regardless of how legitimate they may be from an ethical point of view. This also explains why "factual-constraint" arguments used in support of those system-conformist interests are so conspicuously popular.

2.3.2 *The Ethical Aspects of a Socio-economic Rationality*

As elucidated above, the ideological function of economism consists in double-padlocking the realm of economic-ethical reflection by means of the "factual-constraint" mentality and the reduction of the moral principle to the market principle. The critique of economism is therefore the systematic prerequisite for what would then be the next step: to consider the normative orientation aspects of a rational economy, as regarded within the context of the life-world. Here, one can differentiate between two fundamental questions in the development of a life-serving economy: (i) the question of underlying purpose and (ii) the question of legitimacy.

(i) *The question of underlying purpose* is directed against the "self-purpose" of the factual-constraint logic of market competition. All economic activities should be judged by the yardstick of their contribution to the good life, thus providing insight into the cultural motives and ideas which give meaning to the economic "value-creation" – motives and ideas which economism simply reduces to benefit or profit maximization. Under which model of the good life is the form of our economic activities supposed to make sense? Modern conceptions which are appropriate to an open society will favor personal life-plans made by free individuals in the framework of a philosophical concept of political liberalism.

Without going into the difficulties inherent in a modern philosophical ethics of the good life, we state the basic purpose of the economy is to secure the means of human subsistence. Provision with the fundamental means of life (food, clothing, shelter, health care, education) corresponds to man's general nature as a being of need. The moral right of all human beings to the guarantee of what is necessary for life must be presupposed. Every economy based on the division of labor must therefore be understood as a context of solidarity.

At a more advanced stage, the purpose of economic activities might be to provide persons with diverse, autonomously chosen means to enhance the abundance of human life. Due to the above-sketched structural partiality of market logic, however, we are faced with the problem that in an entirely "free" competition of lifestyles and cultures (!) there is never any question as to who will win: the "life entrepreneurs" who invest more or less all of their energy into continually increasing their competitiveness and improving their market position (Ulrich 2008, p. 207 ff.). This is the primary reason why the real freedom of individuals to pursue other dimensions of the good life is available only within a political framework that sets limits on the factual-constraint character of the "free" market. An economy aimed at the abundance of life will never automatically emerge from economic growth and the abundance of goods, but it will only arise from the socio-political will to develop a different kind of economic culture, one directed at vital aspects of life quality.

(ii) *The question of legitimacy* is directed against the "morality" of the market, which is clearly partial. It places the organization of the economy within the context of the rules of just human coexistence. In this way it calls attention to an aspect ignored by economism: the social-conflict character of the economic process and the distribution of its results. What model of a well-ordered society of free citizens is to serve as an orientation for a legitimate politico-economic order (i.e., the framework of legitimate private striving for profit or other economic benefit)? This question reveals economic and business ethics as an element of political philosophy and ethics. Here its fundamental and foremost task is to counteract the economist reduction of ethically reflected political liberalism (Rawls 1993) to pure economic liberalism and to elucidate the fundamental difference between civic freedom and market freedom: Not the "free" market but rather strong and general civil rights are the basis for the real freedom of all, regardless of their purchasing power and competitiveness on the market. As Dahrendorf (1995, p. 33) summed it up: "Citizenship is a non-economic term. It defines the human status independently of the relative value of their contribution to the economic process."

Seen from this point of view, the development of modern civic rights has by no means been concluded even in the advanced liberal-democratic societies. Still missing are the economic and social citizenship rights which really render the citizens free to lead their lives independently. Really free citizens need – and deserve – to be protected from the structurally imposed helplessness of being unable to secure their existence by means of their own performance because they might come up losers in the economic rat race. More and more people are being subjected to this humiliating circumstance – as a consequence of the nationally and internationally widening income and wealth gap and the tendency towards the social disintegration of society ("two-thirds society"). This state of affairs is incompatible with the ethical principles of a "decent" society, as Margalit (1996) has shown, to say nothing of an even remotely just society. In view of the mighty socio-economic upheavals presently in progress, the primary focus must be on the further development of the civil society and a market economy which is correspondingly "civilized." (See also Chapter 5.)

2.4 The Loci of Socio-economic Responsibility

The act of designing conceptual models of a purposeful and legitimate market economy is one thing; identifying the entities which are to be made responsible for actively adhering to these models is another. Unless we ascertain the "loci" of moral reasoning and responsibility with respect to economic or politico-economic behavior, business-ethical postulates remain literally utopian; i.e., in the classical Greek sense: placeless. The task of economic-ethical topology is to make moral standards and responsibilities assignable to certain players and to make these players accountable to them.

In view of the inherent constraints of market competition, in which (nearly) all of us – as economic agents – are caught up, the central problem connected with this task is the interdependence between individual and institutional ethics. On the one hand it is important not to overtax the good will of individuals to act responsibly, but rather to support it with "institutional backing." On the other hand, without citizens who develop a certain degree of civic spirit and take a share of responsibility for the public cause, it is literally impossible to form a state. Without such civic virtue, the liberal-democratic society's task of shaping an ethically sound economic order would remain unfulfilled.

It is essential that the ethical self-commitment of the economic players and the institutional rules be mutually supportive. Concepts which aim to relieve the economic agents more or less entirely from every moral burden and which postulate the political framework of the market as the only systematic locus of socio-economic responsibility (Homann & Blome-Drees 1992, p. 20 ff.) are as inadequate as the converse – purely individual-ethical concepts which count solely on the ethical self-limitation of the economic players in the "free" market. Of primary significance from the point of view of integrative business ethics is the reciprocal enhancement of three systematic loci of socio-economic responsibility: the economic players as individual citizens, the policies governing the public order, and the business enterprises as "corporate citizens."

2.4.1 Civic Ethics for Economic Players

The economic agents, in all of their roles, must first of all be approached as citizens who acknowledge certain moral duties: as reflective consumers and capital investors, as critically loyal "organization citizens" in the working world, and as citizens of the state. As good citizens they should regard sound politics as making "public use of reason" (Kant 1783/1990; Rawls 1993, p. 212 ff.), taking a share of responsibility for the "res publica," the public cause of the just coexistence of free and equal citizens. Understood in this way, the republican ethos is indivisible. And it is also expressed in the fundamental willingness of the individual to pursue only those private goals which are compatible with the legitimacy conditions of a well-ordered society of free and equal citizens.

As leading historians (Pocock 1975) and legal philosophers (Michelman 1986) have shown, good liberal constitutions have always been borne by republican civic virtue. The significance of the civic-ethics element should also be recognized to a greater degree in connection with business ethics: Republican-minded citizens recognize and support the obligation of the state to integrate the forces of the market into the principles and rules of a well-ordered civil society. The consequence is the political philosophy of *republican liberalism*, which consistently links the principles of political liberalism with the republican ethos (Ulrich 2008, p. 276 ff.; cf. also Ulrich 2009a/b, and the debate on it). Quite obviously, republican liberalism of this kind is diametrically opposed to the old Hobbesian dream of radical market-liberalism according to which the liberal society is to be conceived of entirely as a "system of ordered egoism" (Habermas 1996, p. 90).

2.4.2 Politico-economic Ethics

From the perspective of republican liberalism it is essential to counteract the politico-economic order dictated by economism and reduced by that school of thought to policies of competition in the manner of the neo-liberal doctrine. Competition policies defined as policies intended to keep the market open and ensure workable competition are no doubt indispensable – but they are only one aspect of the politico-economic order. Market competition cannot "know" of its own accord what it is supposed to be efficient for; it needs normative instructions of an extra-economic kind, concerned with the manner in which the competitive dynamic serves the necessities of life and society.

To this end, it is important to adopt an ordoliberal approach to develop the systematic precedence of "Vitalpolitik" – i.e., policies aimed at "vital" prerequisites for a good life – over competition policies. What is meant here is a politico-economic order which "takes into account all factors on which human happiness, well-being and contentment are really dependent" (Rüstow 1955, p. 74). In the words of Röpke (1958, p. 174; own transl.), the second herald of ordoliberalism, Vitalpolitik must guarantee "that we do not make competition the predominant principle" but rather "[...] delimit and [...] moderate [...] competition and the market economy."

From the ordoliberal point of view, Vitalpolitik and competition policies are by no means mutually exclusive, but rather to be understood as a two-level conception of the politico-economic order (Table 2.2, p. 28). Vitalpolitik holds the systematic and normative primacy: it provides normative orientation and determines the boundaries of the market dynamic according to the relevant criteria of its expediency to human life. In principle, these normative prerequisites can consist of the civic rights of the economic agents and all those affected by their activities, the calculative norms applied to individual economic calculations, and the marginal norms limiting the market (Ulrich 2008, p. 352 ff.).

In a liberal-democratic society, the substantive development of the "vital order" is not the task of economic experts but of public discussion (deliberative politics). In this process we are challenged not only as citizens of a state but, increasingly, as world citizens – to the extent that the economy becomes globalized, the tasks required of the political order shift to a supranational level. There, however, the agencies of the systematic "vital-political" integration of the global markets – as opposed to those of supranational competition policies (WTO) – have not yet been adequately institutionalized. (See also Chapter 9.)

Table 2.2 *The Two-level Conception of the Politico-economic Order*

---

1. *'Vitalpolitik'* (A. Rüstow)

= The embedding of the market system "into a higher overall order, which cannot be based on supply and demand, free prices and competition" (W. Röpke)

= Orientation and limitation of "blind" market forces according to ethical aspects of their expediency to life by means of
- Civic rights (with regard to socio-economic living conditions)
- Calculative norms (aimed at internalization of external effects)
- Marginal norms (as limiting values or thresholds)

2. Competition policies

= The assertion of open markets and workable competition *within the framework* of the preconditions of *Vitalpolitik*

= Efficient employment of market competition *with a view to* "vital" purposes of good life and just coexistence

---

2.4.3 Corporate Ethics

The extent to which corporate ethics grows in significance corresponds to the extent to which above all the "global players" among the business corporations are able to evade constitutional integration by the politico-economic regulations of individual states, as well as the extent to which no adequate supranational framework yet exists. Just as it is expected of every republican-minded citizen, the companies must also be required to act as "good corporate citizens." This includes the autonomous self-commitment to principles of business integrity in dealings with all stakeholders, as well as republican-ethical co-responsibility for the overall and industry-specific framework conditions of each company's own business activities. Integrative corporate ethics is thus, in turn, also to be conceived of in two stages (Figure 2.3).

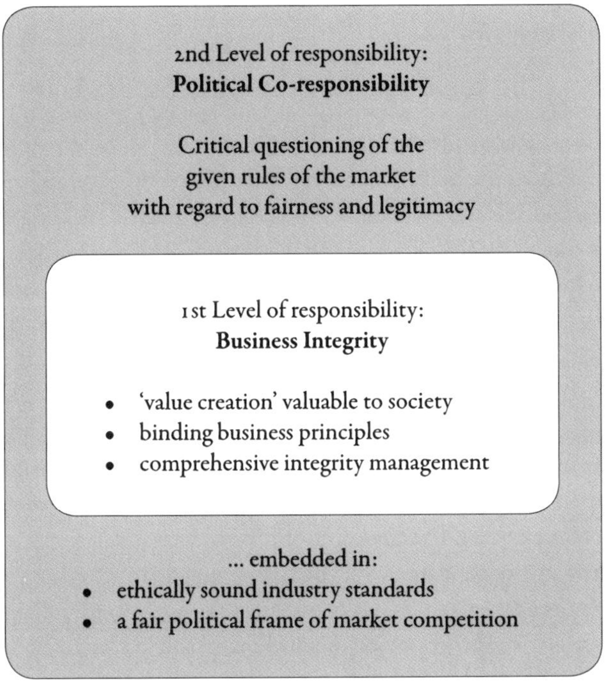

Ethics and Economics

> **2nd Level of responsibility:**
> **Political Co-responsibility**
>
> Critical questioning of the
> given rules of the market
> with regard to fairness and legitimacy
>
> > **1st Level of responsibility:**
> > **Business Integrity**
> >
> > - 'value creation' valuable to society
> > - binding business principles
> > - comprehensive integrity management
>
> ... embedded in:
> - ethically sound industry standards
> - a fair political frame of market competition

Figure 2.3 *Two-level Conception of Corporate Ethics*

Effort is being applied increasingly to the development of entrepreneurial programs of integrity management (first level) both in theory and in practice (Maak/Ulrich 2007). An intelligent form of constitutional integration, as exemplified specifically by the United States Federal Sentencing Guidelines, can contribute significantly to encouraging the willingness of the enterprises to adopt such programs into their corporate policies. But in order for such guidelines to become established, responsible management must learn to appreciate them as a support for the pursuit of their own well-understood interests and be prepared to demonstrate active political commitment to their establishment (second level). In this context it once again becomes clear how strongly practicable business ethics is dependent upon the mutual reinforcement of individual, corporate, and regulatory measures. (See also Chapter 5.)

2.5 Conclusion

The deep-rooted attitude that Max Weber referred to as "economic rationalism" is still the most decisive driving force of the mighty socio-economic upheavals in which we are caught up. The normative logic of the market penetrates our daily lives to an ever more comprehensive extent, spreading across the entire surface of the world in the name of globalization and subjugating politics through the competitive struggle for favorable business locations all over the world. Even intellectual thought – into the remotest corners of the social sciences and social philosophy – is slowly but surely succumbing to the analytical charm of the economic approach and allowing itself to be colonized by it. The logical constraints of economism have taken hold of the "Zeitgeist" at almost the same tempo as the factual constraints of market competition have taken hold of society.

Business ethics cannot merely postulate a little more ethical obligation within the already existing market economy. Rather, it should conceive of itself as a critical ethics of economic reasoning as such. Its first task is therefore the belated enlightenment of economic rationalism (economism); "belated" because of the fact that prevailing ("neo-liberal") economic thought – as opposed to politico-philosophical thought – never developed beyond the stage of a pre-modern metaphysic of the market. The "demystification of the world," as Weber (1920/1988) dubbed the process of culture's and society's modernization and rationalization, is just now getting underway in the area of economic thought. Great efforts will be required from a society to begin the process of civilizing the "demystified market" (Ulrich 2002). And that means: integrating it into the sensible cultural and political framework of a well-developed world citizens' society.

A "civilized" market economy; i.e., one embedded in a well-ordered society of free and equal citizens: This could be the sensible ideal for the future beyond the obsolete alternatives of market deification on the one hand and state deification on the other. It is the ideal of republican liberalism.

The best contribution which can be made by economic and business ethics to the realization of this ideal probably consists in its persistent work on a comprehensive perspective of a life-serving, socio-economic rationality. What we are alluding to here is a fundamental transformation of economic reason (Ulrich 1993) – away from the form of economic rationality which went off on a path of its own and which believes in nothing but itself, and towards an ethically integrated idea of economic reason. The Aristotelian triad of ethics, politics, and economics – in this order – remains essential. On this basis, integrative economic ethics can fulfill its foremost task: to renew the ethical foundation of a modern political economy and to readjust the role of business in society.

References

Albert, H. (1972) *Ökonomische Ideologie und politische Theorie* (1st edn 1954). Göttingen: Schwartz.
Aristotle (2000) *Nicomachean Ethics*. Crisp, R. (transl. and ed.). New York: Cambridge University Press.
Aristotle (1984) *The Politics*. Lord, C. (transl.). Chicago: University of Chicago Press.
Arrow, K. (1994) Methodological Individualism and Social Knowledge. *American Economic Review*, vol. 84, no. 2, pp. 1–9.
Becker, G. S. (1976) *The Economic Approach to Human Behavior*. Chicago: University of Chicago Press.
Bohnen, A. (1964) *Die utilitaristische Ethik als Grundlage der modernen Wohlfahrtsökonomik*. Göttingen: Schwartz.
Boulding, K. E. (1969) Economics as a Moral Science. *American Economic Review*, vol. 59, pp. 1–12.
Buchanan, J. M. (1975) *The Limits of Liberty: Between Anarchy and Leviathan*. Chicago: University of Chicago Press.
Buchanan, J. M. (1987) *Economics between Predictive Science and Moral Philosophy*. College Station: Texas University Press.
Bürgin, A. (1996) *Zur Soziogenese der politischen Ökonomie: Wirtschaftsgeschichtliche und dogmenhistorische Betrachtungen*. 2nd edn. Marburg: Metropolis.

Cortina, A. (1992) Ethik ohne Moral. Grenzen einer postkantischen Prinzipienethik? In: Apel, K.-O. and Kettner, M. (eds) *Zur Anwendung der Diskursethik in Politik, Recht und Wissenschaft*. Frankfurt a. M.: Suhrkamp, pp. 278–295.

Dahrendorf, R. (1995) Über den Bürgerstatus. In: van den Brink, B. and van Reijen, W. (eds) *Bürgergesellschaft, Recht und Demokratie*, Frankfurt a. M.: Suhrkamp, pp. 29–43.

Gauthier, D. (1986) *Morals by Agreement*. Oxford: Clarendon Press.

Habermas, J. (1996) *Between Facts and Norms*, transl. Rehg, W. Cambridge, MA: MIT Press.

Hausman, D. M. and McPherson, M. S. (1996) *Economic Analysis and Moral Philosophy*. Cambridge: Cambridge University Press.

Homann, K. (1993) Wirtschaftsethik: Die Funktion der Moral in der modernen Wirtschaft. In: Wieland, J. (ed.) *Wirtschaftsethik und Theorie der Gesellschaft*. Frankfurt a. M: Suhrkamp, pp. 32–53.

Homann, K. (1996) Wirtschaftsethik: Angewandte Ethik oder Ethik mit ökonomischer Methode. *Zeitschrift für Politik*, vol. 43, pp. 178–182.

Homann, K. and Blome-Drees, F. (1992) *Wirtschafts- und Unternehmensethik*. Göttingen: Vandenhoeck & Ruprecht.

Homann, K. and Suchanek, A. (2000) Ökonomik: *Eine Einführung*. Tübingen: Mohr.

Kant, I. (1783/1982) Beantwortung der Frage: Was ist Aufklärung? In: *Immanuel Kant Werkausgabe*, vol. 11, ed. Weischedel, W. 6th edn. Frankfurt a. M.: Suhrkamp 1982, pp. 51–61 (Engl.: *Foundations of the Metaphysics of Morals*, incl. 'What is enlightenment?', transl. Beck, L. W. New York and London: Collier Macmillan, 1990).

Kirchgässner, G. (1988) Ökonomie als imperial(istisch)e Wissenschaft: Zur Anwendung des ökonomischen Verhaltensmodells in den benachbarten Sozialwissenschaften. *Jahrbuch für Neue Politische Ökonomie*, vol. 7, Tübingen: Mohr, pp. 128–145.

Koslowski, P. (1998) *Ethik des Kapitalismus*. 6th edn. Tübingen: Mohr.

Koslowski, P. (2001) *Principles of Ethical Economy*, transl. Lutz, D. W. Dordrecht: Kluwer.

Maak, Th. and Ulrich, P. (2007) *Integre Unternehmensführung: Ethisches Orientierungswissen für die Wirtschaftspraxis*. Stuttgart: Schäffer-Poeschel.

Macpherson, C. B. (1962) *The Political Theory of Possessive Individualism: Hobbes to Locke*. Oxford: Oxford University Press.

Margalit, A. (1996) *The Decent Society*. Cambridge, MA: Harvard University Press.

Meyer-Faje, A. and Ulrich, P. (eds) (1991) *Der andere Adam Smith: Beiträge zur Neubestimmung von Ökonomie als Politischer Ökonomie*. Bern: Haupt.

Michelman, F. I. (1986) The Supreme Court 1985 Term. Foreword: Traces of Self-Government. *Harvard Law Review*, vol. 100, pp. 1493–1537.

Mill, J. S. (1836/1967) On the Definition of Political Economy. In: Robson, J. M. (ed.) *Collected Works*. Toronto: University of Toronto Press, pp. 309–337.

Mittelstraß, J. (1990) Wirtschaftsethik oder der erklärte Abschied vom Ökonomismus auf philosophischen Wegen. In: Ulrich, P. (ed.) *Auf der Suche nach einer modernen Wirtschaftsethik: Lernschritte zu einer reflexiven Ökonomie*. Bern: Haupt, pp. 17–38.

Myrdal, G. (1932/1953) *Das politische Element in der nationalökonomischen Doktrin-bildung*, 2nd edn (1st edn Berlin 1932). Bonn-Bad Godesberg: Verlag Neue Gesellschaft 1976 (Engl.: *The Political Element in the Development of Economic Theory*, transl. Streeten, P. London: Routledge & Paul, 1953).

Pocock, J. G. A. (1975) *The Machiavellian Moment: Florentine Political Thought and the Atlantic Republican Tradition*. Princeton, NJ: Princeton University Press.

Polanyi, K. (1944) *The Great Transformation*. New York: Farrar & Rinehart.

Rawls, J. (1971) *A Theory of Justice*. Cambridge, MA: Harvard University Press.

Rawls, J. (1993) *Political Liberalism*. New York: Columbia University Press.

Röpke, W. (1958) *Jenseits von Angebot und Nachfrage*. 2nd edn. Erlenbach-Zürich and Stuttgart: Rentsch (Engl.: *A Humane Economy*, transl. Henderson, E. Chicago: Henry Regnery Co., 1960).

Rüstow, A. (1955) Wirtschaftsethische Probleme der sozialen Marktwirtschaft. In: Boarman, P. M. (ed.) *Der Christ und die soziale Marktwirtschaft*. Stuttgart and Cologne: Kohlhammer, pp. 53–74.

Schumpeter, J. A. (1908) *Das Wesen und der Hauptinhalt der theoretischen Nationalökonomie*. Leipzig: Duncker & Humblot.

Sen, A. (1987) *On Ethics and Economics*. Oxford and New York: Blackwell 1987.

Smith, A. (1759/1976) *The Theory of Moral Sentiments*. Raphael, D. D. and Macfie, A. L. (eds). Oxford: Oxford University Press.

Smith, A. (1776/1976) *An Inquiry into the Nature and Causes of the Wealth of Nations*, Campbell, R. H., Skinner, A. S. and Todd, W. B. (eds). 2 vols. Oxford: Oxford University Press.

Sunstein, C. R. (1988) Beyond the Republican Revival. *Yale Law Journal*, vol. 97, pp. 1539–1590.

Thielemann, U. (1996) *Das Prinzip Markt: Kritik der ökonomischen Tauschlogik*. Bern: Haupt.

Tugendhat, E. (1994) *Vorlesungen über Ethik*. 2nd edn. Frankfurt a. M.: Suhrkamp.

Ulrich, P. (1993) *Transformation der ökonomischen Vernunft: Fortschrittsperspektiven der modernen Industriegesellschaft*. 3rd edn (1st edn 1986). Bern: Haupt.

Ulrich, P. (2002) *Der entzauberte Markt: Eine wirtschaftsethische Orientierung*, Freiburg i. Br.: Herder (completely revised 3rd edn: *Zivilisierte Marktwirtschaft: Eine wirtschaftsethische Orientierung*, Bern: Haupt 2010).

Ulrich, P. (2006) John Stuart Mills emanzipatorischer Liberalismus. In: Ulrich, P. and Aßländer, M. S. (eds) *John Stuart Mill: Der vergessene politische Ökonom und Philosoph*. Bern: Haupt, pp. 253–282.

Ulrich, P. (2008) *Integrative Economic Ethics: Foundations of a Civilized Market Economy*. Cambridge: Cambridge University Press 2008 (pb. edn 2010).

Ulrich, P. (2009a) Republican Liberalism versus Market Liberalism. In: Zsolnai, L., Boda, Z. and Fekete, L. (eds) *Ethical Prospects: Economy, Society and Environment*. Berlin: Springer, pp. 255–259.

Ulrich, P. (2009b) Reply: Republican Liberalism and Its Implications for Business Ethics. In: Zsolnai, L., Boda, Z. and Fekete, L. (eds) *Ethical Prospects: Economy, Society and Environment*. Berlin: Springer, pp. 280–285.

Weber, M. (1930) *The Protestant Ethic and the Spirit of Capitalism*, transl. Parsons, T. London: Unwin Heyman.

Weisser, G. (1934) *Wirtschaftspolitik als Wissenschaft: Erkenntniskritische Grundfragen der praktischen Nationalökonomie*. Stuttgart: Kohlhammer.

Weisser, G. (1954) Die Überwindung des Ökonomismus in der Wirtschaftswissenschaft. Reprinted in: Weisser, G. (1978) *Beiträge zur Gesellschaftspolitik*. Göttingen: Schwartz, pp. 573–601.

LASZLO ZSOLNAI
(CORVINUS UNIVERSITY OF BUDAPEST)

3 The Moral Economic Man

3.1 Economic Behavior
    3.1.1 The Ultimatum Bargaining Game
    3.1.2 Choices in Prisoner's Dilemma Situations
    3.1.3 Lost Letter Experiment
    3.1.4 Contribution to the Public Good
    3.1.5 Trust

3.2 Problems of Rationality
    3.2.1 Bounded Rationality
    3.2.2 Myopic and Deficient Choices
    3.2.3 Rational Fools
    3.2.4 The Strategic Role of Emotions
    3.2.5 Social Norms
    3.2.6 The Communitarian Challenge
    3.2.7 Feminist Criticism

3.3 The "I & We" Paradigm

3.4 The Ethical Fabric of the Economy

3.5 Conclusion

Abstract

Economic behavior is multifaceted and context-dependent. However, the so-called Homo Oeconomicus model states that agents are perfectly rational, self-interest-maximizing beings. This model can be criticized on both empirical and normative grounds. Understanding economic behavior requires a more complex and dynamic framework.

In the "I & We" paradigm developed by Amitai Etzioni, economic behavior is co-determined by utility calculations and moral considerations. Two major factors can explain the ethicality of economic behavior; namely, the moral character of the agents and the relative cost of ethical behavior.

Economic agents are moral beings, but the ethical fabric of the economy determines which face of the Moral Economic Man predominates.

Keywords: economic behavior, rational choice, "I & We" paradigm, ethical fabric of the economy

3.1 Economic Behavior

It is a common belief in our age that people are motivated by their *own material well-being* when taking economic actions. This is the well-known Homo Oeconomicus image that depicts economic agents as rational, self-interest-maximizing beings. However, economic behavior is much more complex than the Homo Oeconomicus model suggests. People have rather different motivations, which may determine their economic choices (Jolls, Sunstein and Thaler 2000; Bowles and Gintis 2011).

Overwhelming empirical evidences suggest that

(i) people care about their *own material payoffs*;
(ii) people consider the interest of *others* they *know well*;
(iii) people are willing to *sacrifice* their own material well-being to *help* those who are *kind* to them and to *punish* those *unkind* to them;

The Moral Economic Man 37

(iv) people take into account the *well-being* of *strangers* whose interests are *at stake*;
(v)   people are interested in their *reputations* – what others think about their behavior;
(vi) people care about their *self-conceptions* – what kind of persons they wish to be. (Jolls, Sunstein and Thaler 2000)

Some interesting experimental results aptly illustrate the above-noted behavioral features (i) to (vi). The following famous studies provide strong *counter-evidences* for the Homo Oeconomicus model. They suggest that *people* are *moral beings* in their economic actions.

3.1.1 The Ultimatum Bargaining Game

The ultimatum bargaining game has two players, an allocator and a receiver. The allocator is given ten dollars to distribute between the receiver and herself or himself. The receiver has two options: accepting the offer, in which case each player gets the amount proposed by the allocator; or rejecting the offer, in which case each player gets nothing. The players play the game only once.

The Homo Oeconomicus model presupposes that the allocator will propose $9.99 for herself/himself and only $.01 to the other player, and that the receiver will accept this offer on the grounds that the utility of one penny is greater than zero. But this is not what happens in reality. Offers usually average between three and four dollars. Offers less than two dollars are often rejected. Frequently there is a fifty–fifty division. These results cut across diverse cultures and the level of stakes. (Sunstein 2000)

3.1.2 Choices in Prisoner's Dilemma Situations

The Homo Oeconomicus model predicts that people will always defect in a prisoner's dilemma game situation. Each player may believe that it would pay more if she or he were non-cooperative since the other player is also expected to be non-cooperative.

Robert H. Frank and his colleagues conducted their prisoner's dilemma experiment with real money several hundred times. The subjects met in groups of three. Each was told that she or he would play the game once only with each of the other two subjects. Confidentiality was maintained so that none of the players would learn how their partners had responded in any play of the game. The rate of *cooperation* ranged between 40 and 62 per cent.

To refine their experiment Frank and his colleagues asked subjects whether they would cooperate or defect in a one-shot prisoner's dilemma game if they *knew* with certainty that their *partner* was going to *cooperate*. The answers for cooperation ranged between 42 and 66 per cent. (Frank et al. 1993)

3.1.3 Lost Letter Experiment

Anthony M. Yezer and his colleagues conducted the so-called "lost-letter" experiment (Yezer et al. 1996). The letter was placed in an unsealed, stamped, plain white envelope, with a single name and address on the front and no return address. Inside were ten $1 bills along with a brief handwritten note indicating that the enclosed currency was for repayment of an informal loan.

Thirty-two letters were left in upper level economics classes; an equal number of letters were left in upper level classes in other disciplines such as psychology, political science, and history. The Homo Oeconomicus model predicts that people will not return the lost letters. Contrary to this expectation, 31 to 56 per cent of the letters were *returned*.

This experimental evidence indicates that people display *respect* for the *interests* of *strangers*. The returned envelopes also provided some qualitative evidence on student reactions to the lost letters. In two cases, students added messages indicating that they had made extraordinary efforts to locate the addressee, including checking the student directory, the telephone directory and the university registrar. (Yezer et al. 1996)

3.1.4 Contribution to the Public Good

In their pioneering study, *Gerald Marwell* and *Ruth Ames* designed an experiment where subjects were given some initial endowment of money that they were to allocate between two accounts, the "public" and the "private". Money deposited in the subject's private account was returned to the subject dollar-for-dollar at the end of the experiment. Money deposited in the public account was pooled, multiplied by a factor greater than unity, and finally distributed equally among all subjects.

The Homo Oeconomicus model anticipates a subject putting the entire endowment into the private account. From a social point of view the optimal behavior is to put the entire endowment into the public account. Marwell and Armes found that subjects *contributed* an average of 20 to 49 per cent of their initial endowment into the *public account*. Certainly subjects were "concerned with fairness" when making their decisions. (Marwell and Ames 1981)

3.1.5 Trust

In a game of trust, *Edward Glaeser* and his collaborators paired-off players, some of who knew each other in real life. The first player received $15, of which he or she could give any part to the second player, hidden from view. The amount transmitted was doubled by the researchers, and the second player then sent any part he wished of the new amount back to the first player. Here the trusting outcome is for the first player to send the full $15 to the second. Then, provided that the second player is worthy of the first's trust, both can walk away with $15. Nevertheless, the Homo Oeconomicus model predicts that the first player will keep the entire $15.

The first players *sent* an average of $12.41 to their partners, who *returned* an average of 45 per cent of the doubled sum. The existence of a *previous acquaintance* affected behavior: both the amount initially sent, and the percentage returned by the second player, rose in proportion to the length of time the players had known each other. (Glaeser et al. 2000)

3.2 Problems of Rationality

The *rational choice model* has been widely used in economics, political science, and other social sciences as a basic model of human choice behavior. The model states that the *agent* should *maximize* her or his *utility function* to be considered rational.

Agents are considered rational if their preferences are transitive and complete and they choose what they most prefer among the available alternatives.

The rational choice model does not presuppose anything about the preferences people have. They may have self-centered, altruistic, or even sado-masochistic preferences. The rational choice model represents a *formal theory* that says nothing about what people prefer or should prefer. Hereafter this model is referred as the *weak form* of *rationality*.

In economics and also in political science we can find a much stronger version of rationality where the assumptions of *self-interest* and *perfect knowledge* are added to the weak form of rationality. Hence we get the already discussed *Homo Oeconomicus* model according to which individuals are rational, exclusively self-interested, and have perfect knowledge about the consequences of their choices. The Homo Oeconomicus model does have *substantive assumptions* about what people want and the manner in which they want it. This model is hereafter referred to as the *strong form* of *rationality*. (Zsolnai 2009)

3.2.1 Bounded Rationality

Herbert A. Simon has been a relentless critic of the rational choice model for decades. He states that the model has overly strong claims on human beings. Real people have poor cognitive capacity and the information available to them is rather limited in most cases.

Agents in the real world are not capable of maximizing their utility function. Instead of maximizing, they usually make "satisficing" decisions.

They usually choose the first available alternative that is good enough for them in the sense that it satisfies their aspiration level. This is the main message of the *theory* of *bounded rationality* for which Simon received the Nobel Prize in Economics.

Simon writes, "Faced with a choice situation where it is impossible to optimize, or where the computational cost of doing so seems burdensome, the decision maker may look for a satisfactory, rather than an optimal alternative. Frequently, a course of action satisfying a number of constraints, even a sizeable number, is far easier to discover than a course of action maximizing some function." (Simon 1982, p. 244.)

The question arises of how a decision maker may set the level of criteria that define "satisfactory." "Psychology proposes the mechanism of aspiration levels: if it turns out to be very easy to find alternatives that meet the criteria, the standards are gradually raised; if the search continues for a long while without finding satisfactory alternatives, the standards are gradually lowered. Thus, by a kind of feedback mechanism, or 'tatonement', the decision maker converges toward a set of criteria that are attainable, but not without effort. The difference between the aspiration level mechanism and the optimization procedure is that the former calls for much simpler computations than the latter." (Simon 1982, p. 244.)

During the last decades abundant empirical evidence has been produced by economists and psychologists that shows that bounded rationality is important in real-world situations.

3.2.2 Myopic and Deficient Choices

Psychologist *Daniel Kahneman* criticizes the rational choice model on the basis of research findings, which indicate that people are *myopic* in their decisions, may lack skill in predicting their future tastes, and can be led to *erroneous choices* by fallible memory and incorrect evaluation of past experiences. (Kahneman 2011)

Kahneman differentiates between experienced utility and predicted utility. The *experienced utility* of an outcome is the measure of the hedonic experience of that outcome. The *predicted utility* of an outcome is defined as the individual's beliefs about its experienced utility at some future time. Predicted utility is an *ex ante* variable, while experienced utility is an *ex post* variable in the decision-making process.

According to the rational choice model, decisions are made on the basis of predicted utility. If experienced utility greatly differs from predicted utility then this may lead to sub-rational, or even irrational choices.

The problem of predicted utility raises the question: "Do people know what they will like?" The answer is a definite "No." The accuracy of people's hedonic predictions is generally quite poor.

Experimental studies suggest two conclusions: (i) people may have little ability to forecast changes in their hedonic responses to stimuli; and (ii) even in situations that permit accurate hedonic predictions, people may tend to make decisions about future consumption without due consideration of possible changes in their tastes. (Kahneman 2011)

Discrepancies between *retrospective utility* and *real-time* utility should also be addressed. This leads to the question: "Do people know what they have liked?" The answer is again a definite "No." Psychological experiments show that retrospective evaluations should be viewed with greater distrust than introspective reports of current experience.

The results of these studies support the following two empirical generalizations: (1) *The Peak – End Rule*: global evaluations are predicted with high accuracy by a weighted combination of the most extreme affect recorded during the episode and of the affect recorded during the terminal moments of the episode. (2) *Duration Neglect*. The retrospective evaluation of overall or total pain (or pleasure) is not affected by the duration period. (Kahneman 2011)

Since individuals use their evaluative memories to guide them in their choices toward future outcomes, deceptive retrospective evaluations may lead to erroneous choices.

Kahneman identifies two major obstacles to the maximization of experienced utility required by the rational choice model. People lack skill in the task of predicting how their tastes might change. It is difficult to describe as rational agents who are prone to large errors in predicting what they will want or enjoy next week. Another obstacle is a tendency to use the affect associated with particular moments as a proxy for the utility of

The Moral Economic Man

extended outcomes. Observations of memory biases are significant because the evaluation of the past determines what is learned from it. Errors in the lessons drawn from experience will inevitably be reflected in deficient choices for the future. (Kahneman 2011)

3.2.3 Rational Fools

Nobel Laureate economist Amartya Sen concluded that if real people behaved in the way that is required of them by the rational choice model then they would act like "rational fools."

Sen criticizes both the weak and strong forms of rationality. He refers to the weak form as "internal consistency of choice" and to the strong form as "maximization of self-interest."

He states, "It is hard to believe that internal consistency of choice can itself be an adequate condition of rationality. If a person does exactly the opposite of what would help achieving what he or she would want to achieve, and does this with flawless internal consistency (always choosing exactly the opposite of what will enhance the occurrence of things he or she wants and values), the person can scarcely be seen as rational. (...) Rational choice must demand something at least about the correspondence between what one tries to achieve and how one goes about it." (Sen 1987, p. 13.)

Sen uses the term "*correspondence rationality*" to describe the correspondence of choice with the aims and values of the agent. He states that this kind of correspondence must be a necessary condition of rationality, regardless of whether or not it is also the sufficient condition. Correspondence rationality might be supplemented by some requirements on the nature of the reflection regarding what the actor should want and value. (Sen 1987, pp. 13–14.)

It might well be arguable that rational behavior must demand some consistency, but consistency itself can hardly be adequate to ensure the rationality of choice. Internal consistency is not a guarantee of a person's rationality.

Rationality as *self-interest maximization* has additional problems. Sen asks, "Why should it be uniquely rational to pursue one's own self-interest to the exclusion of everything else?" Sen argues that the self-interest view of rationality "involves inter alia a firm rejection of the 'ethics-based' view of motivation. Trying to do one's best to achieve what one would like to achieve can be a part of rationality, and this can include the promotion of non-self-interested goals which we may value and wish to aim at. To see any departure from self-interest maximization as evidence of irrationality must imply a rejection of the role of ethics in actual decision making." (Sen 1987, p. 15.)

According to Sen, "universal selfishness as actuality may well be false, but universal selfishness as a requirement of rationality is patently absurd." (Sen 1987, p. 16.)

Rationality can be interpreted broadly as the discipline of subjecting one's choice – of action as well as objectives, values, and priorities – to reasoned scrutiny. In the light of this definition, reasonable economic choices should not necessarily satisfy the criteria of "internal consistency of choice" or "maximizing self-interest". Economic choices should be subjected to the demands of reason. (Sen 2002)

3.2.4 *The Strategic Role of Emotions*

Behavioral economist *Robert Frank* developed a model that emphasizes the role of the emotions in making choices. Frank argues that *passions* often *serve our interest* very well indeed because we face important problems that are simply unsolvable by rational action. "Emotions often predispose us to behave in ways that are contrary to our narrow interests, and being thus predisposed can be an advantage." (Frank 1988, pp. 4–7.)

Human behavior is directly guided by a complex psychological reward mechanism. Rational calculations are the input for the reward mechanism. "Feelings and emotions, apparently, are the proximate causes of most behavior. (...) The reward theory of behavior tells us that these sentiments can and do compete with feelings that spring from rational calculations about material payoffs." (Frank 1988, pp. 51–53.)

The modular brain theory supports Frank's ideas. According to the modular theory, the brain is organized into a host of separate modules.

Each module has its own capacity for processing information and motivating behavior. Most of these brain modules do not "speak"; they simply do not have language capability. Even more importantly, these non-language modules are not equally well connected to the central language module of the brain. Perhaps this is the cause of the seeming disparity between different methods of assessing motivation.

Modular brain theorists view the language module of the brain as the center of our rational consciousness, obsessed with rationalizing all that we feel and do. However, there is a great deal of information that enters the central nervous system that cannot be accessed by the language module. The modular brain theory suggests, "that when economists talk about maximizing utility, they are really talking about the language module of the left hemisphere, however, it does not account for all of our behavior. (...) The rational utility-maximizing language module of the brain may simply be ill-equipped to deal with many of the most important problems we face." (Frank 1988, pp. 205–211.)

Frank's main conclusion is that persons *directly motivated* to *pursue their self-interest* are often doomed to *fail* for exactly that reason. Problems can often be solved by persons who have abandoned the quest for maximal material advantage. The *emotions* that lead people to *behave* in *irrational ways* can indirectly lead to *greater material well-being*. (Frank 1988, pp. 258–259.)

3.2.5 Social Norms

After a decade-long preoccupation with the rational choice model, sociologist *Jon Elster* developed an alternative theory that he calls the *theory* of *social norms* (Elster 1989, 2007). Elster contrasts rational action with norm-guided behavior. Rational action is outcome-oriented. Rationality says: "If you want to achieve X, do Y." Elster defines social norms as devices that are not outcome-oriented. Social norms say "Do X" or "Do not do Y" or "If you do X then do Y" or "Do X if it would be good if everyone did X."

"Rationality is essentially conditional and future-oriented. Its imperatives are hypothetical; that is, conditional on the future outcomes one wants to realize. The imperatives expressed in social norms are either unconditional or, if conditional, not future-oriented. In the latter case norms make the action dependent on past events or (more rarely) on hypothetical outcomes." (Elster 1989, p. 98.)

Not all norms are social. There are two requisite conditions for norms to be considered *social*. First, they must be shared by other people and second, partly *sustained* by their approval or disapproval. "In addition to being supported by the attitudes of other people, norms are sustained by the feelings of embarrassment, anxiety, guilt and shame that a person suffers at the prospect of violating them, or at least at the prospect of being caught violating them. Social norms have a grip on the mind that is due to the strong emotions their violations can trigger. (...) A norm, in this perspective, is the propensity to feel shame and to anticipate sanctions by others at the thought of behaving in a certain, forbidden way." (Elster 1989, pp. 99–100 and p. 105.)

Elster argues for the reality and autonomy of social norms. By the *reality* of *norms* he means that norms have independent motivating power. Norms are not merely ex post rationalization of self-interest. They serve as ex ante sources of action. Autonomy of norms means their *irreducibility* to *optimization*. Norms are partly shaped by self-interest because people often adhere to the norms that favor them. However, norms are not fully reducible to self-interest. The unknown residual is a brute fact. (Elster 1989, p. 125 and p. 150.)

3.2.6 The Communitarian Challenge

Communitarian thinkers criticize the *liberal conception* of the *self* that is at the heart of the rational choice model.

Philosopher *Charles Taylor* has argued that the liberal conception of the self is basically an *atomistic conception* of the person and that of human agency focusing exclusively on will and freedom of choice. Taylor defends a *relational, inter-subjective* conception of the self that stresses the social, cultural, historical, and linguistic constitution of personal identity. By rejecting the voluntaristic conception of human agency he has formulated a cognitive conception that emphasizes the role of critical reflection, self-interpretation, and rational evaluation. (Taylor 1985)

Catholic philosopher *Alasdair MacIntyre* defends a teleological and contextualist view of human agency. According to him, moral conduct is characterized by the *exercise* of *virtues* that aims at realization of the good. No agent can properly locate, interpret, and evaluate her or his actions except by participating in a moral tradition or in a moral community. (MacIntyre 1988)

3.2.7 Feminist Criticism

In feminist literature the rational choice theory, and especially the strong form of rationality, is often criticized for presupposing an *androcentric, male-biased* conception of the human person, the so-called *separative self*. (Ferber and Nelson 1993; Nelson 2006)

In her book "Beyond Self-Interest", *Jane J. Mansbridge* offers an alternative theory of choice that is inspired by feminine values. She distinguishes three forms of motivation, namely *duty, self-interest*, and *love*. Starting with her own case she says, "I have a duty to care for my child, and I am happy by his happiness, and I get a simple sensual pleasure from snuggling close to him as I read him a book. I have a principled commitment to work for women's liberation, and I empathize with women, and I find a way to use some of my work for women as background to a book that advances my academic career. Duty, love (or empathy), and self-interest are intermingled in my actions in a way I can rarely sort out." (Mansbridge 1990, p. 134.)

Mansbridge favors the coincidence of duty and love with self-interest. She says that both forms of non-self-interested motives (empathic feelings and moral commitments) are embedded in a social context, which makes them susceptible to being undermined by self-interested behavior on the part of others. Arrangements are required that generate some self-interested return for non-self-interested behavior to create an "ecological niche" for sustaining such behavior. Arrangements that make the absence of self-interested behavior less costly in self-interested terms increase the degree to which individuals feel that they can afford to indulge their feelings of empathy and their moral commitments. (Mansbridge 1990, pp. 136–137.)

Based on the criticisms reported above we can say that the rational choice model is *empirically misleading* and *normatively inadequate*. For understanding economic behavior, a more complex and dynamic framework is needed.

3.3   The "I & We" Paradigm

Amitai Etzioni developed a theory that he calls *socio-economics*. He introduced the so-called *I & We paradigm* that "sees individuals as able to act rationally and on their own, advancing their self or 'I', but their ability to do so is deeply affected by how well they are anchored within a sound community and sustained by a firm moral and emotive personal underpinning – a community they perceive as theirs, as 'We.'" (Etzioni 1988)

Etzioni presents a new model of decision making in which people typically choose means largely on the basis of emotions and value judgments, and only secondarily on the basis of logical-empirical considerations.

In Etzioni's model, two irreducible sources of valuations play a role, namely *pleasure* and *morality*. "Individuals are, simultaneously, under the influence of two major sets of factors – their pleasure, and their moral duty (although both reflect socialization). (...) There are important differences in the extent each of these sets of factors is operative under different historical and societal conditions, and within different personalities under the same conditions." (Etzioni 1988, p. 63.)

The relationship between pleasure and morality is that while both affect choice, they also affect one another. However, each factor is only partially shaped by the other; that is, each factor has a considerable measure of autonomy. This co-determination model is shown by Figure 3.1.

The Moral Economic Man 49

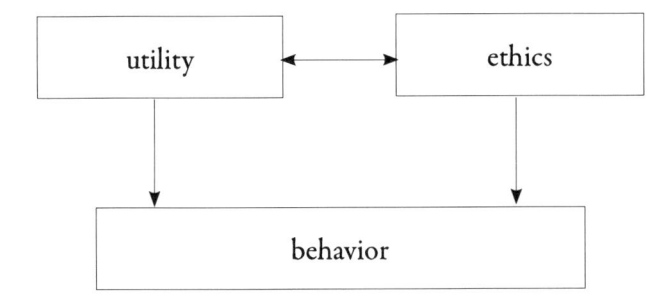

```
  ┌──────────┐          ┌──────────┐
  │ utility  │◄────────►│  ethics  │
  └────┬─────┘          └─────┬────┘
       │                      │
       ▼                      ▼
  ┌─────────────────────────────────┐
  │            behavior             │
  └─────────────────────────────────┘
```

Figure 3.1 *Etzioni's Socio-economic Model*

Etzioni states that "people do not seek to maximize their pleasure, but to balance their service of the two major purposes – to advance their well-being and to act morally." (Etzioni 1988, p. 83.)

3.4 The Ethical Fabric of the Economy

Economic behavior is co-determined by utility calculations and moral considerations. The *major factors* that can help in understanding behavior can be identified:

(i) the moral character of the agents;
(ii) the relative cost of ethical behavior.

Moral character refers to the strength of the moral beliefs and commitments of the agents. In a given situation, the *relative cost* of *ethical behavior* is determined by the cost of an ethical option compared against the cost of the unethical option in terms of transaction cost and opportunity loss.

We can predict the ethicality of economic behavior by combining the moral character of the agents and the relative cost of ethical behavior. If the moral character of the agents is strong and the relative cost of ethical behavior is low, then ethical behavior can be expected. If the moral character of the agents is weak and the relative cost of ethical behavior is high, then unethical behavior can be expected (Figure 3.2).

strong moral character ⟶ ethical behavior
low relative cost of ethical behavior ⟶

weak moral character ⟶ unethical behavior
high relative cost of ethical behavior ⟶

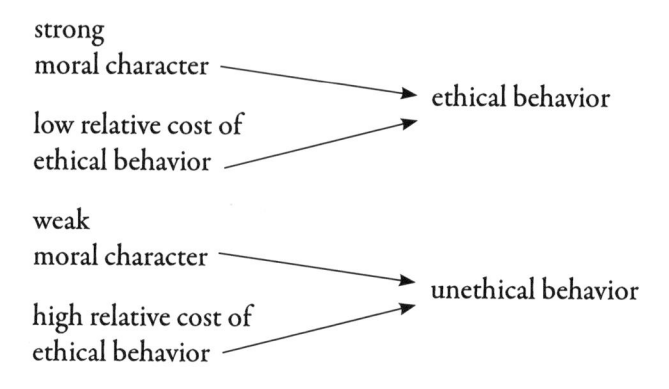

Figure 3.2 *Determinants of the Ethicality of Behavior*

The level of corruption in different countries is a good illustration. *Transparency International* produces the corruption ranking of countries year by year. Their ranking for 2011 is shown in Table 3.1.

Table 3.1 *Corruption Indices of Selected Countries in 2011*
Source: Transparency International 2011: Corruption Perceptions Index 2011

Rank	Country	Score
1	New Zealand	9.5
2	Denmark	9.4
2	Finland	9.4
4	Sweden	9.3
5	Singapore	9.2
6	Norway	9.0
7	Netherlands	8.9

8	Australia	8.8
8	Switzerland	8.8
10	Canada	8.7
...		
24	United States	7.1
25	France	7.0
...		
50	Oman	4.8
50	Seychelles	4.8
54	Hungary	4.6
...		
177	Sudan	1.6
177	Turkmenistan	1.6
177	Uzbekistan	1.6
180	Afghanistan	1.5
180	Myanmar	1.5
182	Korea (North)	1.0
182	Somalia	1.0

A corruption index measures the likelihood that a particular economic transaction involves corruption in a given country. New Zealand, Denmark, Finland, Sweden, Singapore, and Norway are countries where corruption is virtually nonexistent. In these countries, economic agents have high moral expectations and at the same time, it is *easy* to *behave ethically*. In the most corrupt countries – such as Sudan, Turkmenistan, Uzbekistan, Afghanistan, Myanmar, North Korea, and Somalia – economic agents have low moral expectations, and at the same time it is *difficult* to *behave ethically*.

3.5 Conclusion

Economic agents are moral beings. The context determines which face of the Moral Economic Man predominates. Some hypotheses can be generated about the conditions, which mitigate the behavior of the Moral Economic Man for better or worse.

(i) The stronger the collective belief in the ethical norms by the economic actors, the less one can expect unethical behavior from them.
(ii) The stronger the pro-social orientation of the economic actors, the more one can expect ethical behavior from them.
(iii) The greater the social costs of transgression by the economic actors, the less one can expect unethical behavior from them.
(iv) The greater the transparency and accountability of the economic actors, the more one can expect ethical behavior from them.

Collective belief in the ethical norms, pro-socialness of agents, high cost of transgression, as well as transparency and accountability, are all major conditions for the proper functioning of the Moral Economic Man.

References

Bowles, S. and Gintis, H. (2011) *A Cooperative Species: Human Reciprocity and Its Evolution*. Princeton, NJ: Princeton University Press.
Elster, J. (1989) *The Cement of Society*. Cambridge: Cambridge University Press.
Elster, J. (2007) *Explaining Social Behavior: More Nuts and Bolts for the Social Sciences*. Cambridge: Cambridge University Press.
Etzioni, A. (1988) *The Moral Dimension*. New York: The Free Press.

Etzioni, A. (1992) Normative-Affective Factors: Toward a New Decision-Making Model. In Zey, Mary (ed.) *Decision Making: Alternatives to Rational Choice Models*. Newbury Park, CA: Sage Publications, pp. 89–111.
Ferber, M. A. and Nelson, J. A. (eds) (1993) *Beyond Economic Man*. Chicago and London: University of Chicago Press.
Frank, R. (1988) *Passions Within Reason*. New York and London: W. W. Norton.
Frank, R. H., Gilovich, T. and Regan, D. T. (1993) Does Studying Economics Inhibit Co-operation? *Journal of Economic Perspectives*, Spring, pp. 159–171.
Glaeser, E. L. et al. (2000) Measuring Trust. *Quarterly Journal of Economics*, 115 (3): pp. 811–846.
Jolls, C., Sunstein, C. R. and Thaler, R. H. (2000) Overview and Prospects. In: Sunstein, C. R. (ed.) *Behavioral Law and Economics*. Cambridge: Cambridge University Press, pp. 13–58.
Kahneman, D. (2011) *Thinking, Fast and Slow*. New York: Farrar, Straus and Giroux.
MacIntyre, A. (1988) *Whose Justice? Which Rationality?* Notre Dame, IN: University of Notre Dame Press.
Mansbridge, J. J. (1990) On the Relation of Altruism and Self-Interest. In: Mansbridge, J. J. (ed.) *Beyond Self-Interest*. Chicago and London: University of Chicago Press, pp. 133–143.
Marwell, G. and Ames, R. (1981) Economists Free Ride, Does Anyone Else? *Journal of Public Economics*, 15: pp. 295–310.
Nelson, J. A. (2006) *Economics for Humans*. Chicago and London: University of Chicago Press.
Sen, A. (1987) *On Ethics and Economics*. Oxford: Blackwell.
Sen, A. (2002) *Rationality and Freedom*. Cambridge, MA: Harvard University Press.
Simon, H. A. (1982) *Models of Bounded Rationality*. Cambridge, MA and London: MIT Press.
Sunstein, C. R. (2000) Introduction. In Sunstein, C. R. (ed.) *Behavioral Law and Economics*. Cambridge: Cambridge University Press, pp. 1–10.
Taylor, Ch. (1985) *Philosophical Papers*. Cambridge: Cambridge University Press.
Thaler, R. H. (1991) *Quasi Rational Economics*. New York: Russell Sage Foundation.
Transparency International (2011) *Corruption Perceptions Index 2011*. Berlin: Transparency International.
Yezer, A. M., Goldfarb, R. S. and Poppen, P. J. (1996) Does Studying Economics Discourage Co-operation? Watch What We Do, Not What We Say or How We Play. *Journal of Economic Perspectives*, 10 (1): pp. 177–186.
Zsolnai, L. (2009) *Responsible Decision Making*. New Brunswick, NJ and London: Transaction Publishers.

ALOY SOPPE
(ERASMUS UNIVERSITY ROTTERDAM)

4 Ethics and the Theory of the Firm

4.1 Introduction: Finance and Ethics

4.2 Theory of the Firm
    4.2.1 Neoclassical Approach
    4.2.2 The Firm as a Nexus of Contracts
    4.2.3 Ethics and the Theory of the Firm

4.3 An Ethical Framework
    4.3.1 Virtue Ethics
    4.3.2 Deontological ethics
    4.3.3 Teleological Ethics

4.4 Alternative Approaches in Finance
    4.4.1 Behavioral Approaches
    4.4.2 Corporate Social Responsibility
    4.4.3 In Search of an Ethical Theory of the Firm
    4.4.4 Virtue Ethics and Finance
    4.4.5 Finance and Ethics

4.5 Conclusion

Abstract

The shareholder paradigm is no longer a suitable concept in the current stage of market capitalism. The traditional theory of the firm is too restrictive to incorporate ethical values into the financial framework. In the property rights model, it is the shareholder that holds the residual risk and therefore receives the residual profit. The company is considered as a set of direct investments projects that converts inputs into outputs. From this materialistic viewpoint, a company is not a system of cooperating persons but a contracting institute that produces cash flow. From this perspective no social responsibility is involved. This neoclassical approach is justified by selecting the shareholders as the optimal stakeholders in order to reduce the agency cost. This line of argument denies any explicit relationship between social cohesion and operational efficiency.

In the "ethical finance" approach, the neoclassical paradigm is replaced by a broader view. In addition to the necessity of competition and profitability, it includes care for the environment, the social and physical health of the employees, and a moral responsibility for the risk run by creditors and other stakeholders. Unbridled competition encourages operational efficiency, but at the same time it is not a well-balanced allocation mechanism. Sustainable behavior often requires increasing governance costs and therefore higher agency costs. On the other hand, in a safer and more stable environment, contracting costs may fall and create additional wealth for society overall.

Keywords: shareholder paradigm, ethics and finance, virtue ethics, deontological ethics, teleological ethics, sustainable growth

4.1 Introduction: Finance and Ethics

In 2007, financial capitalism in the USA and Europe entered the stage of the Roller Coaster Economy. The collapse of Lehman and Brothers, the US bailout of AIG, and the takeover of Bear Stearns by JP Morgan Chase, for example, stressed the international financial markets in such a way that governments all over the world felt obliged to bail out major local banks. The resulting depression in the US economy negatively influenced the global economy. Moreover, the 2010 European debt crisis, triggered by countries like Greece, Portugal, Ireland, Italy, and Spain, intensified the Western financial crisis. While banks have problems with sound solvency and liquid money markets, this sector can be considered a catalyst of negative economic cycles and depressions. The lack of trust in the financial sector seriously threatens the global economy.

Finance and ethics: contradiction or paradox? Despite the rapidly growing interest in business ethics, the development of finance and ethics as a topic is relatively slow. It seems that the intervention of money in economic transactions alienates humans from the moral implications of economic trade. Traditional financial theory reduces economic relations to the behavior of "rational economic man." From that perspective, human behavior can be represented by neoclassical utility functions where agents optimize their individual preferences. The Neumann & Morgenstern axioms facilitate a set of strict assumptions in financial theory that enable a smooth, quantitative approach wherein more is always better than less. At first sight, the resulting mathematical and econometric approach seems to be value free and morally neutral. When we take a closer look at the underlying ethical values, however, we must conclude that the finance-scientific approach is inherently normative.

An alternative approach to describing human behavior is provided by Aristotle. He was the first to analyze the influence of money and prices in the chain of the physical production process. He stated that money could never be an end in itself for "a virtuous man," but should always be a means towards a higher end (Meikle 1995, p. 96). Although this statement is more than 2,000 years old, it is relevant today. Money and the role of financial institutions have been debated throughout history (see Davies 1994). The discussion on "Usury" in the late Middle Ages reflects the natural connection between money and ethical values. Even today, religions have well-developed views on how to cope with money (see Chapter 12).

Surveying the financial industry over the last four decades, we must realize that fundamental changes have taken place. First there was the *communications revolution* that facilitated the financing sector in such a *globalizing* way that it changed its culture from a servicing character into a leading position in the process of economic growth. Making money for the sake of making money has become a well-accepted goal. The investment industry, for example, used to be a gentlemen's business that primarily served its clients, based on high standards of honesty, integrity, care, and diligence. In the profession nowadays, the entry barriers have disappeared and the key employees are creative, risk-taking, success-driven, analytical, and intelligent people who lack training in the common ethical values of the profession (Caccese 1997). Before the 2008 banking crisis, many company treasurers acted as if capital should be more productive than the real economic activities on the asset side of their company's balance sheet. This attitude, including the bonus culture, is now heavily criticized.

A second important aspect of the changing financial environment is the *securitization process* of international financial markets. Since the 1990s a gradual change took place as market traded assets became more important than traditional bank lending instruments. Financial and cultural change influenced the increasing role of the international institutional investors and the necessary risk diversification and reinsurance processes. The introduction and success of special purpose vehicles (SPV) and credit default swaps (CDS) facilitated the mortgage bubble that existed prior to the banking crisis. Closely related to this trend was the substantial rise of the trade of off-balance-sheet products or derivatives. The inherent volatility of underlying assets prices required an adequate set of financial instruments to manage the financial exposure.

A third important factor regarding the responsibility for social welfare is the growing influence of the *civil society*. During the last decades, Europe in particular can be characterized by sizable privatization projects of industries that traditionally belonged to the domain of the public sector. The increase in private competition created a competitive advantage for the private sector over the public sector. The major question is whether financial market liberalization encouraged this more politically engaged process, or whether the trend towards national privatization was driven by political liberalization and globalization. The fact is that a growing number of companies do realize that they have not only an economic responsibility, but also a responsibility towards other stakeholders.

Behavioral economics and the banking crisis have encouraged alternative approaches to corporate governance and globalization. From these perspectives the shareholder paradigm is considered to be a normative choice in favor of agents that primarily represent the interests of the production factor capital. Section 4.2 describes the existing *theories of the firm*, especially the shareholder paradigm and the stakeholder approach to the company. We provide some arguments for a stronger integration of ethics. In section 4.3 an ethical framework is introduced in order to benchmark the normative character of finance as a discipline. This uses the teleological, the deontological, and the virtue-ethical approach (e.g., see Baron et al. 1997). Section 4.4 presents several alternative perspectives of finance and corporate governance, and section 4.5 summarizes the relationship of finance and ethics in the modern market economy. We conclude with the idea of sustainable growth and argue that a virtue-ethical approach is better suited to modern finance than the traditionally used utilitarian ethics.

4.2 Theory of the Firm

Analyzing the market economy basically starts with an analysis of the "theory of the firm." Boatright (1999), for example, suggests that the acceptance of shareholders as owners of the firm is dependent on the theory of the firm that underlies the model. He distinguishes three different theories of the firm. The first, the *property rights model*, is the standard neoclassical approach, which will be explained in section 4.2.1. The other two theories, namely the *contractual theory* and the *social institution theory*, will be discussed in section 4.2.2.

4.2.1 Neoclassical Approach

In his classic paper "The Nature of the Firm" Ronald Coase (1937) explicitly poses the question of why companies exist. He argues that in perfect markets, the company is the cheapest and most efficient way to organize production. Informational costs and transaction costs can be lowered compared with individuals working together. Moreover, long-term contracts are considered good instruments against short-term uncertainty. Later, Alchian and Demsetz (1972) showed that within a company the synergy effects of teamwork are an important element and they argued that shirking behavior can be monitored more easily too. Williamson (1985) then refined and extended these ideas into what is called the "transaction costs economics." He even concluded that minimizing transaction costs through organizational production can be considered a moral justification of the company.

In the *property rights model* – see, for example, Grossman and Hart (1986) – the shareholders are the owners of the firm that chooses to do business in corporate form. Shareholders differ from other constituencies of the firm only by virtue of being residual risk bearers and therefore residual claimholders. The crux of the shareholders wealth paradigm is that shareholders are considered optimally suited to maximize the wealth of society through their natural ability to discipline the management. As owners of the corporation they demand that managers maximize their wealth by investing in all possible positive net present value (NPV) projects. However, the agency theory describes and assumes in the neoclassical model that managers act primarily according to their own interest. It is therefore necessary that monitoring and bonding costs be effectuated in markets in order to discipline the managers (Jensen and Meckling 1976). Since every manager is assumed to be selfish, the incentive for managers to act according to the shareholders' interests is subsequently based on the bonding and monitoring abilities of the shareholders.

The theoretical funding described above dominated the governance paradigm for many decades. The ABN AMRO takeover in 2007 is a good example of the shareholder paradigm. (Box 4.1)

> Box 4.1 *Example of Aggressive Takeover and Unsustainable Behavior*
>
> In 2007, in the turbulence before the Western banking crisis, there was a fierce corporate governance battle between the shareholders and the management of ABN AMRO bank, the 8th largest bank of Europe at that time. In February 2007, one of the bank's shareholders, the hedge fund *The Children's Investment Fund* (TCI), which owned 1 per cent of the shares, put pressure on the management for higher returns on its share by urging it either to split up the company in order to increase shareholder wealth, or to accept a takeover bid. One month later, ABN AMRO announced a merger with Barclays, to create the second largest bank in Europe. Later that year, a consortium consisting of Fortis, Royal Bank of Scotland (RBS), and Banco Santander proved to be the highest bidder and announced their plan to buy ABN AMRO. After the collective takeover they intended to split up ABN AMRO immediately and to divide its activities between the consortium members. he management of ABN AMRO preferred Barclays' offer despite the lower price, because Barclays was said to have a better "strategic vision." The CEO of the Board of ABN AMRO, Groenink and another board member were expected to join the new board of Barclays. After the announcement of the consortium, the management sold a part of its American activities, the subsidiary LaSalle to Bank of America, making ABN AMRO a less interesting target for a takeover by the consortium.
>
> Nevertheless, the consortium did not withdraw its offer and eventually offered a 9.8 per cent higher price than Barclays. The shareholders chose the highest bidder, being the consortium, despite other preferences of the management. Groenink left ABN AMRO shortly after the takeover. The takeover turned out to be a major contribution to the downfall of Fortis and the performance of RBS during the financial crisis. In 2008, Fortis had to sell their Dutch activities to the Dutch government because of liquidity problems. This case is a prime example of the "Winners Curse" – which is a result of pure financial market competition, but which often leads to social and environmental failures.

The neoclassical finance approach is rational and attractive as it enhances operational efficiency. The problem is that this one-dimensional material approach, as assumed because of its homogeneous expectations, encourages a general perception in society that finance is a purely positive science where rational behavior is the key to personal success. It is important to realize that this general attitude towards finance and financial theory is based on normative assumptions.

4.2.2 The Firm as a Nexus of Contracts

Boatright (1999) makes a case against the view of the shareholder as unique company owner and residual risk-taker. He argues that the shareholder can easily diversify his or her portfolio of stocks to eliminate idiosyncratic downside risk. The highly skilled employee on the other hand, who has developed valuable firm-specific human capital, may possibly assume considerably more residual risk. The labor market is far less efficient and flexible in comparison to the financial markets. Moreover, there is the interest of the environment as a stakeholder. As long as there are no private institutions that act on behalf of the environment, government or non-governmental organizations are its best representatives.

The stakeholder approach is facilitated by what is called the *contractual theory*, in which the corporation is sanctioned by the state to serve general welfare. Boatright (1999, p. 171) states that: "In contrast to the property rights theory, the contractual right theory does not hold that the firm is the private property of the shareholders. Rather, shareholders, along with other investors, employees and the like, each own assets that they make available to the state. Thus, the firm results from property rights and the right of contract of every corporate constituency *and not from the shareholder alone.*" Many other authors criticize the shareholder paradigm (e.g. Engelen 2002). Stout (2002, 2007) empirically shows that lawmakers, managers and even shareholders themselves do not prefer shareholder primacy rules but rather firms with strong board control.

Boatright (1999) also presents the *social institution theory*, which holds that the right to incorporate is a privilege granted by the state and therefore that the "right to incorporate" inherently has a public aspect. This is where politics and ethics explicitly come in. The central theoretical question is, who should be the optimal residual risk bearer of the company (and therefore claimant and responsible for the ultimate gains and losses)? Contracts only concern the consequences of the contracting economic agents. The influence of these contracts on third parties, for example the environment or the welfare of the society, is too often considered to be outside the realm of finance.

4.2.3   Ethics and the Theory of the Firm

The seminal criticisms by Sen (1987, 1993) and Fukuyama (1995) are examples of the major cultural criticisms on financial paradigms. However, there have also been many developments in the finance literature itself. For example, Bovenberg and Klundert (1999) state that neoclassical economics gives little attention to moral values. They fear that such a restricted economic scope encourages the "economizing of the society."

So what is the role of ethics in finance and the theory of the firm? Let us start with the classic yet nevertheless instructive model by Carroll (1996) from business ethics literature. (Figure 4.1, p. 64))

Carroll categorizes the activities of corporations in terms of four types of responsibilities. The *economic* and the *legal responsibilities* of companies are scarcely questioned by anyone in the market economy. The discussion starts with the *ethical* and the *philanthropic responsibilities*. Introducing these elements into economic terminology suggests the acceptance of moral values explicitly in economic actions. This is the crucial difference between the neoclassical approach based on shareholders' value and a broader concept of finance.

```
        Philanthropic Responsibilites
        Be a good corporate citizen
        Contribute resources to the
       community, improve the quality
                of life

         Ethical Responsibilites
              Be ethical
    Obligation to do what is right, just and fair.
              Avoid harm

          Legal Responsibilites
             Obey the law
   Law is societies codification of right and wrong
         Play by the rules of the game

         Economic Responsibilites
              Be profitable
  The foundation upon which all other factors rest
```

Figure 4.1 *Companies' Responsibilities*
Source: Carroll 1996

Because finance is dominated by legal contracts, and contracts always suggest explicit economic agents representing specific contractual institutions, modeling these relationships necessarily restricts itself to the parties involved. In other words, framing human behavior into financial trade is akin to stepping into a suit of armor. At the very moment when human actions are confirmed by contractual relations individual freedom is partially lost and the moral implications change drastically. An ethical approach to finance in this context is defined as a set of thought constructions in which financial transactions consider not only the economic consequences of the subjects in that transaction, but also the moral and the material and/or immaterial aspects of other stakeholders in the economy at hand and that of future generations. Alternatively, formulated in terms of Carroll's CSR (corporate social responsibility) pyramid (Figure 4.1), financial institutes do not just have economic and legal responsibilities, but also ethical and philanthropic responsibilities, which are considered part of a sustainable financial process.

The danger of treating finance as an independent science rather than as an integrated element of trust can be traced back to methodological origins. Contrary to the process of finance becoming a specialized discipline, Figure 4.2 presents a theory development indicating how new theoretical paradigms are implicitly based on a permanent process of historical knowledge-gathering. As in the "multi-model causation framework" used by Dembinski (2009), this figure emphasizes that the development of new theories should be based on integral normative choices with which positive models can be built and that can be transformed into new instruments of analysis. This holistic view of wealth creation links traditional knowledge of the shareholder paradigm to the normative choice of the stakeholder, and emphasizes the role of stewardship theory as an alternative to agency theory.

Past
Observation
– – –
Securitization
Short termism
Hedgefunds

Present
Problem Setting

Future
Developing instruments
– – –
Universal banking
Long termism
Stakeholder participation

KNOWLEDGE

Wealth creation through agency cost reduction

CHOICE

Theory
- Shareholder paradigm
- Agency

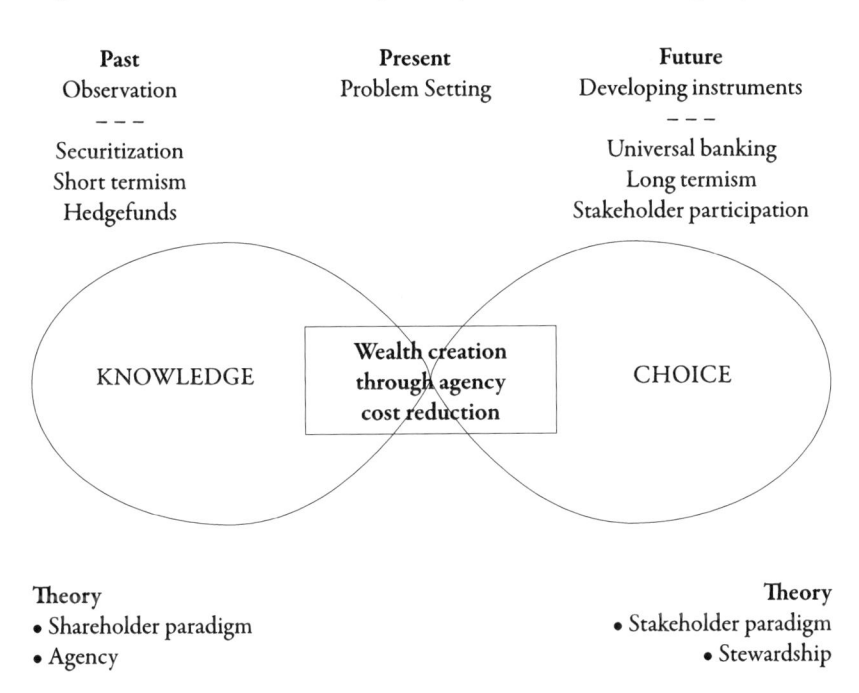

Theory
- Stakeholder paradigm
- Stewardship

Figure 4.2 *A Holistic View of Wealth Creation*
Source: Soppe 2010, p. 455

Dembinski's (2009) interdisciplinary approach to the financial system, which argues that finance is more a deceiver than a servant, is perfectly in line with the holistic approach to the financial system shown above, in which the future, the present, and the past are reconnected by the lemniscates. Dembinski argues that finance as a discipline needs to return to its most basic goals, which are to be a unit of account and a measure of exchange. The eighteenth-century François Quesnay, who along with Adam Smith is considered to be one of the founding fathers of the capitalist economy, compared the economy to a human body. Extending this metaphor, we can compare finance to the blood of a physical human body. Blood flows to and connects every part of the body, from head to toe. In this metaphor, finance can be thought of as the transportation mechanism used in distributing and redistributing wealth among economic agents. From that perspective, sustainable finance (see Soppe 2004) is a crucial element in the search for an ethical theory of the firm.

4.3 An Ethical Framework

It is not just finance practice that is developing; the role of ethics is also permanently debated in the literature. For example, James (2011) deepens ethics literature by introducing and discussing the role of natural selection and human nature. In particular the role of evolutionary and psychological adaptations in human behavior lead James to very interesting options for what is called "the evolutionary realist": learning right from wrong, response dependency, naturalizing virtue ethics, and moral constructivism. James argues, for good or ill, the "biologicalization" of ethics is underway (Jones et al. 2005), thus deepening the discussion on ethics by criticizing and emphasizing the problems of ethics. It is a right claim that business ethics promises far more than it delivers.

For reasons of simplicity, an ethical framework is used in this chapter that is well established in traditional business ethics literature. In accordance with Baron, Pettit, and Slote (1997), Donaldson and Werhane (1996), Boatright (1996), Koslowski (1995), and many others, we use the classical trios of deontological ethics, teleological ethics, and virtue ethics. We start with virtue ethics and Aristotle, its most inspiring representative. Then we discuss the deontological framework, basically inspired by Kant and Locke, and next teleological ethics, as represented by Bentham and Mill.

4.3.1 Virtue Ethics

Virtue ethics is described by Slote (1997, p. 177) as ethics that is *not* based on moral laws, rules and or principles. The focus is on the virtuous individual and on the inner traits, dispositions, and motives that qualify a person as being considered virtuous. Aristotle was one of the first philosophers to emphasize the importance of practical reasoning. For scholars in the Middle Ages, it created a theoretical framework on which to build their Christian perspective on human conduct.

Closely related to economics and finance is the Aristotelian discussion that suggests two products of different dimension must be comparable "in a way" (see Meikle 1995, p. 12). This problem of commensurability is introduced immediately when goods have to be exchanged. Aristotle divides what we call "economic value" into two parts: *use value* and *exchange value*. It is important to notice that the very moment at which use value becomes subordinate to exchange value in the pricing of goods or labor, ethics and virtues become less relevant in the transaction. If we include money in the transaction, by paying the exchange value, the alienation of the idea that we are also exchanging use values is strengthened. In the neoclassical paradigm of the financial market economy, using exchange values as prices, the process of making money has become a goal in itself. This is contrary to the original Aristotelian idea on the neutral use of money. Money can only be used as a means but never as an end, because acquiring money does not fit into Aristotle's notion of the "perfect life."

A recent interpretation of virtue ethics, as applied to business and finance, is provided by Solomon (1996). He describes the Aristotelian approach by using several dimensions. First there is the *community* and the idea that the self-interest in members of a community is largely identical to the greater interest of the group. Secondly, there is *excellence*. It is not enough to do no wrong, something additional called "excellence" is needed. Thirdly, Solomon mentions *role identity*. All ethics is contextual, and one of the problems with all the grand theories is that they attempt to transcend contexts and end up with vacuity. The fourth element is *integrity*. This is judged as the linchpin of all virtues. *Good Judgment*, the fifth element, gives careful consideration to the particularity of the persons and the circumstances involved. Finally, Solomon conveys the concept of *holism*. He criticizes the tunnel vision of business life, which is encouraged by the overly narrow business curriculum and the daily rhetoric of the corporate community. According to Solomon, a broader concept of economic proceedings is needed, and virtues are a simple way of summarizing the ideals that define "good character."

4.3.2 Deontological Ethics

The most prominent deontological theory (the word *deontological* is derived from *deon*, the Greek word for duty) is based on Kant's ethical theory as outlined in his *Fundamental Principles of the Metaphysics of Morals* (1785).

In deontological ethics, duty rather than virtue is the fundamental moral category. Kant characterizes moral rules as imperatives that express what human beings ought to do either hypothetically or categorically. An essential feature of categorical imperatives is the principle of universalizability. This implies that if someone says an act is right for one person, we are then committed to say it is right for all other persons in similar situations. So we should always ask ourselves: "What if everyone acted as I did?" If the act is acceptable for one, it might be acceptable for society. Another important characteristic (Boatright 1996, pp. 65–71) of Kant's work is the focus on human rights and respect for other people. Kant defines a right as "a moral capacity to bind others." Rights are divided by Kant into *innate*, those that belong to everyone and are "by nature," independent of any juridical act; and *acquired*, which depend on some human convention or juridical act. According to Kant, there is only one fundamental innate right, and that is the right to be free from the will of others insofar as this is compatible with a similar freedom for all.

The difference between duties and virtues is complicated. Kant wonders whether ethics and the legal system are based on metaphysical thinking. His answer is a clear yes (Kant 1797/1922, p. 35 Introduction). In his "Metaphysics of Morals" (1797), Kant starts with an extensive description of a country's legal system. This is needed because in the second part (Tugendlehre) he develops the "elementary ethical theory" (Ethische Elementarlehre) in terms of duties. Virtues are therefore laid down in terms of duties based on the legal system of a country. The term "duty" is necessary because of the existing legal control of discretion. It is a moral imperative that forces rational human beings, as a part of Nature, into the armor of duties. According to Kant this is all based on the moral freedom of humans, and we are discussing "ethical duties" which differ from legal duties. Kant distinguishes between "duties towards oneself" and "duties towards others." Well-known examples of duties to oneself include Kant's opinions on suicide and on lying or "truth telling" (Donaldson and Werhane 1996, pp. 131–136). The exchange of sentiments is perceived by Kant as the main factor in social intercourse, and truth telling must be the guiding principle herein. The first social duty is to love others (Kant 1797/1922, p. 448). Love is not meant to be a feeling in this context, but a categorical imperative for welldoing and beneficence. Other examples of "duties towards others" are to simply help others and not to squander one's talents. In Menzer (1924), a wide range of Kant's "oughts and musts" is described extensively within many ethically sensible subjects.

4.3.3 Teleological Ethics

Teleological ethics (*telos* – goal) is a theory stating that the consequences of a moral act determine the value of the act. It is a perception of ethics in which the value of an act is judged with reference to some well-defined end result (as opposed to judging on the basis of the actor's intention, motive, or moral principle). In essence, teleological ethics do not deny or undervalue the importance and existence of both the virtue and the deontological approach to ethics. Despite severe criticism, Pettit (in Baron et al. 1997) claims that the consequentialist answer to questions on rightness are still tenable because of additional important aspects. He states: "The fundamental determinants of rightness are the values on the basis of which the property is predicated of options, and that these values, if they are to satisfy the relevant version of the universalizability test, must ultimately be all neutral in character. What ultimately makes any option the right one for an agent to take or to have taken, as consequentialists say, is the fact that that option best promotes the neutral values that are relevant in the situation on hand" (see Baron et al. 1997, p. 151).

The main strength of the teleological approach is the process of reflection upon all consequences of an act. This thought process in itself gives birth to the creation of a more objective approach to ethics. But this strength is subject to the major objections of the consequentialists. As Pettit discusses extensively (Baron et al. 1997, pp. 151–169), agents acting in accordance with consequentialists' maxims are often required to make decisions that are intuitively wrong or based on wrong arguments.

Table 4.1 summarizes the ethical framework as presented above. In the teleological approach, for example, we see that the motive for human actions involves the consequences of acts rather than the duties and inner freedom found in the deontological and the virtue-ethical approaches respectively. Furthermore, we note that human decisions are based on rationality in the teleological concept where wealth distribution is theoretically obtained by optimizing utility functions. The moral responsibility for the aggregate material wealth is a collective problem because everybody is assumed to behave rationally. In the virtue-ethical approach, on the other hand, the moral responsibility is purely individual because the economic agents voluntarily act in the way they do.

Ethics and the Theory of the Firm

Table 4.1 *Summary of the Ethical Framework*

	Motive of human acting	Human decision mechanism	Instrument for wealth distribution	Moral responsibility
VIRTUES *Voluntary goodness*	Inner freedom	Intuition/ metaphysical	Community thinking	Individual
DUTIES *Enforced goodness*	Duties	Social willpower	Legal supervision	Individual *and* collective
TELOS *Rational goodness*	Consequences/ goals	Rationality	Utility functions	Collective

4.4 Alternative Approaches in Finance

The major question at hand is still why the shareholder should carry the residual risk. As cited in section 4.2, Boatright (1999) argued that any assumption that the shareholder solves the agency costs problem is based on fuzzy logic. Control rights in themselves are varied and diverse. Restricting the agency- and control-relations to shareholder/manager relationships (see Jensen and Meckling 1976) is a far too rigorous assumption of corporate behavior. There is a lot of criticism on the key principles of the property rights theory and its inherent importance with regard to the agency theory (e.g., see Bowie and Freeman 1992; Engelen 2002).

In the following sections we focus on literature that criticizes the pure shareholder paradigm. First we briefly mention the behavioral approach, where models distinguish implicit and explicit claims (section 4.4.1). In section 4.4.2 we briefly look at the concept of social responsibility as the basic paradigm in business ethics. Then, in section 4.4.3, we touch upon the most recent development in governance: to see the firm as a nexus of stakeholders. Section 4.4.4 deals with virtue ethics and the "postmodern approach" of the firm as introduced by Dobson (1999). And finally, in section 4.4.5 we reconsider the opening question of this chapter, finance & ethics: contradiction or paradox?

4.4.1 Behavioral Approaches

The first refinements of the neoclassical approach, as applied in early financial models, were based on the behavioral theory of the firm. In this approach the managers are perceived as human beings who are unable to behave completely rationally and have all manner of interests and motives aside from their formal organizational ones and their narrow self-interest. They can only partially achieve the best interest of their stockholders because they operate from a position of "bounded rationality" (see Simon 1982) rather than complete rationality. Cornell and Shapiro (1987) emphasize the distinction between explicit contractual claims like wage contracts and product warranties on the one hand and implicit claims, such as the promise of continuing service to customers and job security for employees, on the other. They define the distinguishing feature of implicit claims as "too nebulous and state contingent to reduce to writing at a reasonable cost. (...) For this reason, implicit claims have little legal standing." (Cornell and Shapiro 1987, p. 6). They stress that as long as only explicit claims are considered, stakeholders will not play an important role in the financial policy of the company because their explicit claims are generally senior to those of stockholders and bondholders.

Cornell and Shapiro developed what they called an extended balance sheet, on which the "net organizational capital" was added on the asset side, and "organizational liabilities" on the liability side. The organizational capital (OC) is defined as "the current market value of all future implicit claims the firm expects to sell," and the organizational liabilities (OL) equal the "expected costs, from the firm's point of view, of honoring both current and future implicit claims." (Cornell and Shapiro 1987, p. 8). It is clearly very difficult to value both the organizational assets and the liabilities. The value of the implicit claims is dependent on the character of the company, the product market involved, and the nature of its stakeholders. In other words, the value depends on the relevant perception of the cultural and ethical values of the society at hand. Cornell and Shapiro predicted that firms which expect to provide high payoffs on implicit claims would attempt to distinguish themselves *ex ante*. This could be done through an appropriate dividend payout rate or financial structure. It should be noted that this approach explicitly opens the theoretical road to corporate social responsibility (CSR) and the acceptance of ethics in finance.

After its early development literature on behavioral approaches increased rapidly, particularly over the last decade. For example, De Bondt et al. (2008) extensively discuss the state of the art and the expected future of behavioral finance. De Bondt et al. explain that sentiment impacts the prices of all assets and drives the difference between what behavioral and neoclassical finance tell us about the relationship between risk and return. This area of enquiry is sometimes referred to as "behavioral finance," but is also called "behavioral economics." Behavioral economics combines the disciplines of psychology, sociology, and economics to explain why and how people make seemingly irrational or illogical decisions when they spend, invest, save, and, borrow money. De Bondt et al. (2008) conclude that a major paradigm shift is underway that will combine neoclassical and behavioral elements. Notably, the behavioral stochastic discount factor (SDF) approach, as developed by Shefrin (2005, 2008), incorporates the human factor into financial engineering. It is widely accepted that financial risk requires compensation and the premium can take any form in financial markets. However, the neoclassical framework focuses on fundamental risks in which the behavioral approach includes sentiment risks. Behavioral risk premiums serve as a compensation for bearing both fundamental and sentiment risks whereby investors collectively commit errors in their judgment of probabilities, thereby causing some derivatives and their underlying assets to be mispriced. Behavioral mean-variance portfolios aim to explain risk premiums and to replace unrealistic, heroic assumptions about the optimality of individual behavior with descriptive insights tested in laboratory experiments (see De Bondt et al. 2008, p. 17).

4.4.2 Corporate Social Responsibility

Corporate social responsibility (CSR) is a stakeholder's approach wherein the mission statement of the firm is extended. While classical firms define profits as their primary goal, socially responsible firms consider profits only as a necessary condition. In the latter approach, profits are equally important in relation to a healthy environment and a sustainable employee policy. Examples of classical opponents of social responsibility are Modigliani and Miller (1958, 1963), Friedman (1970), and Jensen and Meckling (1976). Their strictly neoclassical approach is firmly based on the shareholder wealth model (SWM). Especially famous is the Friedman (1970) article entitled, "The social responsibility of business is to increase its profits." There he makes the case that firms have to make economic choices that are only concerned with operational efficiency. All social responsibility is deemed a government concern and therefore irrelevant in the realm of business decisions. In the 1970s it was an understandable position, but today, when the deregulation of government tasks and the development of the civil society are ongoing, it is more difficult to accept that opinion.

In academic literature there is a huge ongoing debate over the question of whether socially responsible behavior by corporations increases or decreases the long-term profits of the firm (see, among others, Pava and Krausz 1996; Hamilton et al. 1993). For the time being, only empirical results may answer the question. However, one thing seems clear: the interest of the shareholder is not the same as (or may not even be congruent to) the interest of the firm. Few modern approaches measure financial performance alone; instead, most emphasize the link between competitive advantage and CSR. Porter and Kramer (2006) argue that the prevailing approaches to CSR are so disconnected from business as to obscure many of the greatest opportunities for companies to benefit society. They propose addressing social issues by creating shared value that may lead to self-sustaining solutions which do not depend on private or government subsidies. Shared value is defined by Porter and Kramer (2011) as policies and operating practices that enhance the competitiveness of a company while simultaneously advancing the economic and social conditions in the communities in which it operates. Value is defined as benefits relative to costs, not just benefits alone, whereas traditionally societal issues are treated as peripheral issues. The acceptance of the concept of *shared value* is a step forward in modern CSR development. It is not just companies that are opening up to the social demands of society; governments and judicial power are also increasing social pressure on the financial industry (see, e.g., the verdict by Judge Rakoff as presented in Box 4.2).

Box 4.2 *Changing Moral Opinions*

On 19 October 2011, the US Securities and Exchange Commission (the 'SEC') filed a lawsuit accusing Citigroup of a substantial securities fraud. According to the SEC, Citigroup stuffed a $1 billion mortgage fund that it sold to investors in 2007 with securities that it believed would fail so that it could bet against its customers and profit when values declined. The fraud, the agency said, was in Citigroup falsely telling investors that an independent party was choosing the portfolio's investments. Citigroup made $160 million from the deal and investors lost $700 million. The SEC proposed to settle the case by levying a fine of $285 million on Citigroup and allowing it to neither admit nor deny the fraud findings.

The judge, Jed S. Rakoff of the United States District Court in Manhattan, ruled that the SEC's $285 million settlement was 'neither fair, nor reasonable, nor adequate, nor in the public interest because it does not provide the court with evidence on which to judge the settlement.' He called the settlement 'hallowed by history, but not by reason', since it created substantial potential for abuse because 'it asks the court to employ its power and asserts its authority when it does not know the facts. An application of judicial power that does not rest on facts is worse than mindless, it is inherently dangerous', Judge Rakoff wrote in the case, SEC v. Citigroup Global Markets. 'In any case like this that touches on the transparency of financial markets whose gyrations have so depressed our economy and debilitated our lives, there is an overriding public interest in knowing the truth.' The SEC in particular, he added, 'has a duty, inherent in its statutory mission, to see that the truth emerges.'

'Judge Rakoff carefully treads the line between the deference that judges are supposed to show to regulatory agencies while also ensuring that the court does not simply rubber-stamp decisions', said Barbara Black, a professor at the University of Cincinnati College of Law. 'In a legal dispute between two private parties, they can agree to whatever settlement they desire, but in a case involving a public agency with consequences that affect the public interest, there has to be some kind of acknowledgment that certain things did occur.'

Source: Wyatt, Edward (November 2011) *The New York Times*

4.4.3 In Search of an Ethical Theory of the Firm

The most challenging theory is Wieland's (2011) idea of seeing the firm as a nexus of stakeholders. Wieland argues that the nature of a company can be defined as a contractual nexus of stakeholder resources and stakeholder interests, the function of which is the governance, in other words leadership, organization, and control of the resource owners with the aim of creating economic added value and distributing cooperation rent. Figure 4.3 illustrates the concept. From an economic perspective, stakeholder management is strategic management based on the idea that the economic success or failure of the company is determined by those players that take an interest in the company's success as it helps them to realize their own interest simultaneously. This is stakeholder management as a theory of added value! Of crucial importance in that approach is the identification and prioritization of the distinguished stakeholders.

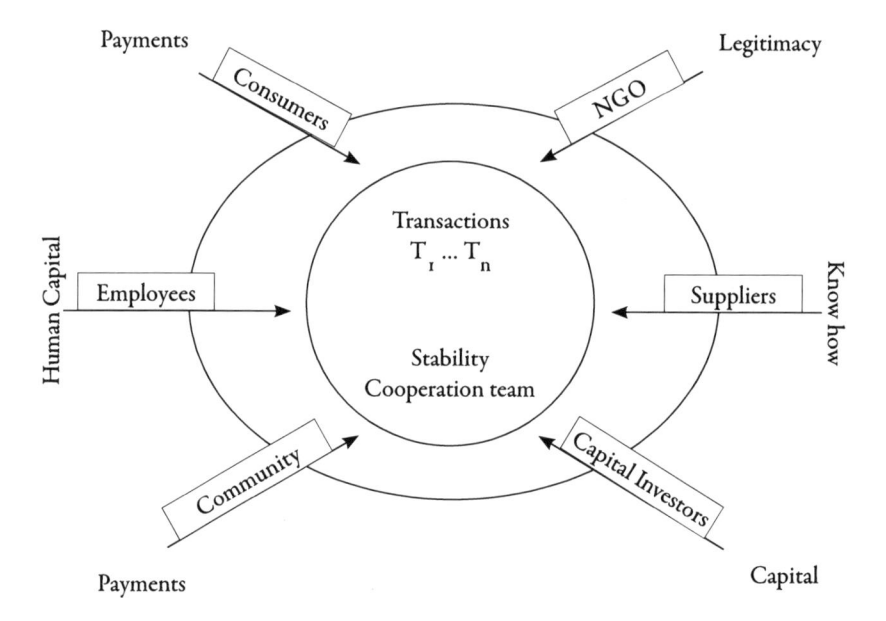

Figure 4.3 *The Firm as a Nexus of Stakeholders*
Source: Wieland 2011, p. 226

In this approach, the governance of cooperation rents leads to alternative definitions of the nature of a firm. Wieland defines the firm as "a project of social cooperation, a nexus of multiple stakeholders with the goal of deploying their resources in the context of market competition" (Wieland 2011, p. 241). From this perspective, modern corporate governance is not limited to a mere monitoring function, but is extended to the management of stakeholders. The trend of intensifying stakeholder management is also a theoretical convergence between managing the corporation on the one hand and running an association and/or cooperation on the other.

A strong opponent of the stakeholder approach is Sternberg (2000). She pointed out that stakeholder theory in practice promotes ethical confusion about the fundamental aims of business. She is the modern representative of the traditional Friedman perspective in which companies should act to maximize profits, within the limits of the law of course. Although the strict liberal reasoning behind this position is theoretically sound, the approach is scientifically limited. In the modern multidisciplinary society, we need an integration and collaboration of sciences instead of splitting business sciences into law, economics, psychology, and other specialized sciences all with their own responsibility and competition. The traditional materialistic approach creates agency costs instead of stewardship fruits like public wealth. An ethical theory of the firm includes interdisciplinary aspects.

4.4.4 Virtue Ethics and Finance

Following the multidisciplinary scientific approach described in the previous sections, it can be argued that virtue ethics are the optimal driver of change in an economy, followed by soft law – a form of duty-based ethical approaches – all within the limits of the firm's utilitarian profitability. Methodologically, this can be seen as a reverse priority to that of the traditional approach, where ethics often start off with utilitarian goals, then proceed with compliance to the law and end up with a culture that reduces virtues to profit making as an acceptable moral intention (virtue). Starting with virtue ethics as a necessary precondition for an ethical theory of the firm is exactly the opposite. Therefore, moral education and individual responsibility are needed to reverse the current trend in free-riding to obtain commercial goals. The combination of virtue ethics and finance has a rather short history. Early advocates of virtue ethics are MacIntyre (1985) and Pincoffs (1988).

Dobson (1999) introduced the "postmodern approach" to business and finance and brought two articles together. The first is John Hasnas's article, "The Normative Theories of Business Ethics: A Guide for the Perplexed", which invokes the shareholder's model as a valid normative theory of business ethics (Hasnas 1998). The second article is Thomas W. Dunfee's "The Market Place of Morality: Small Steps toward a Theory of Moral Choice". In that article Dunfee (1998, p. 142) suggests, "MOM (market place of morality) could provide a unifying framework integrating moral preferences, reasoning, behaviors and organizational context with broader political and economic concepts." Dobson (1999) concludes that both articles suggest that the accepted financial-economic view of the firm is more than able to accommodate ethics. He underlines how the postmodern approach emphasizes business as a type of aesthetic activity, rather than business as a strict science. Dobson advocates virtue ethics and derivatives thereof such as "corporate soul craft" (Johnson 1997) and "craftsmanship ethics" (Klein 1998 and Vogel 2010).

In the Netherlands the Aristotelian approach is firmly supported by van Staveren (1999) in her dissertation *Caring for Economics, an Aristotelian Perspective*. The shortcomings of "Rational Economic Man" are extensively described and the case is made that in order to provide a meaningful explanation of economic behavior, four moral capabilities (Commitment, Emotion, Deliberation, and Interaction) have to be added to economic modeling. Also Graafland (2010a, 2010b) focuses explicitly on virtue ethics and the role of interest in the credit crisis. Without explicitly mentioning the postmodern approach, van Staveren and Graafland pave the same road to reintegrate moral values into economic theory.

4.4.5 Finance and Ethics

Let us return to the opening question of the chapter: finance and ethics: contradiction or paradox? Basically, the question boils down to making a choice on the basis of the "theory of the firm." On the one hand we can define the firm as a "set of investments projects" that generates cash flow. On the other hand we can see the firm as a cooperation of human agents, satisfying both economic and social needs. The transaction cost approach is somewhere in between and considers a company as a "nexus of contract." From that perspective economic (financial) incentives are necessary to motivate agents who are basically selfish. So morality is implicitly present, but it is treated as an exogenous variable and therefore value neutral from the strict economic perspective.

The ethical approach departs from the human cooperation perspective of the firm, where the agents are necessarily committed to economic transactions in order to satisfy their needs. Accepting the moral capabilities of every human agent and the importance of ethics as a guiding line in human financial behavior, financial managers may choose among the *virtues*, the *duty* or the *goal* concepts of morality. Because the virtue concept is the only choice where a purely individual responsibility is assumed, it opens the possibility of improving the moral character of financial behavior. We can conclude that from the virtue-ethical perspective, finance and ethics is a paradox that can be solved by financial managers with an open eye for social consequences and individual responsibility. The current financial crisis in Europe may be helpful in the process of discovering "ethical finance."

4.5 Conclusion

Capital market models are traditionally ruled by the strict quantitative trade-off between expected return and risk. The ethical problem is that it only refers implicitly to fairness. It must be noted that the underlying "theory of the firm" basically boils down to the neoclassical shareholder paradigm, justified by considering the shareholders as the optimal stakeholders to reduce the agency cost.

In the "ethical finance" approach, the general neoclassical paradigm is replaced by a broader view of economics as a discipline. In addition to the necessity of competition and profits, it includes care for the environment and the mental health of the employees, the consumers and that of other stakeholders. Growth and the increase of cash flows are only acceptable if the quality of the new products can be qualified as socially and environmentally sustainable. Severe competition might be healthy because it encourages operational efficiency, but at the same time it could be too limited as an allocation mechanism. The problem with the ethical perspective is that it replaces the strict quantifiable approach of finance with a more qualitative and multidisciplinary one.

In today's modern multidisciplinary society we need the integration and collaboration of the sciences rather than, for example, the splitting of business science into law, economics, psychology, and other specialized sciences, each with its own responsibility and competition. The traditional materialistic approach creates agency costs instead of stewardship fruits such as public wealth. An ethical theory of the firm includes interdisciplinary aspects. The financial industry is based on the worldwide trust of people and economic institutes. An unbalanced growth of the worldwide financial capital on one side versus the human capital, the environment, and the quality and quantity of the physical production on the other, endangers the future. It is primarily the responsibility of financial economists to analyze these developments in relation to the future well-being of a global society.

References

Alchian, A. A. and Demsetz, H. (1972) Production, Information Costs and Economic Organization. *American Economic Review*, December, vol. 62, no. 5, pp. 777–95.

Argandona, A. (1995) *The Ethical Dimension of Financial Institutions and Markets*. Berlin: Springer.

Baron, M. W., Pettit P. and Slote, M. (1997): *Three Methods of Ethics: A Debate.* Oxford: Blackwell.
Boatright, J. R. (1996) *Ethics and the Conduct of Business.* Upper Saddle River, NJ: Prentice Hall.
Boatright, J. R. (1999) *Ethics in Finance.* Malden, MA: Blackwell.
De Bondt, W. F. M., Muradoglu, G., Shefrin, H. and Staikouras, K. (2008) Behavioral Finance: Quo Vadis. *Journal of Applied Finance,* Fall/Winter, pp. 7–21.
Bouckaert, L. (red.) (1994) *Interest en Cultuur: Een Ethiek van het Geld.* Leuven: Acco.
Bovenberg, A. L. and van de Klundert, T. C. M. J. (1999) Christelijke traditie en neoklassieke economie in gesprek. *ESB,* pp. 848–852.
Bowie, N. E. and Freeman, R. E. (1992) *Ethics and Agency Theory: An Introduction.* New York: Oxford University Press.
Caccese, M. S. (1997) Ethics and the Financial Analyst. *Financial Analyst Journal,* January/February.
Carroll, A. B. (1991) The Pyramid of Corporate Social Responsibility: Toward the Moral Management of Organizational Stakeholders. *Business Horizons,* 34, pp. 39–48.
Coase, R. H. (1937) The Nature of the Firm. *Economica,* No. 4, pp. 386–405.
Cornell, B. and Shapiro, A. (1987) Corporate Stakeholders and Corporate Finance. *Financial Management,* pp. 5–14.
Davies, G. (1994) *A History of Money: From Ancient Times to the Present Day.* Cardiff: University of Wales Press.
Dembinski, P. H. (2009) *Finance: Servant or Deceiver?* Basingstoke: Palgrave Macmillan.
Dobson, J. (1999) Defending the Stockholder Model: A Comment on Hasnas, and on Dunfee's MOM. *Business Ethics Quarterly,* 9, pp. 337–345.
Donaldson, T. and Werhane, P. H. (1996) *Ethical Issues in Business: A Philosophical Approach.* New York: Prentice Hall.
Dunfee, W. T. (1998) The Market Place of Morality: Small Steps towards a Theory of Moral Choice. *Business Ethics Quarterly,* 8, pp. 127–146.
Engelen, E. (2002) A Conceptual Critique of Shareholder Ideology. *Economy and Society,* vol. 31, no. 3, pp. 391–413.
Friedman, M. (1970) The Social Responsibility of Business is to Increase Its Profits. *New York Times Magazine,* 13 September, p. 33.
Fukuyama, F. (1995) *Welvaart: De grondslagen van het economisch handelen.* Amsterdam: Contact.
Graafland, J. J. (2010a) Do Markets Crowd out Virtues? An Aristotelian Framework. *Journal of Business Ethics,* vol. 91, no. 1, pp. 1–19.
Graafland, J. J. (2010b) Calvin's Restriction on Interest: Guidelines for the Credit Crisis. *Journal of Business Ethics,* vol. 96, pp. 233–248.

Grossman, S. J. & Hart, O. (1986) The Costs and Benefits of Ownership: A Theory of Vertical and Lateral Integration. *Journal of Political Economy*, vol. 94, pp. 691–719.

Hamilton, S., Jo H., and Statman M. (1993) Doing Well While Doing Good? The Investment Performance of Socially Responsible Mutual Funds. *Financial Analyst Journal*, pp. 62–66.

Harman, W. (1998) *Global Mind Change*. San Francisco: Berrett-Koehler.

Hasnas, J. (1998) The Normative Theories of Business Ethics: A Guide for the Perplexed. *Business Ethics Quarterly*, 8, pp. 19–42.

James, M. J. (2011) *An Introduction to Evolutionary Ethics*. Chichester: John Wiley & Sons.

Jensen, M. C. and Meckling, W. H. (1976) Theory of the Firm: Managerial Behavior, Agency Costs, and Ownership Structure. *Journal of Financial Economics*, vol. 3, October, pp. 305–360.

Johnson, E. W. (1997) Corporate Soulcraft in the Age of Brutal Markets. *Business Ethics Quarterly*, vol. 7, no. 4, pp. 109–124.

Jones, C., Parker M., Ten Bos, R. (2005) *For Business Ethics*. Oxford: Routledge.

Kant, I. (1785) *Fundamental Principles of the Metaphysics of Morals*, transl. Abbott, T. K. pp. 1–54, <http://www.gophet.vt.edu:10010/02/107/5>.

Kant, I. (1797/1922) *Metaphysik der Sitten*, Vorländer, K. (ed.). Hamburg: Meiner.

Klein, S. (1998) Don Quixote and the Problem of Idealism in Business Ethics. *Business Ethics Quarterly*, 8, pp. 43–64.

Koslowski, P. (1995) The Ethics of Banking. In: *Argandona (1995)*, ch. 10, pp. 181–232.

MacIntyre, A. (1985) *After Virtue: A Study in Moral Theory*, 2nd edn. London: Duckworth.

Meikle, S. (1995) *Aristotle's Economic Thought*. London: Clarendon Press.

Menzer, P. (1924) *Eine Vorlesung Kants über Ethik*. Berlin: Pan Verlag Rolf Heise.

Modigliani, F. and Miller, M. H. (1958) The Cost of Capital, Corporate Finance and the Theory of Investment. *American Economic Review*, vol. 48, no. 3, pp. 261–275.

Modigliani, F. and Miller, M. H. (1963) Taxes and the Cost of Capital, a Correction. *American Economic Review*, vol. 53, no. 3, pp. 433–443.

Pava, M. L. and Krausz, J. (1996) The Association between Corporate Social Responsibility and Financial Performance: The Paradox of Social Cost. *Journal of Business Ethics*, vol. 15, no. 3, March, pp. 321–357.

Pincoffs, E. L. (1988) *Quandaries and Virtues: Against Reductivism in Ethic*. Lawrence: University of Kansas Press.

Porter, M. E. and Kramer, M. R. (2006) Strategy and Society: The Link between Competitive Advantage and Corporate Social Responsibility. *Harvard Business Review*, December, pp. 68–92.

Porter, M. E. and Kramer, M. R. (2011) Creating Shared Value; How to Reinvent Capitalism – and Unleash a Wave of Innovation and Growth. *Harvard Business Review*, January/February, pp. 62–77.

Shefrin, H. and Statman, M. (1993) Ethics, Fairness and Efficiency in Financial Markets. *Financial Analyst Journal*, November/December, pp. 21–29.

Shefrin, H. (2005) *Behavioral Corporate Finance*. New York: McGraw-Hill.

Shefrin, H. (2008) Risk and Return in Behavioral SDF-Based Asset Pricing Models. *Journal of Investment Management*, vol. 6, no. 3, pp. 1–19.

Simon, H. (1982) *Models of Bounded Rationality*. Cambridge, MA: MIT Press.

Sen, A. (1987) *On Ethics and Economics*. London: Blackwell.

Sen, A. (1993) Money and Value, On the Ethics and Economics of Finance. *Economics and Philosophy*, 8, pp. 203–227.

Solomon, R. C. (1996) Corporate Roles, Personal Virtues: An Aristotelian Approach to Business Ethics. In: *Donaldson and Werhane* (1996), pp. 45–59.

Soppe, A. B. M. (2004) Sustainable Corporate Finance. *Journal of Business Ethics*, vol. 53, pp. 213–224.

Soppe, A. B. M. (2010) Finance: Servant or Deceiver? Financialization at the Crossroads; Paul H. Dembinski, Book Review, *Journal of Business Ethics*, vol. 91, pp. 451–456.

Sternberg, E. (2000) *Just Business: Business Ethics in Action*. Oxford: Oxford University Press.

Stout, L. A. (2002) Bad and Not-So-Bad Arguments For Shareholder Primacy. *Southern California Law Review*, vol. 75, no. 5, pp. 1189–1209.

Stout, L. A. (2007) Mythical Benefits of Shareholder Control. *Virginia Law Review*, no. 3, pp. 789–810.

Van Staveren, I. (1999) *Caring for Economics: An Aristotelian Perspective*. Delft: Eburon.

Vogel, D. (2010) The Private Regulation of Global Corporate Conduct: Achievements and Limitations. *Business & Society*, vol. 49, no. 1, pp. 68–89.

Wieland, J. (2011) The Firm as a Nexus of Stakeholders: Stakeholder Management and Theory of the Firm. In: *Corporate Governance and Business Ethics*, Brink, A. (ed.) Heidelberg: Springer, pp. 225–244.

Williamson, O. E. (1985) *The Economic Institutions of Capitalism: Firms, Markets, Relational Contracting*. New York: Free Press.

THOMAS BESCHORNER AND CHRISTOPH SCHANK
(UNIVERSITY OF ST. GALLEN)

5 The Citizenship and Responsibility of Corporations

5.1 Corporations and Social Responsibility

5.2 "Bourgeois" and "Citoyen"

5.3 The Corporate Citoyen

5.4 Corporate Citizenship and Responsibility in Action

5.5 Conclusion

Abstract

Relationships between business and society and the responsibilities of business towards society have been discussed extensively under umbrella terms such as "corporate social responsibility" (CSR) and "corporate citizenship" (CC). The citizenship role of corporations is a perceived ideal of the integral role of business in society that enables responsible business conduct. Specific expectations of the different actors in society can be developed based on an understanding of the term "citizenship."

Both the liberal and the republican traditions provide an interpretation of the nature of citizenship. While in the liberal tradition the good citizen respects the regulatory framework and protects his or her chartered rights against third parties, other citizens, or the state, the good citizen in the republican tradition takes a more proactive stance and becomes a political actor. While liberalism emphasizes individual rights, republicanism emphasizes duties towards society.

The corporate "citoyen" reflects the republican tradition, acting as an impartible citizen among citizens who is not torn between his or her economic interests and civic duties. From this republican perspective, corporate citizenship goes beyond mere corporate philanthropy and implies responsibility for the company's core business activities along its entire supply chain.

Keywords: corporate social responsibility, corporate citizenship, corporate "citoyen" versus corporate "bourgeois"

5.1 Corporations and Social Responsibility

After several decades of research and attempts toward standardization, there is no consensus on the definition, meaning, and purpose of the concepts of corporate social responsibility (CSR) and corporate citizenship (CC). On the one hand, heightened public awareness in globalized societies is increasingly attributing a "social" role to corporations, in addition to their traditional economic role. On the other hand, the definitional ambiguity of these concepts is what most likely attracts academics, practitioners, and the public because it allows each of them to adapt these terms to their own individual understanding and context. Perhaps it is precisely because of this definitional openness that CSR and CC have entered mainstream management literature and research (Matten and Palazzo 2008; Hansen and Schrader 2005).

Even more noteworthy is the rapid growth in popularity of the concepts in corporate practices. An ever-increasing number of corporations use the CSR and CC terminology – sometimes one or the other, sometimes both – as a label to signal their societal responsibility. As a result of this growing popularity, however, they run the risk of being reduced to an empty shell. In particular, the arbitrariness, or at least the ambiguity, in the use of CSR as opposed to CC has become apparent. While in academic literature the two concepts are sometimes treated as different terms describing equal things, each one is also often seen as a part of the other. Nevertheless, both concepts differ from the approaches found in today's prevailing and rather abstract literature on business ethics. More specifically, the concepts share a less normative, but more pragmatic approach to responsibility (Göbel 2006, p. 200). In addition, the metaphor of the good citizen is often used to personify an organization as an actor who has a mind, soul, and consciousness (Schrader 2011, p. 309).

One of the most cited contributions dealing with the ambiguity of the definitions of CC and CSR is the work of Archie B. Carroll. In his 1991 classic work, Carroll calls on corporations to establish themselves as good citizens. Without explicitly using the term CC, he defines it as the optional philanthropic top layer of a four-stage pyramid of CSR (Carroll 1991). (See also Figure 4.1, Chapter 4.) This leaves CC as subordinate to CSR. However, in 1998 Carroll equated both concepts and replaced the term CSR with CC (Carroll 1998). This juxtaposition exemplifies the continuing ambiguity of definitions that circumscribe the relationship between business and society. For example, the question as to whether philanthropy and charitable donations deserve to be called corporate responsibility is left unanswered.

5.2 "Bourgeois" and "Citoyen"

The discourse in Western political philosophy surrounding the rights and duties of citizens originates from liberalism and republicanism. Thomas Hobbes and John Locke constituted the role of the citizen in liberalism, the "bourgeois," through the idea of ownership (Schrader 2006). As such, the liberal tradition emphasizes the individual rights of the citizen in order to protect him or her from others and from the state. Isaiah Berlin (1958) called this notion of an individual's rights "negative liberty," meaning "the freedom *from* something" as opposed to "the freedom *for* something" (positive liberty). In this context, property rights are one of the key rights of citizens, protected by law and order. Thus, the bourgeois as a private actor is explicitly allowed to pursue his or her own individual interest as long as he or she remains within the collectively accepted regulatory framework of the state and the "rules of the game." From this perspective, respecting the law is the only relevant duty of a citizen. Applied to corporations, it means that the law and regulations must be respected at all times, but within this legal framework individual interests can be pursued vigorously.

This interpretation of the citizen as a bourgeois seems to be appealing to corporations for various reasons. On the one hand, it reflects a tradition that seeks to prevent state intervention in corporate practices, while a philanthropic approach to responsibility tries to obviate such interventions before they are carried out. On the other hand, the right to an unconditional pursuit of profits and the utilization of these profits is seen as paramount. Consistent with this approach are interpretations of CSR that classify the realization and the utilization of profits as two distinct categories. This understanding of corporate responsibility as charity may lead corporations to react to legitimate societal demands for moral integrity in their business conduct by frequently and haphazardly engaging in philanthropy, without reflecting on the moral legitimacy of their core business model (Ulrich 2008, pp. 376–442). In other words, corporate responsibility interpreted as charity claims that the way corporations spend their profits has nothing to do with the way they make their profits in the first place. Therefore, it is difficult to see how any corporate responsibility strategy merely focusing on charity and negative liberty is promoting the common good. The liberal approach does not require any serious interaction between a company's core business and its civic engagement (Moon et al. 2003, pp. 7 f.).

The bourgeois in liberalism's counterpart is the "citoyen," the citizen of the state, in republicanism. Having its roots in the political thinking of Aristotle, Rousseau, and Kant, the republican tradition's influence is strongly reflected in the understanding of corporate responsibility found in German business ethics literature, as illustrated by the works of Peter Ulrich, Horst Steinmann, and Albert Löhr, among others. From this perspective, the citoyen is an actor who does not see his or her private interest as more important than the common good. Rather, pursuing common interests of society is seen as the noblest goal. The role as citizen is not based on negative liberty. Instead, a citoyen voluntarily accepts his or her duties toward society. While the core of good citizenship in liberalism is respecting the law, in republicanism good citizenship is measured by its contribution to the common good. Given its focus on an overarching regulatory framework that protects individual rights, liberalism is generally critical of the state. In contrast, republicanism and the citoyen are defined by their active political participation in governing and being governed (Aristotle 1994, p. 135).

Political orientation towards public welfare is also explicitly valid within the sphere of the market. Therefore, good citizens consider themselves to be both citizens and business people at the same time (Ulrich 2005, p. 14). In doing so, a citoyen is the inseparable from the actor who is oriented towards balancing private interest and public welfare. Thus, as Peter Ulrich points out in Chapter 2 of this book, a good citizen wishes to pursue "only those private goals which are compatible with the legitimacy conditions of a well-ordered society of free and equal citizens." Business strategies therefore need to be publicly evaluated in order to qualify as morally legitimate. However, their evaluation does not rely on the state as the primary representation of society. Communitarianism, for example, emphasizes the relationships between citizens. Communitarians see citizen engagement as a means to overcome the deficits in the regulatory framework governed by the state. In an era of increasingly globalized societies and economic activity, such regulatory deficits have become very much apparent (Schrader 2011, p. 308). From a republican perspective, a good citizen does not take advantage of weak regulatory frameworks in order to ensure his or her negative liberty. Instead, he or she will unconditionally pursue and promote only those freedoms that contribute to public welfare, knowing full well that he or she can never be fully independent from the demands and requirements of third parties.

5.3 The Corporate Citoyen

Apart from the theoretical differences between the two theories of citizenship, they share a common understanding of the role of the citizen that is particularly relevant to corporate citizenship.

However, attributing citizen status to corporations is quite complex. Organization theory, having made central theoretical contributions to economics, facilitates an approach to this problem. From this perspective, the smallest building blocks of an organization are the individuals and institutions that act therein (North 1992, p. 5). These "participants" of an organization follow its original purpose and the mutual objectives that brought about the organization's existence in the first place. The organization's constitution as a legal entity, the assignment of individuals belonging to that organization, and the binding institutional arrangements (including the act of creation) all allow for the permanent separation of the corporation and its environment, just as much as it is self-evident for natural persons. This separation also holds for artificial constructs such as organizations. Consequently, the distinction between members and non-members, and the internal and external spheres, are key characteristics of autonomous and stable organizations, including profit-oriented corporations (Schreyögg 1999, p. 9).

Based on these considerations it becomes not only possible, but even necessary to regard corporations as collective actors. Corporations pursue objectives which are framed within a "formal and legitimized process" (Kieser and Walgenbach 2003, p. 8) and executed via coordinated and joint activities. As such, in their entirety, corporations are not a diffuse construct, but are actors clearly separable from their surrounding environment. Moreover, actions and their consequences can be explicitly attributed to a particular corporation. Zsolnai's (2009) contribution clearly illustrates that companies can foster ethical decision-making within the boundaries of their organizational structures.

Schrader (2011, p. 309; 2006, p. 226) states that in order to function as good citizens, corporations must develop a consistent corporate identity. This identity, however, does not merely imply a separate entity in relation to the external environment. In addition, it entails an overall picture of the corporation where core business operations and philanthropic activities are not separated from each other. CC therefore is not something limited to the distribution of profits after they have been generated. Instead, it is about how these profits have been generated in the first place.

From a CC perspective, this approach still seems to be tied to a *corporate bourgeois* understanding of the role of corporations. In a republican theory of citizenship, however, it becomes possible to attribute a societal status to corporations as corporate citizens. This includes the voluntary acceptance of societal responsibilities to increase overall public welfare. Nonetheless, as has been emphasised by Moon et al. (2003, p. 20 f.), a complete equalization of the natural and the corporate citizen is not necessary: "Corporations could reasonably claim to act as if they were metaphorically citizens in that their engagement in society resembles the key process of citizenship, participation."

Therefore, a corporation that wants to be seen as a *corporate citoyen* in the republican sense needs to pay explicit attention to its political activities. This implies refraining from lobbying in a classical sense. Instead, the explicit participation of the corporation in public governance is key (Pfriem 2004, p. 190). At its core, this requires not only making use of legitimate rights provided by the state, but also most importantly accepting voluntary duties that contribute to the constitution of a functioning society (see also Marsden 2000, p. 11). This is because societal expectations towards corporations go beyond economic profitability and acting lawfully. They extend to aligning the private interest of making profits with the public interest of contributing to common welfare. This extension cannot be made when considering CC only as an act of charity.

From this perspective, the political influence of corporate citizens illustrates a rather complex relationship between a company and the political communities and the state in which it operates. This complex relationship has brought about harsh criticism focused on private companies' overreaching political influence. Clearly, powerful transnational corporations are influential actors not only in the economic, but also the political, social, and cultural, spheres. As such, in many cases they have tried to influence political processes in their favour, which has been critically discussed in political, economic, and legal literature.

This criticism is not new. As early as in the nineteenth century, US Chief Justice Marshall (Dartmouth College v. Woodward, 4 Wheat. 518, 636 (1819)) pointed out that: "A corporation is an artificial being, invisible, intangible, and existing only in contemplation of law. Being the mere creature of law, it possesses only those properties which the charter of creation confers upon it, either expressly, or as incidental to its very existence. These are such as are supposed best calculated to effect the object for which it was created." Since then, legal scholars have critically discussed the legal nature of business entities like corporations. From this perspective, corporate citizenship is a rather new phenomenon in business literature, and it has not yet been sufficiently scrutinized in constitutional jurisprudence and political philosophy. From a legal perspective, one might argue that there is no place for corporate citizens in the constitutional system of a modern representative democracy and, therefore, corporations should play only a limited role in the political arena.

This is certainly a valid critique. However, it is valid only if we interpret the notion of citizenship strictly from a legal perspective and apply it to the self-interested *corporate bourgeois* we have outlined above. In contrast to that perspective, a *corporate citoyen* adhering to a normatively well-grounded understanding of good CC in the republican tradition is defined precisely by the fact that it does not wish to take advantage of its power to influence the political process only to promote its self-interest. This has large-scale implications for management practices, which might not even be fully utilized by most corporations. Good CC requires that corporations stop manifesting their societal engagement only in philanthropic activities that are unrelated to their core business. Rather, the entire range of business activities (i.e., the creation of profit along the whole value chain) needs to contribute to public welfare. The pursuit of economic self-interest is only legitimate as long as it does not conflict with the overall interest of society, that is to say, without violating the moral rights of any stakeholder.

The regulatory framework administrated by the state is only an initial guideline, and is insufficient. At the same time, CC releases corporations from their defensive discourse. As a collective of fully-fledged citizens, corporations are no longer just addressees of expectations; they are explicitly called upon to contribute to the political sphere. Naturally, this implies developing a new perspective on the purpose of an organization and the underlying organizational logic. Exhausting any legitimate possibility to make a profit is still subject to qualification from the corporation's citizenship duty. From this point of view, we can derive several further interpretations.

First, an understanding of the term CC either as corporate giving or corporate volunteering, common in the German-speaking regions, only represents a limited perspective. Corporate giving refers to different forms of either contribution in kind or monetary donations provided by the corporate bourgeois. Corporate volunteering refers to societal engagement of any kind by members of the organization (potential differentiations of corporate citizenship can be found in Weber 2008, p. 44; Schrader 2011, p. 304; Damm and Lang 2001; Dresewski et al. 2004). If restricted to the output of societal engagement, i.e. for example the aggregated number of hours of social activities by members of a corporation, corporate volunteering can merely be understood as another form of corporate giving, in other words: giving "time." The critical measure, however, for an adequate understanding of citizenship in the above-mentioned sense should be the impact of a social activity, i.e. whether it has contributed to solving a certain problem in a dual sense: (i) True interaction of citizens with each other; not the voluntary painting of a classroom by employees of a corporation, but the planning, procurement, and the painting of the classroom itself together with disadvantaged students represents an important exercise, and may induce a mutual learning process, and (ii) such experiences by corporate employees in unfamiliar contexts may lead to a reconsideration of the initial purpose of the organization.

Second, the republican understanding of CC provides a fertile ground to outline an ideal conception of the relationship between the corporation and the government as well as the civil society. Its abstractness and distance from real ethical problems in actual business conduct, however, represents a structural weakness. Nevertheless, it is possible to conceptualize the above-mentioned relationship by using the notion of responsibility.

It may come as a surprise that the notion of responsibility is, from a philosophical perspective, relatively young. As Kurt Röttgers (2007, pp. 17ff.) comprehensively illustrates, until the beginning of the twentieth century, the notion of responsibility was not even present in the philosophical handbooks or dictionaries available. The reason, Röttgers argues, was that the notion of duty became obscure in the twentieth century. He adds that, in principle, the same structure characterizes the imperative of duty and the rhetoric of accepting responsibility for a higher entity. However, the Kantian concept of *Vernunft* (reason) ultimately failed to comprehensively outline that there are no "real," which means unsolvable, conflicts of duty (Röttgers 2007, p. 21). The establishment of the social sciences and sociology in particular in the twentieth century added to this picture, as they shifted their focus from contemporary philosophical approaches to social relationships and interactions, reflected in particular in the works of Max Weber.

Today, responsibility basically means the intensification of a "response" towards something, and it includes a preceding question that needs to be answered. The classic formula is "someone being responsible for something towards someone else" (Küpers 2008, p. 313). Originally, the notion of responsibility meant being pushed towards a point where one would not go voluntarily, such as a situation where one has to account for something, or even oneself (Röttgers 2007, p. 18). Nowadays, we often assume that individuals tend to – more or less voluntarily – accept responsibility based on a moral rather than a legal connotation. These interpretations reflect a backward-looking notion of responsibility, and the literature calls these interpretations retrospect or ex-post responsibility, or responsibility based on liability (see Küpers 2008, p. 312ff.; Lautermann and Pfriem 2010, p. 296ff.). From the backward-looking types of responsibility we can distinguish a more future-oriented interpretation of responsibility, which is referred to as *prospective responsibility*. It does not lock the stable door after the horse has bolted, but instead is an essential part of any future-oriented strategy of social actors, including corporations. As such, prospective responsibility is centred on the individual, i.e. there is a subject of responsibility, or someone who is taking responsibility, respectively; it refers to something tangible, i.e. there is an object of responsibility, or responsibility for something is taken; it addresses a particular audience, i.e. there is an instance of responsibility, or responsibility is taken towards someone. Moreover, prospective responsibility is based on the republican ideal of citizenship, that is, it implies an understanding of a citizen who wants to be responsible for the society in which he lives. (See also Chapter 7.)

Our interpretation of the notion of responsibility in terms of "being responsible for something" does not imply a specific content of responsibility. Instead, the content (i.e., the concrete actions of responsibility to be taken) is to be defined by the parties directly involved or affected. In this context, it is important that, firstly, the historic-cultural context is taken into account, and secondly, that the inclusion of stakeholders is not "negotiated" on strategic grounds alone, or influenced by power relations, but that an inclusive discourse takes place "at eye level". Lautermann and Pfriem (2010, p. 295) state: "Whenever a situational, problem-oriented solution is required that takes into account heterogenous, but in principle equally valuable perspectives about what is good or just, the most useful ethical concept is that of temporary and concretely applicable relation of responsibility." The contents of responsibility are then defined along concrete societal problems, and the respective subjects of responsibility; they are also, most importantly, based on discourse between the affected parties.

This extension of the concept of responsibility outlined above is critical for an adequate understanding of CSR in order to address the central question of how to mobilize corporations so that they contribute to the public interest. It is not about how to distribute donations or how to avoid bad practices such as corruption or fraud, but about the opportunities and limits in the realization of good corporate practices. Adequate concepts are necessary to answer questions of how to shape future societies, and we argue that a future-oriented understanding of responsibility allows us to deal with these questions.

5.4 Corporate Citizenship and Responsibility in Action

A good corporate citoyen in the republican understanding is not supposed to ruthlessly maximize profits by morally illegitimate strategies, and then spend some of these profits on charity. Instead, the moral quality of the core business model, meaning how profits actually are being made, is what matters. This focus on corporations' responsibility for their "core strategy" has recently been recognized by the *European Commission's* new policy on *Corporate Social Responsibility* (European Commission 2011, p. 6): "To fully meet their corporate social responsibility, enterprises should have in place a process to integrate social, environmental, ethical, human rights and consumer concerns into their business operations and core strategy in close collaboration with their stakeholders, with the aim of: maximising the creation of shared value for their owners/shareholders and for their other stakeholders and society at large; identifying, preventing and mitigating their possible adverse impacts." While this position marks a significant improvement over previous CSR policies on the European level, the new policy (European Commission 2011, p. 3) still seems to argue from an instrumentalist point of view: "A strategic approach to CSR is increasingly important to the competitiveness of enterprises. It can bring benefits in terms of risk management, cost savings, access to capital, customer relationships, human resource management, and innovation capacity." Clearly, these arguments are supposed to act as incentives for companies that are still reluctant to jump on the CSR bandwagon. The Commission appeals to corporations' enlightened self-interest, thus framing CSR as an instrument for financial success. We would argue, however, that such an approach only takes into account the mindset of a corporate bourgeois. A corporate citoyen, on the other hand, does not need a financial incentive to do the right thing. Instead, such a company would try to actively promote the public interest by challenging those companies that only strive for their own short-term gain. (Box 5.1)

> Box 5.1 *Apple and its Withdrawal from the US Chamber of Commerce*
>
> In October 2009, Apple Inc. resigned its membership in the United States Chamber of Commerce. In its letter of resignation (Johnson 2009a), the company stated: "We strongly object to the Chamber's recent comments opposing the [Environmental Protection Agency's] effort to limit greenhouse gases. ...Apple supports regulating greenhouse gas emissions, and it is frustrating to find the Chamber at odds with us in this effort. We would prefer the Chamber take a more progressive stance on this critical issue and play a constructive role in addressing the climate crisis. However, because the Chamber's position differs so sharply with Apple's, we have decided to resign our membership effective immediately."
>
> The background to Apple's decision (cf. Galbraith 2009) was that the Environmental Protection Agency had suggested new greenhouse gas regulation, and the Chamber of Commerce lobbied against the proposed regulation on behalf of its member companies which, one might argue, is precisely what the Chamber was supposed to do. From a corporate bourgeois perspective, companies are supposed to maximize profit, and the Chamber of Commerce is supposed to protect its member companies from state regulation (as the concept of negative liberty suggests). Why, then, would Apple not be interested in being protected by the Chamber anymore?
>
> Perhaps it had something to do with the fact that time and time again Apple had been criticized by Greenpeace for its allegedly poor environmental record (Deleon 2009)? After all, Greenpeace (2009) applauded Apple's resignation from the Chamber. Maybe it had a lot to do with the fact that "Apple has been trying to embrace its image as a green computing company for the past year" (Schwartz 2009; Johnson 2009b)? Or perhaps it was environmentalist Al Gore, a member of Apple's board, who influenced the company's decision (Berkow 2012).

> Given Apple's highly secretive approach to strategy making, we will probably never know for sure what led to the decision. It is possible, however, that the company intentionally said goodbye to the old model of the corporate bourgeois and openly embraced a republican understanding of corporate citizenship. As a good corporate citoyen, Apple would not be interested in merely saving cost in the short term. Instead, it would try to influence its political context in a way that promotes the public interest. The company's resignation from the Chamber of Commerce therefore might provide an example of the consequences of this understanding of corporate citizenship.

5.5 Conclusion

The discussion about the responsibility of corporations is gaining momentum in academia as well as among business practitioners. This alone calls for a reconsideration of the two popular concepts of CSR and CC and their relationship to each other. We have shown how good CC can be understood as a challenging concept, the complete fulfilment of which by corporations could be seen as an ideal level of responsibility. We see this ideal level mirrored in corporations that consider themselves an integral part of society, and which are not, therefore, trying to avoid societal demands, but trying to proactively fulfil them by utilizing reflection, anticipation, and interaction. Given that a corporation accepts and consistently follows a republican understanding of citizenship, it will not only face duties that promote public welfare, but it will acquire a concrete mandate to proactively shape society.

The approximation of actual business practices to the republican ideal of good CC represents an enormous task for corporations, civil society, and governments. In particular, attention needs to be shifted towards the interactionist momentum of proactive responsibility, wherein bearers and addressees of responsibility are brought together in discourses about concrete problems. CC, if not just understood as a defensive concept to avoid negative publicity or to mitigate governmental regulation, has the potential to shape such discourses. In doing so, it contributes to creating a self-image of corporations as good corporate citizens.

References

Aristotle (1994) *Politik*. Reinbek: Rowohlt.
Berkow, J. (2012) Did Al Gore force Apple to quit the U.S. Chamber of Commerce? *Financial Post*. 10 January. <http://business.financialpost.com/2012/01/10/did-al-gore-force-apple-to-quit-the-u-s-chamber-of-commerce/> accessed 28 September 2012.
Berlin, I. (1958) *Two Concepts of Liberty*. Oxford: Clarendon Press. Repr. in: Berlin, I. (2002) *Liberty*. Oxford: Oxford University Press, pp. 166–217.
Carroll, A. B. (1979) A Three-Dimensional Conceptual Model of Corporate Performance. *Academy of Management Review*, vol. 4, no. 4, pp. 497–505.
Carroll, A. B. (1991) The Pyramid of Corporate Social Responsibility: Toward the Moral Management of Organizational Stakeholders. *Business Horizons*, vol. 34, no. 4, pp. 39–48.
Carroll, A. B. (1998) The Four Faces of Corporate Citizenship. *Business and Society Review*, vol. 100, no. 1, pp. 1–7.
Damm, D. and Lang, R. (2001) *Handbuch Unternehmenskooperation. Erfahrungen mit Corporate Citizenship in Deutschland*. Bonn: Stiftung Mitarbeit.
Deleon, N. (2009) Apple quits U.S. Chamber of Commerce over environmental policy. 6 October. <http://techcrunch.com/2009/10/06/apple-quits-u-s-chamber-of-commerce-over-environmental-policy/> accessed 28 September 2012.
Dresewski, F., Kromminga, P., von Mutius, B. (2004) Corporate Citizenship oder: Mit solcher Verantwortung gewinnen. In: Wieland, J. (ed.) *Handbuch Wertemanagement*. Hamburg: Murmann, pp. 489–526.
European Commission (2011) A Renewed EU Strategy 2011–14 for Corporate Social Responsibility. <http://ec.europa.eu/enterprise/policies/sustainable-business/corporate-social-responsibility/index_en.htm> accessed 28 September 2012.
Galbraith, K. (2009) Apple Resigns from Chamber over Climate. *The New York Times*, 5 October. <http://green.blogs.nytimes.com/2009/10/05/apple-resignes-from-chamber-over-climate/> accessed 28 September 2012.
Göbel, E. (2006) *Unternehmensethik*. Stuttgart: Lucius & Lucius.
Greenpeace (2009) Bravo Apple: Company Slams Lobby Group over Climate Change. <http://www.greenpeace.org/international/en/news/features/apple-leaves-us-chamber-071009/> accessed 28 September 2012.
Hansen, U. and Schrader, U. (2005) Corporate Social Responsibility als aktuelles Thema der Betriebswirtschaftslehre. *DBW*, vol. 65, no. 4, pp. 373–395.
Johnson, K. (2009a) Apple quits Chamber of Commerce over Climate Spat. *The Wall Street Journal*, 5 October. <http://blogs.wsj.com/digits/2009/10/05/apple-quits-chamber-of-commerce-over-climate-spat/> accessed 28 September 2012.

Johnson, K. (2009b) Happy, shiny people: Apple's big drive for green credibility. *The Wall Street Journal*, 29 September. <http://blogs.wsj.com/environmentalcapital/ 2009/09/29/happy-shiny-people-apples-big-drive-for-green-credibility/> accessed 28 September 2012.

Kieser, A. and Walgenbach, P. (2003) *Organisation*. Stuttgart: Schäffer-Poeschel.

Küpers, W. (2008) Perspektiven responsiver und integraler "Ver-Antwortung" in Organisationen und der Wirtschaft. In: Heidbrink, L. (ed.) *Verantwortung in der Marktwirtschaft*. Frankfurt a. M.: Campus, pp. 307–338.

Lautermann, C. and Pfriem, R. (2010) Corporate Social Responsibility in wirtschaftsethischen Perspektiven. In: Raupp, J., Jarolimek, S. and Schultz, F. (eds) *Handbuch Corporate Social Responsibility. Kommunikationswissenschaftliche Grundlagen und methodische Zugänge*. Wiesbaden: VS-Verlag, pp. 281–304.

Marsden, C. (2000) The New Corporate Citizenship of Big Business: Part of the Solution to Sustainability. *Business and Society Review*, vol. 105, no. 1, pp. 9–25.

Matten, D. and Crane, A. (2005) Corporate Citizenship: Toward an Extended Theoretical Conceptualization. *Academy of Management Review*, vol. 30, no. 1, pp. 166–179.

Matten, D. and Palazzo, G. (2008) Unternehmensethik als Gegenstand betriebswirtschaftlicher Forschung und Lehre: Eine Bestandsaufnahme aus internationaler Perspektive. In: *Zeitschrift für betriebswirtschaftliche Forschung*, Sonderheft 58, pp. 50–71.

Moon, J., Crane, A. and Matten, D. (2003) Can Corporations be Citizens? Corporate Citizenship as a Metaphor for Business Participations in Society. 2nd ed. No. 13–2003 *ICCSR Research Paper Series*.

North, D. C. (1992) *Institutionen, institutioneller Wandel und Wirtschaftsleistung*. Tübingen: Mohr Siebeck.

Pfriem, R. (2004) Ein pluralistisches Feld von Governancekulturen. In: Wieland, J. (ed.) *Governanceethik im Diskurs*. Marburg: Metropolis, pp. 183–212.

Röttgers, K. (2007) Verantwortung nach der Moderne in sozialphilosophischer Perspektive. In: Beschorner, T., Linnebach, P., Pfriem, R. and Ulrich, G. (eds) *Unternehmensverantwortung aus kulturalistischer Sicht*. Marburg: Metropolis, pp. 17–31.

Schäfer, C. K. (2009) *Corporate Volunteering und professionelles Freiwilligen-Management: Eine organisationssoziologische Betrachtung*. Wiesbaden: VS-Verlag.

Schrader, U. (2006) Corporate Citizenship – Eine Innovation? In: Pfriem, R., Antes, R., Fichter, K., Müller, M., Paech, N., Seuring, S. and Siebenhüner, B. (eds) *Innovationen für eine nachhaltige Entwicklung*. Wiesbaden: DUV, pp. 231–248.

Schrader, U. (2011) Corporate Citizenship. In: Aßländer, M. S. (ed.) *Handbuch Wirtschaftsethik*. Stuttgart and Weimar: J. B. Metzler, pp. 303–312.

Schreyögg, G. (1999) *Organisation: Grundlagen moderner Organisationsgestaltung*. Wiesbaden: Gabler.
Schwartz, A. (2009) Why Did Apple Quit the U.S. Chamber of Commerce? *Fast Company*, 6 October. <http://www.fastcompany.com/blog/ariel-schwartz/sustainability/why-did-apple-quit-us-chamber-commerce> accessed 28 September 2012.
Ulrich, P. (2005) *Zivilisierte Marktwirtschaft: Eine wirtschaftsethische Orientierung*. Bern: Haupt.
Ulrich, P. (2008) *Integrative Economic Ethics*. Cambridge: Cambridge University Press.
Weber, M. (2008) Corporate Social Responsibility: Konzeptionelle Gemeinsamkeiten und Unterschiede zur Nachhaltigkeits- und Corporate-Citizenship-Diskussion. In: Müller, M. and Schaltegger, S. (eds) *Corporate Social Responsibility. Trend oder Modeerscheinung?* Munich: oekom, pp. 39–51.
Zsolnai, L. (2009) *Responsible Decision Making*. New Brunswick, NJ and London: Transaction Publishers.

JOSEP M. LOZANO
(ESADE BUSINESS SCHOOL, RAMON LLULL UNIVERSITY)

6 Organizational Ethics

6.1 Organizational Ethics as an Opportunity for Learning and Innovation
    6.1.1 A Context for Social Change
    6.1.2 A Context of Corporate and Professional Changes
    6.1.3 What is the Organizational Ethics Horizon?

6.2 From Culture to Identity
    6.2.1 Organizational Culture or Organizational Ethics?
    6.2.2 Organizational Ethics Should Be Learning and Process-oriented

6.3 Reflective Organizational Ethics
    6.3.1 Structuring Components
    6.3.2 How to Understand the Process?

6.4 Real-world Examples
    6.4.1 Danone
    6.4.2 Interface

6.5 Conclusion

Abstract

Organizational ethics refers to the set of values that identifies an organization either as it is perceived by those working in the organization or by those who have dealings with the organization. Organizational ethics can be considered in a broad sense (that is, as the set of values which structures the organization and its practices) or in a narrow sense (that is, as only those values that express the vision, the "raison d'être" and the commitments of the organization, and which are linked to its identity).

We can speak of organizational ethics on the basis of various focal points: (i) the organization's practices – identifying the values which in fact structure organizational functioning; (ii) formal statements – studying the discourse which is proposed as a value reference for the organization; (iii) the processes which permit continual reinterpretation of the relationship between statements and practices; and (iv) the project – stressing what is relevant to the creation and renewal of corporate identity.

These four perspectives are not mutually exclusive. However, we can recognize them as evolutionary sequences of organizational ethics. This chapter conceives organizational ethics as an opportunity for learning and innovation. Organizational ethics is here viewed not merely as a process of awareness but as a project through which organizations reflect on themselves.

Keywords: values, corporate culture, organizational learning, organizational citizenship

6.1 Organizational Ethics as an Opportunity for Learning and Innovation

We talk about organizational ethics as an opportunity for learning and innovation because the organizational ethics issues do not exist in a vacuum. Rather they form both catalysts for the social and organizational changes and their products as well.

6.1.1 A Context for Social Change

Over the last few years, there have been substantial changes in both the discourse on corporations and society's expectations regarding them. One of the defining features of these changes consists in seeing corporations as simultaneously playing both economic and social roles. We could say that a view of corporations from both market and societal standpoints has emerged. This change has already materialized in various initiatives such as institutional proposals, the creation of new methodologies for auditing or accountability, the launching of new indices and rankings, the development of new investment tools, and social campaigns against corporate actions perceived as unacceptable.

This trend is inseparable from the deep transformations our economies and societies are undergoing. To be more precise: We believe that the debate about a new understanding of the relationships between corporations and society is an intrinsic part of these transformations. Beyond the clichés, terms such as globalization, knowledge society, or network society indicate that the whole world has become the frame of reference for corporations. Knowledge and talent are the key resources – linked to people and their learning processes – and the most suitable paradigm for understanding organizations is no longer the factory or the hierarchical bureaucracy but networks.

In an interdependent world, ICT and social networks pose new challenges to organizations' legitimacy. Here, legitimacy is understood as the need to build and win acceptance in society within the framework of diverse values and beliefs. Accordingly, it may be useful to recall Suchman's (1995) distinction between three types of legitimacy: pragmatic, cognitive, and moral. Pragmatic legitimacy is linked to a calculation of the interests of each party within the context of stakeholder relations. Cognitive legitimacy is the result of accepting certain generic assumptions – taken-for-granted frameworks and values – that enable one to plausibly construct organizations rhetorics (Castelló and Lozano 2011). Morality here enshrines a positive, normative evaluation of the organization and its activities. While all three dimensions should be borne in mind, one can only speak of organizational ethics if one incorporates moral legitimacy.

In this context, "organizational ethics" is the name we give to the way in which each organization reconstructs and responds, through practice, to the question on how these complex structures and new corporate responsibilities and social demands should be acknowledged and managed.

6.1.2 A Context for Corporate and Professional Changes

A series of questions has emerged through the process of redefining the role of corporations in society – along with the creation of issues that transcend the corporation's impact on society or its concomitant contributions. Precisely because the understanding of the role of corporations in society is changing, firms are asking themselves what a corporate identity actually means in a changing world. Some professionals are beginning to wonder how their personal view of life and corporate projects can be squared with their personal and professional integrity on the one hand and the consistency between their personal projects and professional and corporate projects on the other. Weick (1995) showed sensemaking's importance to organizations. Sensemaking is not an option, it is a process inherent in the organizational dynamic and takes both operational and existential forms.

Corporations are wondering how they can structure their organizations and foster corporate identity. Their task is made harder by the increased job mobility of professionals, multiculturalism, and transnational operations. Corporations' interactions with social actors are becoming increasingly more complex, requiring lengthy public justifications for their activities. This legitimizing process, related to the development of professional and corporate identities, has converged with the growing importance given to the formulation of corporate values and to finding management models and styles based explicitly on the commitment to fundamental values.

From this point of view organizations should be creative and innovative not only with regard to technologies and processes, but also with regard to establishing values to fuel corporate practices. We are considering the organization as a learning and ethical space where one can develop personal and corporate values. The task is thus to provide an axiological competence, which enables people and organizations to move freely within changing social and cultural contexts, characterized by the lack of a fixed set of values.

Organizational ethics implies that organizations are here to create direction, purpose, and meaning. Organizations should not limit themselves to simply speaking of their organizational culture but should also actively work on building their value-based identities.

6.1.3 What is the Organizational Ethics Horizon?

Scharmer (2009) speaks of the inner territory of leadership, which goes beyond mechanically repeating behavior patterns and conventional, well-worn models of thought. He argues the need to connect to the source of one's actions. This gives rise to practical and existential questions such as "Who is my self?" or "What is my work?".

It is not only individuals who should ask themselves these questions. Organizational ethics could lead companies "to pay attention to corporate existential matters such as: 'Who are "we"?', 'What do we stand for?', 'What are our core values?', 'How should we reflect upon our identity and responsibilities?', 'How should we measure, evaluate and report on our identity, development and success?'" (Pruzan 2001). In other words, organizational ethics is inseparable from the question of, "How can and do corporations contribute to constructing 'the good society'?" (Wood 1991).

We should never forget that any model of organization and management rests on an *anthropological model*. What makes it possible to understand and manage an organization is not only the clear conscience of its aim and strategy, but also the acknowledgement of the anthropological model that it has assumed. We can say that organizational ethics concerns the recognition that in pursuing their own ends, corporations ultimately promote and foster specific models of the individual and of society.

6.2 From Culture to Identity

6.2.1 Organizational Culture or Organizational Ethics?

Understanding organizations from the cultural point of view amounts to a radical shift in analyzing and managing them. Morgan (1986) points out that understanding organizations as cultures mainly hinges on two aspects. First, the cultural viewpoint pays attention to the symbolic – and even magic – meaning of the organization's life, which is inexplicable from a rational perspective. Secondly, it stresses that an organization also depends on a system of shared meanings and interpretation schemes. It is reasonable to conclude that company development involves (re)creating the meaning that shapes the company.

Schein offers an approach that allows us to better understand how to deal with organizational ethics. He states that organizational culture is the pattern of basic assumptions that a given group has invented, discovered, or developed in learning to cope with its problems of external adaptation and internal integration, and that have worked well enough to be considered valid and, therefore, to be taught to new members as the correct way to perceive, think, and feel in relation to those problems (Schein 1984, p. 3). In addition, he proposes a scheme that distinguishes three levels of culture, together with their interactions (Figure 6.1).

Organizational Ethics

Artifacts and Creations

- Technology
- Art
- Visible & Audible
- Behavior Patterns

Visible but Often Not Decipherable

Values

Greater Level of Awareness

Basic Assumptions

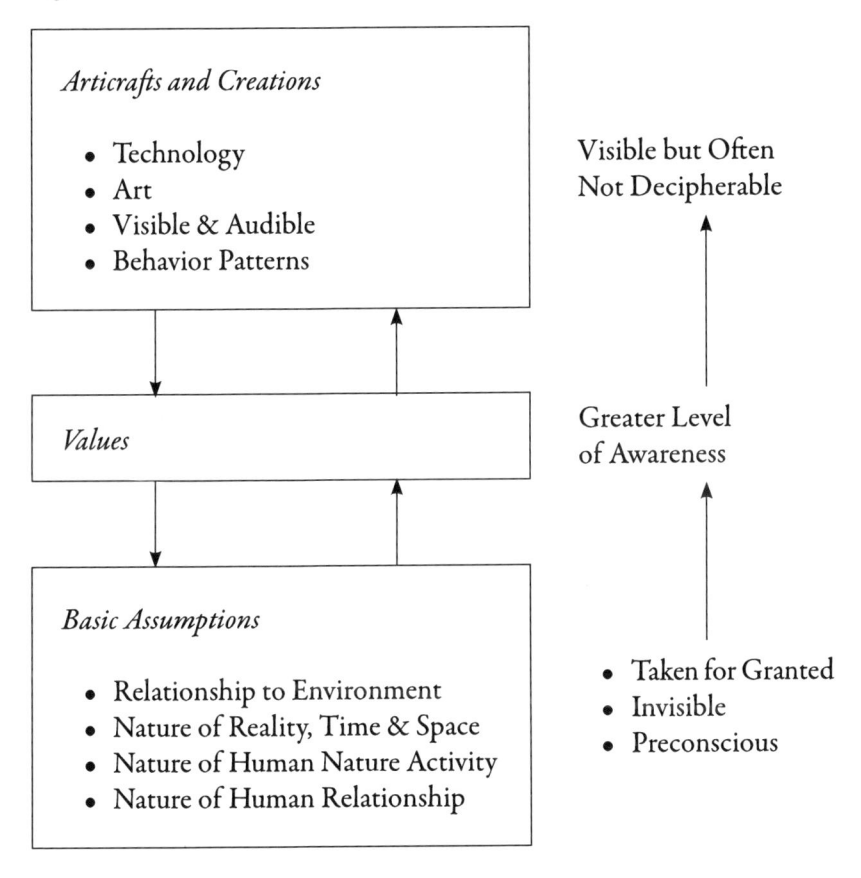

- Relationship to Environment
- Nature of Reality, Time & Space
- Nature of Human Nature Activity
- Nature of Human Relationship

- Taken for Granted
- Invisible
- Preconscious

Figure 6.1 The Levels of Culture and Their Interaction
Source: Schein 1984, p. 4.

Figure 6.1 reveals two things: (1) that it is not always easy to escape the temptation to reduce the development of an organizational culture to the level of artifacts and creations; and (2) that values play a crucial role in this process. It is for these reasons that Gagliardi (1986) argues that the maintenance of a corporation's cultural identity, through paying special attention to values, constitutes one of the most important management tasks. It is one of the most important tasks but also one of the most difficult ones. Torbert (2004) stresses the difference between single-, double-, and triple-loop awareness: The first focuses on behaviors and operations; the second on strategy, structure, and goals; the third on attention, intention, and vision. Consciously placing oneself in the third loop allows one to link practices in the other two with the construction of identity and sense.

What really makes sense is "a cultural perspective on changing and developing organizational ethics" (Trevino 1990), where the emphasis is precisely on organizational ethics and on the willingness to turn it into a project for corporate identity. In developing a moral culture a corporation must formulate clear ethical strategies and structures, taking into account opportunities and risks, resources and competencies, personal values and preferences, and economic and social responsibilities. Such a corporate process includes ethical codification; ethical training programs; extended stakeholder representation; ethical audits; new ways and methodologies to bring accountability; clear, open, and continuous communication and consultation at all levels; and appointing corporate officers to develop corporate ethics policies. These and other activities enable the corporation to systematically reflect upon the moral relevance of its functioning in order to arrive at a position suitable for ethical decision-making.

6.2.2 *Organizational Ethics Should Be Learning and Process-oriented*

Organizational ethics could be understood as a *shared value horizon* that facilitates transformation and orients organizational practices, simultaneously creating both significant and ethical meanings (Pruzan and Thyssen 1990). An organizational process that integrates ethical dimensions should make it possible to create this shared value horizon and live within it continuously. Considering this as a process is tantamount to assuming that it is not something given from the outset but something that must be created and constructed, with all the members or the organizations sharing in its creation as well as in its construction.

It is from this context that "we view learning as the bridge between working and innovating" (Brown and Duguid 1991). The type of innovation we need today refers to more than products, services, and processes. We also need to learn how to innovate in terms of institutions, values, and attitudes. In the emergent knowledge society, organizations will have to learn to build their own legitimacy (since it will be given to them from the outside), and they will have to decide how they want to be recognized. And how to do this is a question clearly linked to identity. "The pragmatic 'goods' for business organizations are defined in terms of the 'goods' of effectiveness and performance but there are also ethical 'goods' in terms of what serves corporate purpose, and moral 'goods' in the sense of just decisions. [...] It is for this reason that a theory of organizational ethics requires both substantive and procedural elements" (Collier 1998, p. 634). That is, organizational ethics needs to rely simultaneously on contents and processes; processes express the contents while contents give meaning to the processes. This is why clarifying organizational purpose has been put forward as one of the most important tasks in reviewing CSR and corporate values (Gentile and Samuelson 2005).

6.3 Reflective Organizational Ethics

Reflective organizational ethics is an approach. We can ask ourselves what traits shape this approach. We shall confine ourselves here to considering just three: first, a theoretical perspective that aims at integrating the ethical and corporate elements; second, a set of organizational ethics structuring components; and third, a way of understanding the process that structures a reflective organizational ethics.

6.3.1 Structuring Components

Here we refer to those elements that we need to consider in order to grasp the nature of organizational ethics in an organization.

A negative component. This refers to all those organizational approaches aimed basically at avoiding actions that might be considered reprehensible.

These approaches concern risk avoidance and penalties. When these approaches prevail, they encourage reactive attitudes. Here we include everything related to reputation management, to the extent that it might ultimately reflect a desire to avoid a bad reputation.

A normative component (of a legal nature). This refers to all those organizational approaches that reflect how organizations square themselves with both the spirit and the letter of the law. This also includes their consistency in dealing with different demands and legal frameworks in the countries where they operate.

A normative component (of a fundamental nature). This refers to the relevance that an appeal to Human Rights has in corporate actions and policies, which can range from passive conformity to active commitment. We believe that on this point "the need for organizational ethics becomes visible as a link between legality and legitimacy" (Pruzan and Thyssen 1990).

A propositional component. This refers to the instruments (codes, formal statements, etc.) available to organizations in explicitly proposing a frame of reference for its actions. This enables a positive approach, but when the statements are taken out of context they can become irrelevant or, worse still, a PR whitewash.

A personal component. This refers to the possibility – and the challenge – of increasing human quality in the organizational context. The question is not only how to avoid the corrosion of character but also how to promote character-building as an intrinsic component of professional development. This implies a system of acknowledgement and reward for behavior that is consistent with corporate values.

A procedural component. This refers to the way in which decision-making processes are managed as well as the way in which tensions and the diversity of criteria are dealt with. It also covers the creation of a corporate tradition in decision-making procedures, a tradition enabling the corporation to manage conflicts over incompatible options reflecting equally desirable values.

An institutional component. This refers to the range of instruments (for example, from allocating specific responsibilities to training programs) designed to create new corporate spheres in which values and practices are made explicit, learned, and integrated in daily work.

A relational component. This refers to building relationships with stakeholders, which includes the values at stake. Accordingly, relationships should not be reduced to merely managing interests or to information gathering. The relationship with stakeholders should be based on dialogue and partnership. This can be especially relevant in the knowledge society where the limits of organizations are more like permeable membranes than sea walls.

An accountability component. This refers to the need to find procedures to identify, evaluate, and give an accounting of the correlation between corporate practices and values. "The first point to make is that if ethical auditing is to create ethical *knowledge* about the impacts of companies on the ability of their employees, customers, communities and other stakeholders to lead good and flourishing lives. [...] However useful empirical data is, it is only half the story. The other half, the half that is required if ethical auditing is to create ethical knowledge, is a process of *experimentation and theory building*" (Mackenzie 1998, p. 1397).

Pruzan and Thyssen rightly summarize the point: "Developing and employing organizational ethics is a demanding strategic task for the autopoietic organization. The focus is on the dynamic interplay between conflict and consensus in an ongoing conversation between the organizations and its stakeholders. The ideal of ethics is action, which is rationally accepted for all the parties involved. This ethical principle forms a basis for operational directives as to such far reaching areas as the organization's and its stakeholders' identity and values, the development of the company's ethical codex and Ethical Accounting Statement, the ethical design of the organization, the dissolution of intra-, inter-, and systemic conflicts, and finally formal procedures for conflict solving when conflicts cannot be dissolved by consensus. [...] It is often said that ethics cannot co-exist with free market competition. Our conclusion is the opposite: only if the enterprise develops – and lives up to – an organizational ethics can private initiative survive in the long run" (Pruzan and Thyssen 1990, p. 151).

6.3.2 How to Understand the Process?

An organization not only produces goods and services but in doing so, it shapes itself. Consequently, a reflective organizational ethics should attend to its processes as well as its contents. These processes should enable us to answer the questions: What are the values shaping our identity? With whom do we want to identify ourselves and how do we want to be identified? What do we want to commit ourselves to and how?

Such reflective and practical development of corporate values and identity follows a sequence that can take various forms directly related to specific methodologies and instruments. The forms these assume depend on the nature of each organization and its circumstances. Nevertheless, the process tends to go through certain stages (Figure 6.2).

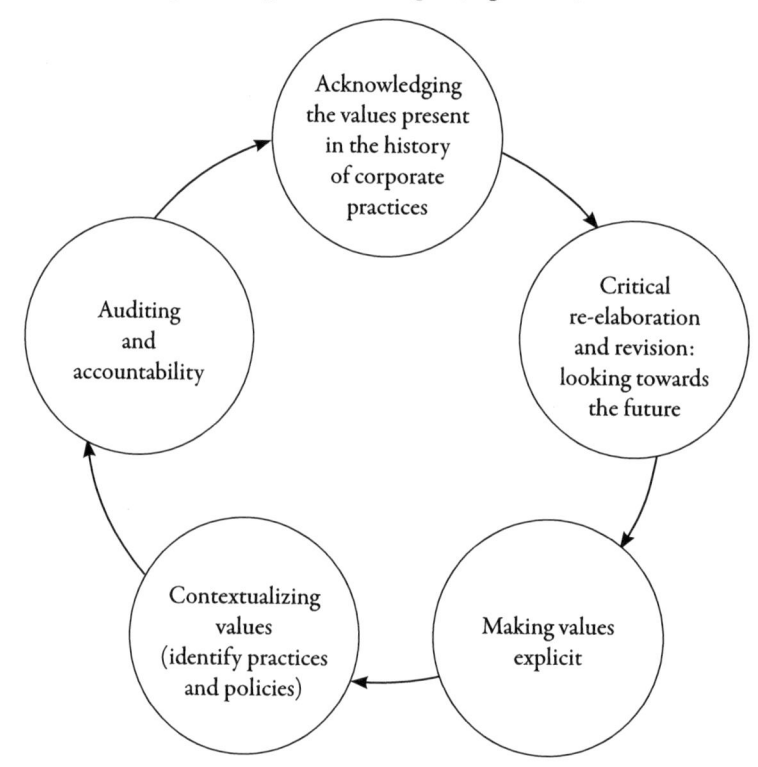

Figure 6.2 *The Development of Corporate Values*

From this sequence, which characterizes the entire organizational ethics, we would like to underscore the following:

We should avoid the temptation to believe that we start from scratch. On the contrary, it is very important to allow the opportunity to make explicit the diversity of values concerning the organization's history and development. This explication process should make it possible not only to remember the formal statements but also to bring to the surface the implicit values identified as present in prevailing practices, attitudes, and tendencies. In this context, it is also very important not to fall into the trap of moralizing but to instead let the organization's values surface, whatever we happen to think of them.

The critical reformulation of the predominant values in the existing organization should not be approached in a confrontational fashion but should rather be directed towards building a consensus that makes values explicit. This consensus should not be reduced to an agreement on the least common denominator but should instead show the path ahead, emphasizing that it represents a shared project. It should also take into account the contribution that the organization makes to society: It is vital not to turn reflective organizational ethics into an inward-looking corporate process.

Values only make sense in a context. A reflective organizational ethics aims at turning the organization into a shared ethical space. For this reason creativity and innovation become indispensable, as an exercise enabling us to identify and formulate the specific practices and policies giving shape to corporate identity. Clarity in the orientation should be compatible with trust and with respect for individual differences: The objective is to generate identity and cohesion, not homogenization and control.

The entire process makes no sense without some form of auditing and accountability, which will make it possible to resume the process and to turn the commitment to values into a key for corporate improvement and innovation, and into an opportunity to build stable and transparent relations with stakeholders.

From all of the above it follows that a key question for corporate identity is to decide on whom one gives a voice in the various stages of the process. We refer here both to voices within and without the organization (internal dialogue and stakeholder dialogue). We believe that the question should always be raised because the answer we give will define the process itself.

To summarize the perspectives in organizational ethics, we can underscore two main orientations (Figure 6.3).

Normative and downward	Someone with authority establishes the values	The result establishes the identity and gives legitimacy	Enunciate Communicate Accept Assume Apply	(obedience with participation)
Narrative and diagonal	The formulation process is an intrinsic component of working with values	The process builds the identity and gives credibility	Enunciate Communicate Accept Assume Apply	(value-building process)

Figure 6.3 Approaches to Organizational Ethics

These two approaches should be considered as general orientations when one engages in the developing organizational ethics. In any case, some form of enunciation, communication, acceptance, assumption, and application of corporate values is certainly required. Reflective organizational ethics almost always requires a narrative and dialogical approach.

Our view of values has to be clarified within the framework of reflective organizational ethics.

We propose a *dynamic* view of values. Values are not inanimate objects but rather the expression of a horizon that directs and gives meaning to our actions. This means that in our organizations, the accent should not be on the definition of our identity (as if this were some fixed essence) but on what we identify with, what our project is, what we have in common, and what we want to achieve.

We propose a *practical* view of values. We do not proceed from formulated values to practices; rather, we enunciate our values when we give direction and meaning to what we do. Values are not holy writ to be carved in stone but a catalyst for innovation and creativity. Any discourse on values within an organization should be linked to the process of making associated improvements explicit, regarding competencies which should be developed and policies that need implementation, if we want to assume these values. This is based on the conviction that a reflective organizational ethics should entail an improvement in and of an organization's quality and cohesion.

We propose a *dialogical* perspective with regard to values. A dialogical perspective can potentially reach all stakeholders. Organizationally, the question is how to go from "my" values to "our" values: it is a process from "me" to "we". This implies that an organizational environment takes into account the individuals' autonomy, sensibility, and values as well as professional ethics. However, this does not mean we should be satisfied with a cacophony of voices. Rather, these views are the point of departure and support for achieving one of the aims of reflective organizational ethics: learning to say "we" instead of "I," alone.

We propose a *committed* perspective with regard to values. That is to say, we believe that reference to values should not be rhetorical but practical. This means that taking care of an organization's core values is one of the fundamental features of the management function and of leadership at all the levels of the organization. Put differently, reflective organizational ethics exists when talk about the future is inextricably bound to our present commitment.

We should recall that a true process of reflective organizational ethics fosters learning, which in turn affects identity, both personal and organizational. This learning is an opportunity for change and transformation, which is reflected in Figure 6.4, p. 118.

```
                          What do we learn?
                         /                \
        Learning to do things          Learning about oneself
        and to work with others
         /            \                   /              \
    To            To achieve        Learning         Learning
    collaborate   objectives        to know          to be
    with other    with other        oneself          oneself
    people        people
    and/or        and/or
    organizations organizations
    (different    (shared
    objectives)   objectives)
```

| As an individual | As a professional | As an organization | As an individual | As a professional | As an organization |

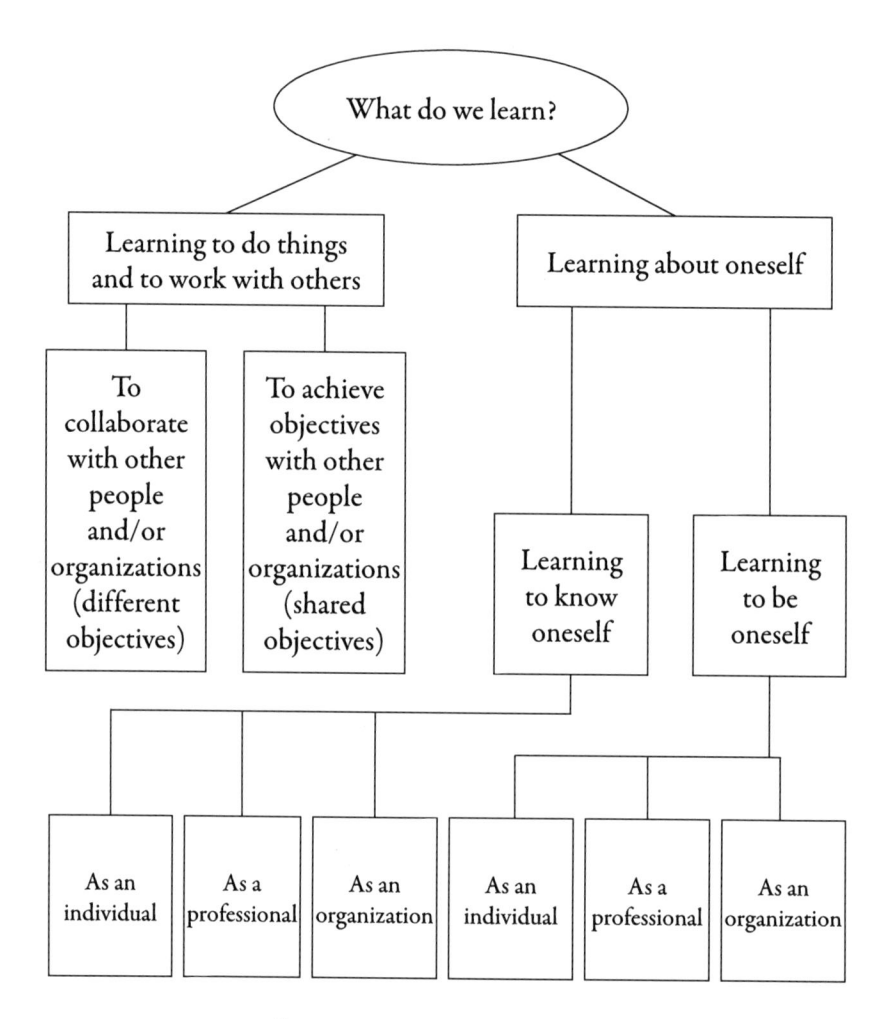

Figure 6.4 *Organizational Learning*
Adapted from Folguera (2000)

Organizational Ethics

6.4 Real-world Examples

Each organization builds its organizational ethics according to its own traditions. Since this construction is basically a process, it contains contradictions and ambiguities. Each organization provides itself with the tools it considers necessary to give shape to its own organizational ethics. We provide two examples below: Danone and Interface. It is worth noting that in both cases, the construction of an identity built on values in inextricably linked to corporate strategy and innovation: values, strategy, and innovation configure corporate identity – they do not run in parallel but rather dovetail. As shown by Vilanova and Dettoni's (2011) study, Danone and Interface share ten special qualities and features that go some way towards explaining their sustainable innovation practices: (1) inspiring leaders; (2) a sustainability vision; (3) a will to survive success; (4) a sustainable innovation culture; (5) sustainable products and services; (6) an engaged workforce; (7) the aim to innovate innovation; (8) a willingness to challenge the organization; (9) optimism; (10) genuineness.

6.4.1 Danone

Danone was created when a French company (BSN) in the food and glass container business merged with a Catalan yogurt firm in 1967. This is significant because Danone was created by Isaac Carasso, a man who was obsessed with making healthy food products (which were initially only sold through pharmacies but were later moved into the retail chain). The BSN part of the company was led by Antoine Riboud, who fervently believed in corporate social responsibility as a key competitiveness factor. In fact, in 1972, just a few years after the merger, Antoine Riboud gave a famous speech in which he said that Danone should undertake a *"double project"*, meaning that it should achieve both financial and social benefits: "Corporate responsibility does not end at the factory gate or at office doors. The jobs a business creates are central to the lives of employees and the energy and raw materials we consume change the shape of our planet. Public opinion is there to remind us of our responsibility in the industrial world of today".

Danone's competitiveness model is built on five pillars. First, focusing on people, including the workers at Danone but also (as Antoine Riboud said in 1972) understanding that they must consider other stakeholders – which means suppliers, customers, communities, and society at large. Second, understanding that as a leading food company one of Danone's central responsibilities is playing a key role in contributing to health. Third, being an innovative company, staying ahead of its competition through "blue sky thinking," (using innovation to power growth, rather than fighting over market shares from competitors). Fourth, reaching as many customers as possible. In this area of "Danone for All," the company reaches 500 million consumers a month and the target is to double that number in four years. Fifth, in the "nature" pillar, Danone wants to reduce its CO_2 emissions by 30 per cent by 1 January 2012, in addition to making some key products that are CO_2 neutral by that same date.

Danone's sustainability strategy focuses on six main fronts: (1) people; (2) water; (3) packaging; (4) agriculture; (5) climate change; (6) biodiversity. Danone Group establishes some general objectives or guidelines for each of these six fronts, but then each country is responsible for turning them into specific policies and practices. Danone sees sustainability as a key competitiveness factor to: "build consumer trust in brands backed by steady flow of investment in product safety, respect for environmental standards and concern for society at large;" "attract talented people looking for a business with a strong culture and value; consolidate internal cohesion through management practices favoring individual progress;" "forge mutually beneficial ties to strategic customers and suppliers."

Some examples of interesting sustainability policies and activities developed at Danone include the development of a factory in Bangladesh to develop yogurt with high nutrition content in a joint venture with Grameen Bank; the establishment of a new partnership in collaboration with the food bank; the institutionalization of the figure of the Carbon Master in each country to supervise and measure the advancements of each subsidiary in achieving CO_2 reduction targets; the restructuring of the company to include a Nature vice-presidency at a global level as one

Organizational Ethics

of the strategic pillars of the company; the development of a sustainability measuring tool called Danone Way Fundamentals; the project to integrate sustainability measuring, particularly in terms of footprint, on their SAP system; accounting sustainability as one third of the bonus evaluation of all executives; eliminating some packaging and distribution systems; creating the Danone Ecosystems Funds; evaluating suppliers on sustainability issues and making four of their top brands carbon neutral.

6.4.2 Interface

Interface is the worldwide leader in design, production, and sales of modular carpet for the commercial, institutional, and residential markets, and a leading designer and manufacturer of commercial broadloom. The company operates in Europe, Middle East, Africa, and India, plus Asia Pacific and the Americas. It is headquartered in Atlanta and has factories in the US, UK, Netherlands, Thailand, Australia, and China.

As in the Danone case, to understand Interface one must start by learning about its founder and CEO, Ray Anderson, who in the mid-1990s shifted the company's strategy, aiming to redirect its industrial practices to include a focus on sustainability without sacrificing its business goals. Anderson wrote a book entitled *Mid-Course Correction* in which he discussed his own awakening, what he called his *"epiphany,"* to environmental concerns and thus presented a model for businesses to achieve sustainability. That explains why today Interface has as its goal "To be the first company that, by its deeds, shows the entire industrial world what sustainability is in all its dimensions: People, process, product, place and profits – by 2020 – and in doing so we will become restorative through the power of influence."

Although Interface is a relatively small company, as multinationals go, it is considered a particularly innovative company in sustainability. For instance, they do not say that they sell modular carpet, but rather "environmentally responsible modular carpet." *Fortune* talks about Interface as one of the "Most Admired Companies in America" and one of the "100 Best Companies to Work For." In fact, Interface has recently leveraged its position as a business leader in sustainability by creating a consulting arm called InterfaceRAISE. The objective is to help other companies develop similar sustainability strategies and products, understanding that collaboration will probably result in greater and speedier change. In its 2009 report Interface claims that three of its key competitiveness strengths are its "innovative capabilities," its "reputation for quality," and its "position as a global sustainability leader."

Interface's dedication to sustainability has evolved into the company's Mission Zero commitment, which is the "promise to eliminate any negative impact Interface has on the environment by 2020." To achieve their goal they have developed a policy based on seven fronts of action: (1) eliminating waste, which aims to eliminate all forms of waste in every business area; (2) benign emissions, to eliminate toxic substances from products, vehicles, and emissions; (3) renewable energy, to reduce energy demands and simultaneously substitute current sources with renewable ones; (4) closing the loop, which aims at redesigning processes and products so that all sources used can be recovered and reused; (5) resource efficient transportation, transporting people and products efficiently, and reducing emissions; (6) sensitizing stakeholders, creating a community around Interface that understands the ecosystem; and (7) redesigning commerce, to focus on the delivery of service and value instead of material.

Some examples of interesting policies and projects developed at Interface are the FairWorks project developed in India; the new business line mentioned earlier called InterfaceRAISE to help other companies become more sustainable; the development of the Emission Zero document with clear goals in terms of timeframes and objectives; the Zelflo project to develop a new cellulose-based material; the institutionalization of the sustainability council; training all Interface employees in sustainability issues; making some Interface employees sustainability *"ambassadors"* for the company; generating products built on bio-based materials; verifying and certifying externally many of their initiatives, such as ISO, green manufacturing, green showrooms, or green products; focusing a lot of their R&D on sustainability concepts such as bio-mimicry (looking at models and processes in nature) which led to the pioneering of random designs; designing products with high recycled content and developing systems to separate and recycle their carpet tiles; and making all their factories run on alternative energies.

6.5 Conclusion

We live in a society composed of organizations. Their impact (both positive and negative) as social actors raises questions concerning the values guiding them and the legitimacy of their actions. Each organization has to create its own network of relationships and decide on the criteria and values that guide its actions and provide its raison d'être. It is for this reason that we have talked about reflective organizational ethics.

We should overcome the implicit division of social responsibility traditionally assumed by organizations in accordance with their genre (corporations, governments, institutions, NGOs, non-profit, etc.). In today's world, responsibilities are shared – we can no longer talk about isolated responsibilities; we need to speak about shared responsibilities. Consequently, the interrelationship between different types of organizations is increasingly important in meeting social challenges. If a genuine dialogue is to arise from such an interrelationship, it is essential that organizations rethink the way they see themselves. In this sense, we think that a partnership approach will be one of the keys to organizational ethics in the future.

The future of organizations is inseparable from the future of society. Accordingly, it is increasingly necessary to speak about *organizational citizenship* as well as organizational ethics. We cannot elaborate a reflection on organizations without also reflecting on their contributions to society. We can illustrate organizational citizenship as the intersection of three elements (Figure 6.5, p. 124).

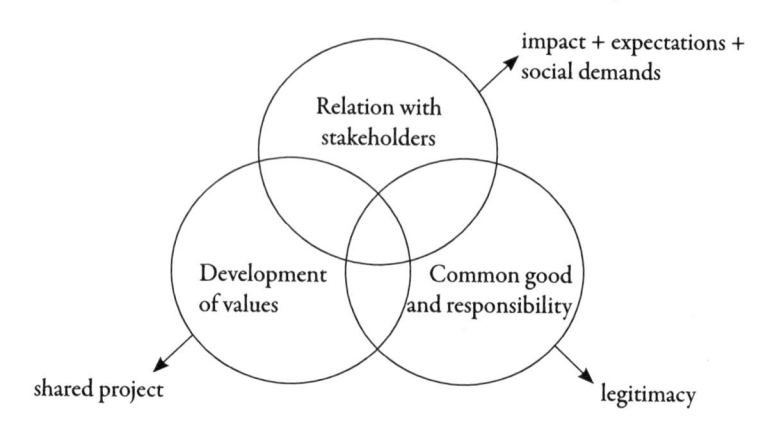

```
                    impact + expectations +
                    social demands
        Relation with
        stakeholders


  Development      Common good
  of values        and responsibility

shared project                          legitimacy
```

Figure 6.5 *How to Situate the Organization in the Social Context*
Source: author, adapted from Zadek, Pruzan and Evans (1997)

Speaking of organizational ethics in this way helps offset the risk of adopting a unilateralist stance. When the development or management of values within an organization is a predominant concern, it means there is a risk of manipulation and indoctrination (to the extent that anyone talking only about values while looking inwards is probably bent on making the organization homogenous and closed). When we find only organizational references to stakeholders, it means the firm runs the risk of seeking an exclusively pragmatic approach based on strategic advantage, while ignoring the need for dialogue. When we find only organizational references to the company's contribution to society, it means that the firm runs the risk of merely carrying out a PR exercise. It is the integration of all three elements that makes organizational ethics appear publicly as organizational citizenship.

In the context of globalization, we should speak of organizational citizenship because governance is a challenge for everyone in an interdependent world. We also need a civil contribution to governance at the micro, meso, and macro levels (Lozano 2010). It is true that some organizations (particularly corporations) contribute, through their actions, to the problems plaguing our world, but all of them should be part of the solution. In this respect, we consider organizational citizenship as a new public manifestation of an advanced and reflective organizational ethics.

Organizational citizenship implies a broader vision of organizations as actors operating within a social context. This means highlighting the role of organizations as social contributors and innovators. This also means that the specific contribution of each organization to society takes the shape of an itinerary when moving from organizational ethics to organizational citizenship.

References

Brown, J. S. and Duguid, P. (1991) Organizational Learning and Communities-of-practice: Toward a Unified View of Working, Learning and Innovation. *Organization Science*, vol. 2, no. 1, pp. 40–57.

Castelló, I. and Lozano, J. M. (2011) Searching for New Forms of Legitimacy through Corporate Responsibility Rhetoric. *Journal of Business Ethics*, vol. 100, pp. 11–29.

Castells, M. (2000) *The Information Age* (3 vols) 2nd edn. Oxford: Blackwell.

Colliers, J. (1998) Theorizing the ethical organization. *Business Ethics Quarterly*, vol. 8, no. 4, pp. 621–654.

Gagliardi, P. (1986) The Creation and Change of Organizational Cultures: A Conceptual Framework. *Organization Studies*, vol. 7, no. 2, pp. 117–134.

Gentile, M. C. and Samuelson, J. F. (2005) The State of Affairs for Management Education and Social Responsibility. *Academy of Management, Learning & Education*, vol. 4, no. 4, pp. 496–505.

Hoffman, W. M. (1986) What is Necessary for Corporate Moral Excellence? *Journal of Business Ethics*, vol. 5, pp. 233–242.

Lozano, J. M. (2000) *Ethics and Organizations. Understanding Business Ethics as a Learning Process*. Dordrecht: Kluwer.

Lozano, J. M. (2010) *The Relational Company. Responsibility, Sustainability, Citizenship*. Oxford: Peter Lang.

Lozano, J. M. and Sauquet, A. (1999) Integrating Business and Ethical Values through Practitioner Dialogue. *Journal of Business Ethics*, vol. 22, pp. 203–217.

Mackenzie, C. (1998) Ethical Auditing and Ethical Knowledge. *Journal of Business Ethics*, vol. 17, pp. 1395–1402.

Morgan, G. (1986) *Images of Organisation*. London: Sage Publications.

Pruzan, P. (2001) Corporate Reputation: Image and Identity. *Corporate Reputation Review*, vol. 4, no. 1, pp. 50–64.

Pruzan, P. (2001) The Question of Organizational Consciousness: Can Organizations Have Values, Virtues and Visions? *Journal of Business Ethics*, vol. 29, pp. 271–284.

Pruzan, P. and Thyssen, O. (1990) Conflict and Consensus: Ethics as a Shared Value Horizon for Strategic Planning. *Human Systems Management*, vol. 9, pp. 135–151.

Scharmer, O. (2009) *Theory U*. San Francisco: Berrett-Koehler.

Schein, E. H. (1984) Coming to a New Awareness of Organizational Culture. *Sloan Management Review*, Winter, pp. 3–16.

Sinclair, A. (1993) Approaches to Organisational Culture and Ethics. *Journal of Business Ethics*, vol. 12, pp. 63–73.

Smirlich, L. (1983) Concepts of Culture and Organizational Analysis. *Administrative Science Quarterly*, vol. 28, pp. 339–358.

Suchman, M. (1995) Managing Legitimacy: Strategic and Institutional Approaches. *Academy of Management Review*, vol. 20, pp. 571–610.Torbert, B. (2004) *Action Inquiry*. San Francisco: Berrett-Koehler.

Trevino, L. K. (1990) A Cultural Perspective on Changing and Developing Organizational Ethics. *Research in Organizational Change and Development*, vol. 4, pp. 195–230.

Vilanova, M. and Dettoni, P. (2011) *Sustainable Innovation Strategies*. Barcelona: Institute for Social Innovation.

Weick, K. E. (1995) *Sensemaking in Organizations*. Thousand Oaks, CA: Sage Publications.

Wood, D. J. (1991) Corporate Social Performance Revisited. *Academy of Management Review*, vol. 16, no. 4, pp. 691–718.

KNUT J. IMS AND LARS JACOB TYNES PEDERSEN
(NHH NORWEGIAN SCHOOL OF ECONOMICS)

7 Personal Responsibility and Ethical Action

7.1 Introduction and Central Issue

7.2 State of the Art of Current Theories
    7.2.1 Ethical and Unethical Action
    7.2.2 Various Conceptions of Responsibility
    7.2.3 Responsible Decision Making

7.3 New Approaches and Solutions
    7.3.1 Personal Responsibility
    7.3.2 Shared Responsibility

7.4 Real-world Examples
    7.4.1 Exit as Responsible Action
    7.4.2 Whistle-blowing as Responsible Action
    7.4.3 Moral Whispering as Responsible Action

7.5 Conclusion

Abstract

There is a close connection between responsibility and ethicality. We provide an insight into the role of personal responsibility in promoting ethical action in business organizations. Assuming an action-oriented perspective on human actors, the importance of deep emotions like empathy and justice is emphasized. Personal responsibility is contrasted with role-mediated behavior and common morality. The perspective can be broadened by introducing the concept of shared responsibility. Personally responsible action almost always includes conflicting loyalties in organizations. Using Hirschman's distinctions between "exit", "voice," and "loyalty," real-world cases are discussed: Inge Wallage's decision to leave her job in Statoil ("exit"), Per-Yngve Monsen's whistle-blowing in Siemens ("voice"), and Storebrand's shareholder strategy as a form of moral whispering ("loyalty"). The cases provide an insight into alternative strategies for personally responsible action in organizational life.

Keywords: personal responsibility, shared responsibility, conflicting loyalties in organizations

7.1 Introduction and Central Issue

In this chapter, we discuss the nature of personal responsibility and ethical action – two concepts that are central to business ethics both in theory and practice. A main concern of business ethics is to distinguish between ethical and unethical decisions or actions in business, i.e. identifying ethically relevant differences between acts that are justifiable from an ethical point of view and those that are not. One of the objectives of such analyses is to assess whether a particular act constitutes *responsible behavior*.

Assessments of responsibility are often retrospective, in the sense that to a large extent they focus on the *accountability* of the decision maker for decisions and activities that have been carried out. The focus is typically the degree to which they: (1) comply with or breach important moral principles (deontological ethics); (2) produce a positive or negative surplus of consequences (utilitarian ethics); or (3) are consistent or inconsistent with conceptions of virtuous character and practice (virtue ethics). (See also Chapter 4.)

However, in line with Hans Jonas's (1984) emphasis on the continuous increase of power that follows from technological progress and the corresponding vulnerability of nature, business ethics also needs to focus on the *prospective responsibility* of individuals and organizations. Prospective responsibility, argues Zsolnai (2009), implies that the moral actor has a duty or obligation to ensure that something occurs. Hence, responsibility is *future-directed* – it deals with the question of *what to do* in order to achieve certain desired outcomes or to avoid certain undesirable outcomes. Already, at this point in distinguishing between ethically justifiable and unjustifiable acts, we can see the close connection between questions of ethicality and questions of responsibility – notions that are inextricably intertwined. As the chapter progresses, we will further explore the question of how responsibility and ethical action relate to each other.

We will also emphasize how an action perspective should be distinguished from a decision perspective in the sense of processes and outcomes. There may be decisions without actions and actions without any prior decisions. While the decision paradigm indicates rational oriented actors, an action paradigm is more mundane in the sense of assuming non-heroic individuals who may be seriously torn between conflicting claims and duties, and ultimately have to choose one of them. Such processes of choice are not necessarily driven by one-sided rational thoughts but may be partly based on deep emotions like empathy and compassion.

We aim to give an insight into the role of personal responsibility in promoting ethical action in business organizations. Moreover, we will discuss several different strategies for assuming personal responsibility in order to shed light on the different meanings and ways of acting responsibly in business. We will discuss how this involves acting in a manner that is both (1) *other-directed*, in the sense that it takes into account important norms and the interests of stakeholders, and (2) *self-directed*, in the sense that it is compatible with the personal values and life-project of the individual moral actor. This leads us to the central issue: how individuals in organizations can act responsibly with regard to the organizations of which they are a part, the stakeholders who are influenced by their decisions and acts, and towards themselves. Often, their objectives will conflict, creating dilemmas and loyalty problems for the individual. This is a core problem when attempting to act responsibly. For what and towards who are you responsible – and how do you make priorities in practice?

The chapter is structured as follows. In Section 7.2 we outline contemporary theories of responsibility and what they tell us about what constitutes ethical action. In Section 7.3 we discuss novel perspectives on promoting personal responsibility in organizational life. In Section 7.4 we present real-world examples in order to illustrate the theoretical points discussed throughout the paper. For purposes of illustration, we choose the individual's decision of whether or not to blow the whistle following the realization that one's organization is doing something blameworthy. We will discuss three different strategies – exit, voice, and loyalty (cf. Hirschman 1970) – as decision alternatives facing the individual, and discuss them in the light of personal responsibility and the ethicality of the action. Finally, we briefly outline our conclusions (Section 7.5).

7.2 State of the Art of Current Theories

In this section, we outline central contemporary perspectives on responsibility and ethical action. First, we discuss the nature of ethical action. Second, we outline various conceptions of responsibility. Third, we discuss a framework for responsible decision making. Thereby, we provide the reader with a broad perspective on responsibility in organizational life.

7.2.1 Ethical and Unethical Action

Ethical actions are typically exercised in situations where there are multiple values at stake and where important values can be realized or protected by the choice and behavior of the individual. This means that the individual as a moral actor needs to understand that he or she is faced with an ethical problem, to make a responsible decision and to carry out that decision in actual behavior (cf. Vetlesen 1994). First, this requires moral sensitivity – the ability to recognize that important values are at stake in the situation and that the action alternatives between which he or she must choose have different value implications for the various involved parts or stakeholders (Pedersen 2009). In such a situation, the person considers: (1) what is at stake, and (2) for whom. Thus, he or she identifies stakeholders – amongst them *himself* or *herself* – to which he or she must attend, as well as their diverse interests or needs. Moreover, in order to act ethically, the individual needs the ability to reflect on the ethically relevant dimensions of the problem and arrive at a justifiable decision about what should be done. Finally, the individual needs the moral character to carry out the decision even if it entails personal costs. As discussed by Zsolnai (2002), moral character is necessary for ethical action in most situations, since there is often a high cost in acting ethically. This is a characteristic of many, but not all, ethical actions. The fact that costs are often associated with such an act implies that the most comfortable course of action is often not the ethical one.

Another important characteristic of both ethical and unethical action is that the individual may *unconsciously* carry out an act. This implies that he or she may act ethically or unethically without considering the act from an ethical point of view at all, or equally the (un)ethical act may be the outcome of a conscious, deliberative process. Opdal (2011) describes the different types of unconscious motivations for individuals and propagates the importance of knowing more about such motives in order to tackle important problems like the climate crisis. He draws the conclusion that we do not like to be responsible when the consequences of our decisions are likely to be unacceptable to us (Opdal 2011, p. 36). Generally, we hold individuals responsible for the choices they make and the acts they carry out, whether or not those acts are the outcome of a conscious ethical judgment. In the following paragraphs we outline relevant perspectives on responsibility in organizational life.

7.2.2 Various Conceptions of Responsibility

Responsibility is a concept at the heart of ethics. However, it is a concept with multiple meanings, which are interchangeable and overlapping. According to Bovens (1998, pp. 24–26), five forms of responsibility can be distinguished and give an indication of the broadness of the concept.

First, we may talk of *responsibility as a cause*, i.e. that people, things, or circumstances may cause the emergence of certain outcomes. We refer to this as causal responsibility. Second, we may talk of *responsibility as accountability*, i.e. moral, political, and/or legal liability for the outcomes of a behavior carried out by the agent. This means that moral responsibility is closely linked to the concept of accountability, which implies giving an account of why a given behavior was carried out (Messner 2009). Using the terms of Jonas (1984), this might be called formal responsibility. Third, we may talk of *responsibility as capacity*, i.e. the responsibility (or lack thereof) that follows from being *able to* exercise a certain amount of responsibility (either due to power, knowledge, or mental ability, or the lack thereof; (Sen 2002). This is what is reflected in the notion "noblesse oblige" or "with great power comes great responsibility." It implies that an individual's responsibility is a function of the degree to which he or she has the means to take responsibility. Fourth, we may talk of *responsibility as task*, i.e. the obligations or functions that follow from having a particular role or position. This is closely related to role-mediated or professional responsibility. Finally, we may talk of *responsibility as virtue*, i.e. the value-laden individual character trait that inclines the individual to act responsibly.

As the five forms of responsibility indicate, we variously use the concept of responsibility to denote features of: (1) the individual and his or her capacities and character, (2) his or her role or professional affiliation, or (3) his or her agency in a particular situation. However, Jonas (1984) uses several distinctions that should be mentioned. For one thing, we have contractual responsibility, where we assume that two partners are more or less on an equal footing. This implies a kind of horizontal responsibility. In addition, we also have a kind of vertical, non-reciprocal responsibility, of which the parent-child relationship is the paradigmatic case. The same paradigm should be used for man's relationship to nature and to future generations. Jonas's (1984) central concept is *substantive responsibility*, which is for what matter you are responsible. In this way, Jonas extends the horizon of responsibility, and lays a positive duty of power on human beings.

For the remainder of the chapter, we will focus on the individual's *moral responsibility* and will build on several of the above different forms in our discussion. Moreover, as noted in the introduction, it is useful to distinguish between retrospective and prospective responsibility (Jonas 1984). In our discussion of personal responsibility we will focus on the latter, because personal responsibility in organizational life is largely oriented towards acting in a manner that ensures that acts and outcomes are aligned with the individual's personal beliefs, values, and life-projects.

7.2.3 Responsible Decision Making

In light of the multitude of meanings of responsibility, there is a need for a concrete and more operational framework for making responsible decisions. Zsolnai (2009) offered a comprehensive framework for responsible decision making that comprises three dimensions of responsibility for managerial decision making. According to Zsolnai responsible decisions integrate *rationality* in goal attainment, *respect* for stakeholders, and *reverence* for ethical norms.

This framework implies that decision makers should balance three different objectives in order to promote responsible decisions. First, the decision maker must formulate the goal and find the most efficient means to achieve it, i.e. maximize the goal attainment value of the decision problem. Second, the relevant ethical norms related to the decision must be identified, and the manner in which the norms constrain the decision must be taken into account. Third, the relevant stakeholders and their interests must be identified, and the implication of respecting their interests for the decision must be understood.

Decision makers make trade-offs along these three dimensions, which are seldom in harmony. According to Zsolnai's model (2009, p. 116), responsible decision-making involves a multidimensional evaluation of any decision alternative based on three types of value. First, the decision should be evaluated with regard to whether it is rational for adequately achieving the desired goal. Second, it should be evaluated based on the degree to which it complies with relevant ethical norms. Finally, it should be evaluated based on the degree to which the decision respects the interests of affected stakeholders. The decision rule that is suggested in order to ensure the most responsible decision is the *maximin* rule (cf. Rawls 1971), i.e. the decision maker should choose the least worst alternative when all three dimensions are taken into account. This means that the worst aspect of the chosen alternative is better than the worst aspect of any other decision alternative.

Zsolnai's (2009) framework for responsible decision making provides an insight into the multidimensional nature of responsible decisions as ethical action, and it makes explicit how trade-offs between different dimensions of one's responsibility can be carried out in practical decision making.

7.3 New Approaches and Solutions

In this section, we outline novel perspectives on responsibility – and in particular *personal responsibility*. First, we discuss personal responsibility as the individual's active responsibility-taking in organizational life. Second, we develop this perspective on personal responsibility by discussing the concept of *shared responsibility* and what it implies for personal responsibility.

7.3.1 Personal Responsibility

In the business ethics literature, the main emphasis is on corporate social responsibility, which deals with questions relating to the responsibility of business organizations. Central questions in this regard are: (1) For what are they responsible, i.e. their domain of responsibility? (2) Towards whom are they responsible, i.e. the scope of relevant stakeholders? and (3) How far does this responsibility extend, i.e. their horizon of responsibility?

These are important issues in contemporary business. However, there is a danger that such strong emphasis on this organizational responsibility displaces important questions about the *personal responsibility* of individual organizational members. Most importantly, it is a mistake to reduce the personal responsibility of the individual actor to the sum of role-defined responsibilities that he or she assumes as an agent for the organization. While considering the concept personal responsibility, we will move beyond this narrow understanding of the individual's responsibility.

Ims (2006) proposed a threefold model of responsibility, which distinguishes between role-mediated responsibility, common morality, and personal responsibility (see Figure 7.1, p. 136). In a business context, the individual's *role-mediated responsibility* is often the focus and refers to the responsibilities assumed by the individual when he or she takes on a given role in the organization (cf. Bovens's (1998) concept of responsibility as task). These role-mediated responsibilities are professional responsibilities, and they give allowances and limitations to the individual. For example, a surgeon is allowed to cut open other people's bodies because of the surgeon's role, but this role also limits the domain of acceptable actions, such as not being allowed to enter into a romantic relationship with a patient. Therefore, the role determines acceptable and unacceptable types of behavior, and places a set of responsibilities on the individual who takes up the role.

Secondly, Ims (2006) points out that any individual is bound by the *common morality* of his or her community or society. This means that there are moral values and corresponding moral obligations that are shared by a community and society, and the individual is partially bound by these values and obligations. In the debate about professional responsibility there has been strong support for a type of ethics within business that might not be restricted by common morality. A little bluffing in business perhaps should be allowed according to some experts, because everyone in business does it. However, as a general rule, common morality trumps professional ethics when professional and societal values are at stake. Common morality is constantly evolving through dialogue between members of the community and as a result of societal changes.

Finally, and most importantly, however, the individual has a profound *personal responsibility* that is independent of the individual's roles and of his or her being part of a given community. This personal responsibility moreover sets the limits for the individual's role-mediated responsibilities, in the sense that the individual evaluates what types of behavior he or she is willing to engage in as the performer of various roles. Similarly, the personal responsibility of the individual is in constant tension both with common morality and role-mediated moralities. The individual's moral life evolves in the tension between adhering to the moral tradition of the community and making radical value choices that sometimes may conflict with that tradition, which is how common morality evolves over time (cf. Kekes 1991). Similarly, the individual's personal values are in continuous tension with the values inherent in the tasks carried out as part of his or her professional role. Therefore, when the individual experiences a mismatch between the values upon which he or she exercises professional responsibility and his or her own values – or similarly between the values the community expects him or her to adhere to and his or her own values – it is necessary to critically reflect on the conflicts and prioritize before choosing and acting. Personal responsibility exists in context, and reflections on one's own norm-horizon should be seen in relation to shared norm-horizons.

Role-mediated responsibility   Common morality

Personal responsibility

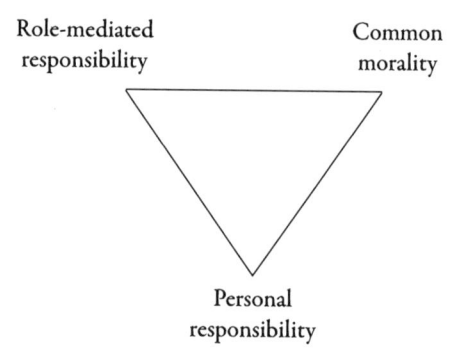

Figure 7.1 *The Triangle of Responsibility*
Source: Ims 2006

Ims's (2006) triangle illustrates a central challenge with regard to acting responsibly in organizations, namely that decision makers typically experience *conflicting loyalties*. In such situations, the individual's personal responsibility may clash with his or her professional responsibility or with a sense of responsibility towards the broader society. For some, these two responsibilities may overlap such as in the case of auditors whose professional responsibility largely coincides with their social responsibility, which is to ensure that the financial information communicated to societal stakeholders is accurate and trustworthy. However, there are many examples of professionals whose organizational responsibilities clash with their own personal beliefs or values. A contemporary example is a group of Norwegian medical doctors who refused to act in line with official governmental policy and recommend pregnant patients to take the swine flu vaccination during the recent epidemic. Even though public health organizations instructed them to give this advice, they refused on the grounds that they felt personally responsible towards the patients and that they were not convinced that existing research gave adequate reassurance that the unborn children would not be harmed.

This cross-pressure of conflicting loyalties can be illustrated in a minimalistic stakeholder model that we may call *the triangle of professional ethics* (see Figure 7.2, p. 138). In the model, the individual agent or professional is at the center of the triangle, and arrows indicate his or her responsibilities towards other key stakeholders. As the model suggests, at any one time a professional is typically responsible in different ways, and to different degrees, to at least one client (e.g. customer, patient), to one's employer, and to society at large. In the case of the medical doctors, their responsibility to the client seemed more important than their employee responsibility to their employer, or their social responsibility for acting in line with publicly regulated guidelines.

```
        CLIENT
         ↑↓
        AGENT
       ↗↖  ↗↘
SOCIETY ←――→ THE COMPANY
```

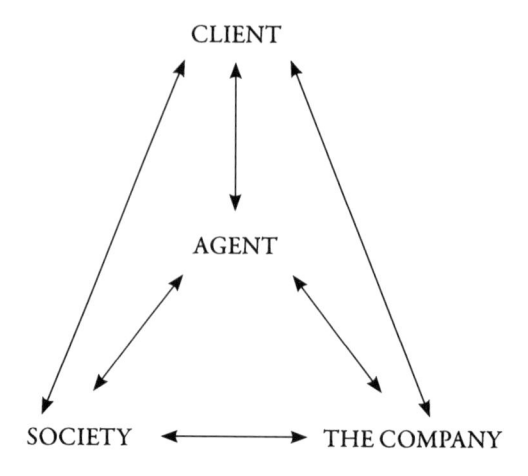

Figure 7.2 *The Triangle of Professional Ethics*

In light of Zsolnai's (2009) framework for responsible decision making, we can interpret the doctors' decision as an application of the maximin principle. In this case, the doctors promoted the goal attainment value of the decision (protecting the health of the pregnant women and their unborn children). Moreover, they prioritized a "do-no-harm" norm over the norm of following public health guidelines – both of which may be seen as important norms. Finally, they made an assessment of the stakeholders involved and their interests, and gave priority to the interests of the pregnant women rather than, for example, the stakeholders who as a consequence were more at risk of becoming infected by swine flu. In this way, we can see how doctors' attempts to resolve conflicting loyalties are compatible with the principles of the responsible decision making framework.

7.3.2 Shared Responsibility

Somewhat paradoxically, the perspective on personal responsibility can be broadened by taking into account the concept of *shared responsibility*. At first glance, this concept may appear contrary to the notion of personal

Personal Responsibility and Ethical Action

responsibility. However, we will argue that there are important implications for personal responsibility by assuming a perspective of shared responsibility.

The basic idea of shared responsibility is that individuals within a community (e.g. within an organization) should see themselves as sharing the blame (i.e. being accountable) for harms perpetrated by, or occurring within, that community with or without their active participation (May 1992, p. 1). This extends the individual's accountability to include acts that he or she has not carried out, but on which the individual may have had some ability to exert influence. Seeing responsibility as shared in a community or an organization implies the awareness that one's personal responsibility transcends one's own choices and behavior. This may cause us to consider our roles, omissions, and attitudes in light of our ethical standards in a similar way to how we consider our actual behavior (May 1992). Hence, such an approach to responsibility implies extending our horizon of responsibility. The perspective is in line with Hannah Arendt's (2003) proposition that to obey and obediently take part in organizational activities should be seen as an active support of that activity. This perspective is also in opposition to Jean-Paul Sartre's existential perspective, wherein all responsibility is laid on the shoulders of the single individual actor.

Thinking in terms of shared responsibility means ascribing responsibility in part based on the *attitudes* of individuals, for example the individual organizational member's attitude of *lenience* toward organizational activities that he or she is not a part of, but does not speak out against. This is a strong form of responsibility, in the sense that it assumes the perspective that individuals who have some degree of ability to influence the activities carried out in an organization thereby carry a responsibility for doing so if it can lead to avoidance of harm or transgressions. As such, this notion gives attention to the fact that we can be personally responsible for acts we contribute to, or facilitate, only in an indirect sense (May 1992). Causally speaking, the individual is part of the causal chain that creates or facilitates the outcome, and therefore has a share in the responsibility for that outcome.

Of course, this does not imply that an individual who is part of an organization or community automatically shares the blame for any wrongdoing perpetrated by that group. As discussed by Williams (1981) and Ims (2006), an individual should not take responsibility for the projects of others, which may conflict fundamentally with his or her own projects. One crucial issue here relates to the individual's degree of power and freedom, i.e. the degree to which the individual could have prevented or influenced the act in question in order to hinder negative outcomes. In such a prospective sense, the extent of the individual's share in the responsibility varies according to the role he or she could have played in avoiding the negative outcome (May 1992). Another crucial issue is: What's at stake? In general, we cannot require supererogatory behavior in the name of ethics – for example require a person to sacrifice his or her own life in order to do what might be right from a utilitarian viewpoint. We should warrant that the agent takes his or her ground projects into account before considering an act that might fundamentally conflict with his or her own deep convictions.

7.4 Real-world Examples

In this section, we outline and analyze some real-world examples that illustrate our perspective on personal responsibility and ethical action. For the purposes of illustration, we focus on the individual's decision of whether or not to blow the whistle following the realization that his or her organization is doing something blameworthy. We will discuss three different strategies – exit, voice, and loyalty (cf. Hirschman 1970) – as decision alternatives facing the individual, and discuss them in light of personal responsibility and the ethicality of the action.

7.4.1 *Exit as Responsible Action*

At the end of 2008, Inge Lisenka Wallage, who at the time was vice president of international communications in the Norwegian oil company StatoilHydro (hereafter referred to as Statoil, which is the company's current name), made a radical and surprising decision. During her two years in communications at Statoil, Wallage had spent a large amount of her time justifying and defending Statoil's controversial oil sands venture in Canada and she had grown increasingly uncomfortable with the task. In spite of her powerful and prestigious position within a major oil company, a role one might imagine many business students and practitioners would envy, Wallage came to an inevitable decision. She resigned from her position in Statoil and started working for Greenpeace – Statoil's main antagonist in the oil sands venture.

Reactions to Wallage's decision were plentiful. Statoil demanded that she left her post immediately. Former Statoil executives questioned her direct transfer to "the enemy," while business professors hailed Greenpeace's new recruit as a strategic coup (Andreassen 2009). Wallage herself explained her decision in an interview, stating that she wanted to be able to look back at her life and say that she had contributed to making the world a better place. Moreover, she asserted: "We only have one planet, and we have to treat the globe with respect" (Kongsnes 2009, p. 6). She emphasized that she had entered her role in Statoil in order to contribute to a sustainable development in the company's operations, but that she had failed to do so. Finally, she explained her choice with reference to her responsibility towards her children, and said: "I hope that my children will grow up able to live on a planet that is still intact and that I have contributed to this through my work life" (Kongsnes 2009, p. 7).

Wallage's decision was – for her – the only ethical action in her situation. She had tried and rejected other action alternatives that were compatible with her fundamental objective of contributing to a sustainable future. Her ethical action was grounded in a deep sense of personal responsibility: (1) *towards* various stakeholders – most notably her children, nature, and future generations, and (2) *for* specific outcomes – most notably a sustainable future. The action alternative that for her was the ethical one was to take her competence to what Statoil considered "the enemy" – Greenpeace – where she could engage in work that was consistent with the values towards which she felt a profound obligation.

We can interpret Inge Lisenka Wallage's reaction to working with Statoil's oil sands venture as resulting from her ability to see the non-technical and ethical dimensions of the case. While Statoil approached the oil sands venture in a techno-centric manner – highlighting their technological advantage over their competitors and de-emphasizing the arguably grave influence of the project on vulnerable ecosystems – Wallage sensed the non-negligible moral implications of the activities of which she was a part. For Wallage, an important ethical issue needed to be addressed, which meant that ethical action was required.

In light of Hirschman's (1970) distinction between exit, voice, and loyalty, Wallage considered the exit strategy to be the most responsible action. To use voice – for instance by criticizing Statoil's practices publicly – would be in conflict with her organizational role as vice president of communications, and would as such be unsustainable and disloyal to her employer. Likewise, the loyalty strategy, which would imply staying in the organization and perhaps aiming to change the organization's practices from the inside, probably appeared unrealistic. In light of this situation, leaving the organization meant that she no longer actively supported the of oil sands practices by being part of the organization (cf. Arendt 1963). At the same time, when leaving the company it allowed her to send a message publicly, which can be powerful, and it also allowed her to use her competence at Greenpeace, where there was alignment between the organization's and Wallage's goals. In this way, Wallage resolved her ethical problem by stepping away from the scene of the problem.

7.4.2 Whistle-blowing as Responsible Action

In 2000, Per-Yngve Monsen was employed as a project economist in Siemens, which is a company with a global presence with approximately 70 billion euros in revenue, 500,000 employees, and representation in more than 190 countries. Monsen was employed in the defense division of the subsidiary Siemens Business Services (SBS). (This section is based on Monsen's book *A Mole in Siemens* (2008).)

In his first months, Monsen and other economists in the organization saw only red numbers on the bottom line. The economists even reported that the result for Siemens was "catastrophically bad." The Norwegian

Personal Responsibility and Ethical Action 143

Defence (Norwegian Armed Forces) invited a tender for a new IT structure for the Norwegian Defence as a whole. The contract would be one of the largest IT contracts in Norway, with a value of more than 100 million euros. During the process, there seemed to be active dialogue between the director in SBS and the Norwegian Defence officials. Monsen thought it was strange that one Defence official had a previous career in Siemens. Obviously, the parties had a good relationship and had even shared an apartment.

The German headquarters subsequently fired the Norwegian CEO due to bad economic results. Monsen was surprised by the use of invoices in December (the invoices meant that the client was debited for undelivered goods). However, due to this "Christmas shopping," the Norwegian Defence was able to use its whole budget for the year. Also, in the following years, Monsen witnessed similar "Christmas shopping." However, Monsen knew that the Norwegian government auditor (Riksrevisjonen) does not permit public institutions to pay in advance.

In late 2000, SBS won the Defence contract, which meant that SBS would be a secure work place for many years. A premise in the contract was that SBS would calculate a maximum margin of 8 per cent on products and that SBS would be paid for services related to planning, installations, the mapping of IT material and logistics, etc. SBS employed a new director who changed the organization, and Monsen was promoted to division economist for the new product division. However, Monsen noticed that the sellers in SBS did not adhere to the 8 per cent margin. Many of the products were sold for a larger profit and, at the same time, Monsen watched the new financial director attempting to hide the illegal profit in the accounting systems by "cooking the accounting books." Inside the organization spirits were high, not least because of the bonuses, which Monsen also received. However, he felt no joy in receiving money from the dirty arrangement between SBS and the Norwegian Defence.

The arrangement continued through 2001 and 2002, and Monsen was able to see where the illegal profit was accounted for. The amount was now significant, since it was more than 2 million euros. He decided to ask the financial director about it, although he knew that criticism of management was a delicate matter at Siemens. The financial director's response was that this was a matter for management and that he would speak with the client at the appropriate time. The tone of the director's response was not at all friendly. Monsen watched the continuation of overbilling and saw how SBS soon disposed of 3 million euros – an amount that in reality belonged to the Norwegian Defence. Monsen again asked the director, who told him it was a matter for senior management.

Subsequently, the corporate headquarters developed business conduct (ethical) guidelines that were to be signed by all employees. It was stated that the consequences of breaking the guidelines could include loss of job and being sued. In addition, all employees received a book entitled *Trust*, which contained ethical and moral admonishments, encouragements, and sayings. Monsen understood that the top executives in Siemens took their ethical codes seriously, and if the overbilling of the Defence continued, it would become a serious problem for him. According to the ethical guidelines, he had a duty to report such matters. If he did not sign the guidelines, it would be the same as handing in his resignation. Monsen experienced a "Catch-22" situation, but signed and submitted the guidelines.

In subsequent years, the annual report was fraudulent, according to Monsen. He was aware of bribery payments from SBS to Defence public officials. In 2004, Monsen decided to write an anonymous letter about the fraud to Siemens headquarters in Germany. Then, Siemens started "hunting the witch." Monsen was interrogated in several meetings and felt a huge pressure, culminating in not being able to sleep and it affecting him physically and mentally. A delegation came from Germany to Norway to investigate the fraud and Monsen wrote a new letter to Germany in which he condemned the way the delegation carried out the investigation. Monsen believed it would destroy the company, and threatened to report what he knew to Siemens AG – the corporate management group.

Soon afterwards, Monsen felt he was in the midst of a tornado. Knowing that he was approaching his last days at SBS, he decided to prepare for probable court proceedings and started printing documentation for his case. Close colleagues pointed him out as the whistle-blower, and condemned him for being disloyal towards management and for destroying the company. In 2004 Monsen was dismissed due to "internal organizational change." Monsen maintained that the dismissal was impartial and sued SBS. In the subsequent year, the story broke in the Norwegian media and readers were told that the Norwegian Defence had been overcharged by 50 million kroner. The case was dealt with in the Norwegian parliament, and both the bribes and the "Christmas shopping" were out in the open.

In April 2005, Monsen won in court and received a compensation of 1.5 million NOK from Siemens due to his dismissal. The Norwegian Defence dismissed officials who were bribed. Monsen sent all his correspondence to the German Stock Exchange authorities. In Norway, a governmental committee investigated the story and concluded that the allegations were true. A consequence was that the Norwegian Defence stated that Siemens was excluded from future public tenders. In 2007, whistle-blower Monsen received an anonymous letter that was seen as a serious threat to him personally and so was investigated by the police. In the same year, he received two prizes for his whistle-blowing, and also published the book *A Mole in Siemens*, where he tells the story of his experiences in Siemens SBS.

Why did Monsen blow the whistle? Clearly, he showed moral courage. But why did he do it? Was he driven by his own deep moral emotions, such as empathy, compassion, and justice? Monsen admits that he could not enjoy a bonus that he perceived as unfair and, it is obvious that he was driven by deep and powerful motives. It appears that for Monsen unconscious motivation was an important part of the picture. In an interesting passage in Monsen's book, he reflects upon the question as to whether he would have done the same after all the pain he had suffered as a whistleblower. Monsen's answer is:

> It is difficult to answer. It is about what one experiences as right and wrong, and which aspects one emphasizes in oneself. I was concerned about my own self-esteem, and for my part this was connected with the beliefs I have of right and wrong. Maybe there might be quite different and less noble feelings which had the same importance, for example pride, stubbornness and anger. Nevertheless, it was unwise to do it considering my role as breadwinner in the family – and not least considering my own health. (Monsen 2008, pp. 159–160; authors' translation)

For Monsen, blowing the whistle was the responsible action. He attempted solving the problem inside the organization, but did not succeed. Thereby, his loyalty to the organization was also undermined. He ended up blowing the whistle first internally, to higher layers of the organization, and subsequently externally, to the Norwegian Defence and to the media. In light of Hirschman's (1970) distinction between exit, voice, and loyalty, voice was the only option for Monsen, and it proved to be a powerful strategy. However, it should be noted that there was a correspondingly heavy personal cost for Monsen following the use of this strategy. This is the pattern that is often seen in whistle-blowing cases – the strategy is effective, but may destroy the individual's professional, and indeed personal, life. Monsen's strategy was to tackle the ethical problem by confronting it head on and being a crusader for the sake of justice. His story, like the story of many other whistle-blowers, shows us the price that is often paid by those who challenge unethical action in business.

7.4.3 Moral Whispering as Responsible Action

In a sense, the concept of moral whispering refers to a weaker form of whistle-blowing. Moral whispering implies that the individual, rather than using the "voice" strategy in order to reveal a blameworthy practice, chooses to discreetly communicate his or her concerns within the organization in order to attempt to influence practice in a positive direction (cf. Bird 2002). As such, it is a subtle influence strategy by means of communication and social interaction. Such behavior is arguably plentiful in organizations, and it is a manifestation of how moral awareness among organizational members may contribute to the organization's avoidance of ethical and reputational crises.

A defining characteristic of moral whispering is its discreetness, because the very strategy it entails is to attempt to promote moral practice without creating noise and uproar outside the organization itself. For this very reason, there are of course fewer known cases of such behavior. Successful moral whispering makes it unnecessary to talk about the case beyond the organization's boundaries. For this reason, we discuss this strategy by means of the example of shareholder activism. Shareholder activism refers to the practice of using shareholder rights and privileges to try to make companies improve their social, ethical and/or environmental performance

(Sandberg 2011, p52). Typically, this strategy is used in order to influence the company so that its practices become more responsible. It is generally executed in one of two ways: either by raising concerns at the company's general assembly or by contacting management directly with one's concerns or claims. The latter form of shareholder activism can be seen as a sort of moral whispering.

In asset management companies of a certain size, shareholder activism is getting increasingly widespread. Among the companies that have employed this strategy successfully is the Norwegian financial institution Storebrand. The shareholder activism in Storebrand includes traditional approaches such as voting and asking questions at general assemblies. Also, however, Storebrand has a more direct and comprehensive approach that involves contacting the management group of companies directly to demand that they alter their irresponsible practices. Storebrand has had considerable success with this strategy, and currently contacts several hundred companies directly each year as part of their shareholder activism strategy (Meisingset and Norum 2011).

Storebrand's approach to shareholder activism can be interpreted as moral whispering if we consider Storebrand to be an internal stakeholder by virtue of their role as a stakeholder. In this sense, they can act as a sort of organizational actor much like an employee. Therefore, in light of Hirschman's (1970) distinction between exit, voice, and loyalty, Storebrand could similarly choose any of the three. Shareholder activism is often done in a very public way, for example at general assemblies or by means of communication in the media. Such a strategy would be considered as "voice," much like whistle-blowing for the organizational actor. In this context the "exit" strategy would be to sell their shares in the companies they consider irresponsible. Storebrand's discreet influence strategy towards the companies in which they invest is rather a form of loyalty, whereby they remain investors in the company but act internally in order to promote ethical business practices (Meisingset and Norum 2011).

Moral whispering can be a powerful strategy in order to develop an ethical culture inside a company. In their shareholder strategy, Storebrand are raising concerns, asking difficult questions, and ultimately giving companies an incentive to move their business activities in a responsible direction.

Otherwise, a company runs the risk of Storebrand selling their share of the company and justifying it with reference to the unethical practices of the company, which from a reputational point of view can be disastrous. In Zsolnai's (2002) vocabulary, Storebrand are increasing the relative cost of *unethical action*, thereby making it more rational for the company to act responsibly.

The case of shareholder activism in Storebrand is of course special in the sense that Storebrand has a great deal of power as big shareholders in the company. As such, making moral whispering effective must be done in different ways by individual organizational members. Regardless, the Storebrand case illustrates how the loyalty strategy can also constitute responsible action in organizations, at least when it is combined with an active attempt at changing existing practices through more or less discreet forms of interaction and communication inside the organization.

7.5 Conclusion

We have discussed the nature of personal responsibility and ethical action and the relationship between the two. We emphasized the desirability of personal responsibility in organizations and proposed a broader notion of personal responsibility that includes the notion of shared responsibility, i.e. that individuals in organizations are in part responsible for acts that they do not actively carry out, but on which they have some ability to exert an influence. Moreover, we have explored the organizational challenge of promoting personal responsibility and ethical action in organizations, and the different forms that personal responsibility can take in organizational life. By discussing responsible action in the light of Hirschman's (1970) distinction between exit, voice, and loyalty, we have also analyzed how different strategies of personal responsibility can be enacted in organizations. We have argued that individuals can assume responsibility in organizations in ways that differ along several important dimensions, but can all be effective in promoting responsible business practices.

The ethical action perspective is important because it illuminates the value of deep moral emotions like empathy and compassion as a foundation for courageous acts like whistle-blowing. Jonas's (1984) substantive responsibility is important for Wallage who left Statoil to join Greenpeace, and the Norwegian whistle-blower Per-Yngve Monsen's acts cannot be explained unless we see him as partly driven by his deep emotions. To act ethically in a situation where the organization actively and brutally tries to stifle one's voice is extremely demanding. For Monsen, there was no money reward waiting for a successful voice – only personal sacrifice. For Monsen, however, his integrity was at stake. Integrity is for some individuals more important than external rewards or punishments. In some sense, Monsen did what was good for its own sake. He took personal responsibility in pursuing the idea of justice in society. We should not forget the subjective side of ethics. Reason has to complement emotion. Emotions are crucial in moral life, and their role is primary in acts of personal responsibility.

References

Andreassen, K. (2009) Oppsiktsvekkende kritikk, Eyeopening criticism. *Stavanger Aftenblad*, 9 June.
Arendt, H. (1963) *Eichmann in Jerusalem: A Report on the Banality of Evil*. New York: Viking Press.
Arendt, H. (2003) *Responsibility and Judgment*. New York: Schocken.
Bandura, A. (1999) Moral Disengagement in the Perpetration of Inhumanities. *Personality and Social Psychology Review*, vol. 3, no. 3, pp. 193–209.
Bird, F. B. (2002) *The Muted Conscience: Moral Silence and the Practice of Ethics in Business*. Westport, CT: Quorum.
Bovens, M. (1998) *The Quest for Responsibility: Accountability and Citizenship in Complex Organisations*. Cambridge: Cambridge University Press.
Hirschman, A. O. (1970) *Exit, Voice, and Loyalty: Responses to Decline in Firms, Organizations, and States*. Cambridge, MA: Harvard University Press.
Ims, K. J. (2006) Take It Personally. In Zsolnai, L. and Ims, K. J. (eds) *Business within Limits: Deep Ecology and Buddhist Economics*. Bern: Peter Lang.

Ims, K. J. and Zsolnai, L. (2006) Shallow Success and Deep Failure. In Zsolnai, L. and Ims, K. J. (eds) *Business within Limits: Deep Ecology and Buddhist Economics*. Bern: Peter Lang.

Jonas, H. (1984) *The Imperative of Responsibility: In Search of an Ethics for the Technological Age*. Chicago: University of Chicago Press.

Kekes, J. (1991) *Moral Tradition and Individuality*. Princeton, NJ: Princeton University Press.

Kongsnes, E. (2009) StatoilHydro-sjef ville ikke forsvare oljesand-prosjekt [StatoilHydro executive would not defend oil sand project]. *Stavanger Aftenblad*, 8 June, pp. 6–7.

May, L. (1992) *Sharing Responsibility*. Chicago: University of Chicago Press.

Meisingset, C. T. and Norum, D. (2011) Bærekraftige investeringer [Sustainable Investments]. *Praktisk økonomi og finans*, vol. 27, no. 3, pp. 19–27.

Messner, M. (2009) The Limits of Accountability. *Accounting, Organizations and Society*, vol. 34, pp. 918–938.

Monsen, P-Y. (2008) *Muldvarp i Siemens: En dokumentar* [Mole in Siemens: A Documentary]. Oslo: Spartacus.

Opdal, L. C. (2011) Responsibility and the Unconscious. In Jakobsen, O. and Pedersen, L. J. T. (eds), *Responsibility, Deep Ecology and the Self*. Oslo: Forlag1.

Pedersen, L. J. T. (2009) *Making Sense of Sensitivity: Moral Sensitivity and Problem Formulation in Business*. PhD dissertation. Bergen: Norwegian School of Economics and Business Administration.

Rawls, J. (1971) *A Theory of Justice*. Cambridge, MA: Harvard University Press.

Sandberg, J. (2011) Changing the World through Shareholder Activism?, *Etikk i praksis (Nordic Journal of Applied Ethics)*, vol. 5, no. 1, pp. 51–78.

Sen, A. (2002) *Rationality and Freedom*. Cambridge, MA: Harvard University Press.

Vetlesen, A. J. (1994) *Perception, Empathy, and Judgment: An Inquiry into the Preconditions of Moral Performance*. University Park: Pennsylvania State University Press.

Williams, B. (1981) *Moral Luck: Philosophical Papers 1973–1980*. Cambridge: Cambridge University Press.

Zsolnai, L. (2002) The Moral Economic Man In Zsolnai, L. (ed.), *Ethics in the Economy: Handbook of Business Ethics*. Bern: Peter Lang. (The updated version is Chapter 3 in this book.)

Zsolnai, L. (2009) *Responsible Decision Making*. New Brunswick, NJ: Transaction Publishers.

DOIREAN WILSON AND LASZLO ZSOLNAI
(MIDDLESEX UNIVERSITY, LONDON/CORVINUS UNIVERSITY
OF BUDAPEST)

8 Gender Issues in Business

8.1 The Women's Disadvantage

8.2 Male-biased Economics and Business

8.3 Feminist Ethics

8.4 The End of Men?

8.5 Conclusion

Abstract

Despite the universal agreement on gender equality women are still in a disadvantageous position in contemporary society. The gender gap between men and women can be seen across many fields of life including business.

Mainstream economics is male-biased as it presupposes an androcentric conception of the human person. With its exclusive focus on productivity, today's businesses tend to undervalue female characteristics, such as care and compassion. However, they like to use women as sex objects in marketing and advertising.

Based on the moral experience of women, Carol Gilligan describes feminist ethics as an ethics of care. For women the self is constructed in relationships and their typical problem-solving strategy is communication. Insights from feminist ethics induce a new model of corporate governance where the key issue is to maintain and manage the firm's relationships in a mutually satisfying way.

The post-industrial economy is more congenial to women than to men. Today's companies require a more feminine management style. Gender equality and feminist ethics are not only important for their own sake. They increase the performance of businesses and economies while also contributing to the quality of life for men and women alike.

Keywords: gender gap, feminist ethics, changing role of men, women-oriented companies

8.1 The Women's Disadvantage

Despite the growing advancement of women, coupled with international agreements declaring gender equality as a fundamental human right, research evidence suggests that women are still being disadvantaged across different fields of life including business.

The World Development Report (World Bank 2011) recognizes that numerous developing countries display significant gender inequalities in employment, education, and health outcomes. Such disadvantages have, and will continue to have, far reaching implications for these countries. Moreover, women who live and work in more affluent societies still experience gender disadvantages. This is more evident among those likely to suffer social exclusion due to, for example, their race, color, sexual orientation, or disability.

The United Nations Development Programme (UNDP) commissioned the independent publication of the Human Development Report (HDR), with the first launched in 1990. These reports examine migration with regard to changing demographics in growth and inequality trends that relate to the movements of peoples within societies and across the globe. It appears that migration occurrence is primarily instigated by the global unequal distribution of capabilities (UNDP 1990–2011). Furthermore, the disadvantages often experienced by women and girls are at the crux of this inequality. The discrimination endured in various sectors, such as education, health, and employment, is evidence of these disadvantages, which in turn can lead to negative repercussions for women's well-being, sense of belonging, and freedom.

The Human Development Report presents an innovative way to measure development. This began as the Human Development Index, referred to as the HDI, which is a combination of life expectancy, educational attainment, and GDP per capita. However, an Inequality-adjusted HDI (IHDI) measure, which focuses on the human development of people in society and takes inequality into account, was introduced in the 2010 HDR report. A new measure of inequalities due to the disadvantages faced by women and girls has also been recently introduced. This latter measure is based on the HDI and IHDI framework, with the intention of depicting any differences in the distribution of achievements between women and men.

Table 8.1 Gender Inequality Index and Related Indicators. Source: Human Development Report 2011

HDI rank		Gender Inequality Index Rank 2011	Gender Inequality Index Value 2011	Maternal mortality ratio 2008	Adolescent fertility rate 2011[a]	Seats in national parliament (% female) 2011	Population with at least secondary education (% ages 25 and older) Female 2010	Population with at least secondary education (% ages 25 and older) Male 2010	Labour force participation rate (%) Female 2009	Labour force participation rate (%) Male 2009	REPRODUCTIVE HEALTH Contraceptive prevalence rate, any method (% of married women ages 15–49) 2005–2009[b]	REPRODUCTIVE HEALTH At least one antenatal visit (%) 2005–2009[b]	REPRODUCTIVE HEALTH Births attended by skilled health personnel (%) 2005–2009[b]	Total fertility rate 2011[a]
VERY HIGH HUMAN DEVELOPMENT														
1	Norway	6	0.075	7	9.0	39.6	99.3	99.9	63.0	71.0	88.0	–	–	2.0
2	Australia	18	0.136	8	16.5	28.3	95.1	97.2	58.4	72.2	71.0	100.0	100.0	2.0
3	Netherlands	2	0.052	9	37.8	86.3	89.2	89.5	72.9	69.0	5.1	–	100.0	1.8
4	United States	47	0.299	24	41.2	16.8[c]	95.3	94.5	58.4	71.9	73.0	–	99.0	2.1
5	New Zealand	32	0.195	14	30.9	33.6	71.6	73.5	61.8	75.7	75.0	95.0	100.0	2.1
6	Canada	20	0.140	12	14.0	24.9	92.3	92.7	62.7	73.0	74.0	–	98.0	1.7
7	Ireland	33	0.203	3	17.5	11.1	82.3	81.5	54.4	73.0	89.0	100.0	–	2.1
8	Liechtenstein	–	–	–	7.0	24.0	–	–	–	–	–	–	–	–
9	Germany	7	0.085	7	31.7	91.3	92.8	53.1	66.8	75.0	7.9	–	–	1.0
10	Sweden	1	0.049	5	6.0	45.0	87.9	87.1	60.6	69.2	–	–	–	1.9
HIGH HUMAN DEVELOPMENT														
1	Uruguay	62	0.352	27	61.1	14.6	56.6	51.7	53.8	75.5	78.0	96.0	100.0	2.0
2	Palau	6.9	–	–	–	13.8	–	–	–	–	21.0	100.0	100.0	–
3	Romania	55	0.333	27	32.0	9.8	83.8	90.5	45.4	60.0	70.0	94.0	99.0	1.4
4	Cuba	58	0.337	53	45.2	43.2	73.9	80.4	40.9	66.9	78.0	100.0	100.0	1.5
5	Seychelles	51.3	–	–	–	23.5	41.2[d,e]	45.4[d,e]	–	–	–	–	–	–
6	Bahamas	54	0.332	49	31.8	17.9	48.5[d,e]	54.5[d,e]	68.3	78.7	45.0	98.0	99.0	1.9
7	Montenegro	–	–	15	18.2	11.1	79.7[d,e]	69.5[d,e]	–	–	39.0	97.0	99.0[g]	1.6

8	Bulgaria	40	0.245	13	42.8	20.8	69.1	70.6	48.2	61.2	63.0	–	100.0	1.6
9	Saudi Arabia	135	0.546	24	11.6	0.0[f]	50.3	57.9	21.2	79.8	24.0	90.0	91.0	2.6
10	Mexico	79	0.448	85	70.6	25.5	55.8	61.9	43.2	80.6	73.0	94.0	93.0	2.2
MEDIUM HUMAN DEVELOPMENT														
1	Jordan	83	0.456	59	26.5	12.2	57.1	74.2	23.3	73.9	59.0	99.0	99.0	2.9
2	Algeria	71	0.412	120	7.3	7.0	36.3	49.3	37.2	79.6	61.0	89.0	95.0	2.1
3	Sri Lanka	74.5	0.419	39	23.6	56.0	57.6	57.6	57.6	75.1	68.0	99.0	99.0	2.2
4	Dominican Republic	90	0.480	100	108.7	19.1	49.7	41.8	50.5	79.8	73.0	99.0	98.0	2.5
5	Samoa	3.8	–	–	–	28.3	4.1	64.2[d,e]	60.0[d,e]	37.9	75.4	25.0	–	100.0
6	Fiji	2.6	–	–	26.0	45.2	–	86.6	88.6	38.7	78.4	35.0	–	99.0
7	China	35	0.209	38	8.4	21.3	54.8	70.4	67.4	79.7	85.0	91.0	99.0	1.6
8	Turkmenistan	–	–	77	19.5	16.8	–	–	62.4	74.0	48.0	99.0	100.0	2.3
9	Thailand	69	0.382	48	43.3	14.0	25.6	–	65.5	80.7	77.0	98.0	97.0	1.5
10	Suriname	2.3	–	–	100.0	39.5	9.8	–	–	38.5	66.0	46.0	90.0	90.0[g]
LOW HUMAN DEVELOPMENT														
1	Solomon Islands	–	–	100	70.3	0.0	–	–	24.2	50.0	27.0	74.0	70.0	4.0
2	Kenya	130	0.627	530	100.2	9.8	20.1	38.6	76.4	88.1	46.0	92.0	44.0	4.6
3	São Tomé and Príncipe	–	–	–	66.1	18.2	–	–	44.5	76.0	38.0	98.0	82.0	3.5
4	Pakistan	115	0.573	260	31.6	21.0	23.5	46.8	21.7	84.9	30.0	61.0	39.0[g]	3.2
5	Bangladesh	112	0.550	340	78.9	18.6	30.8	39.3	58.7	82.5	53.0	51.0	24.0[g]	2.2
6	Timor-Leste	–	–	370	65.8	29.2	–	–	58.9	82.8	22.0	61.0	18.0	5.9
7	Angola	5.1	–	–	610	171.1	38.6	–	–	74.5	88.4	6.0	80.0	47.0[g]
8	Myanmar	96	0.492	240	16.3	4.0	18.0	17.6	63.1	85.1	41.0	80.0	64.0	1.9
9	Cameroon	134	0.639	600	127.8	13.9	21.1	34.9	53.5	80.7	29.0	82.0	63.0	4.3
10	Madagascar	143	–	–	440	12.1	–	–	–	84.2	88.7	40.0	86.0	44.0[g]	4.5

Notes [a] Annual average for 2010–2015 [b] Data refer to the most recent year available during the period specified [c] The denominator of the calculation refers to voting members of the House of Representatives only [d] UNESCO Institute for Statistics (2011) [e] Refers to an earlier year than that specified [f] For purposes of calculating the Gender Inequality Index, a value of 0.1 percent was used [g] Includes deliveries by cadres of health workers other than doctors, nurses and midwives.

The Gender Inequality Index (GII) is based on three dimensions, namely, the labor market, empowerment, and reproductive health. This is an addition to five other indicators: labor force participation, educational attainment, parliamentary representation, adolescent fertility, and maternal mortality (UNDP 1990–2011).

There are various differences in inequality across countries. The ensuing losses in achievement, particularly those that are gender-related, range from 4.9 to 76.9 per cent. Furthermore, societies with unequal distribution of human development, tend to experience high inequality between the sexes and vice versa, that is, countries where there is high inequality among men and women, experience unequal distribution of human development (UNDP 1990–2011).

Table 8.1 (p. 154–155) presents a Gender Inequality Index and its related indicators, such as labor force participation rate, and the population of men and women aged twenty-five and over with at least secondary education. The table depicts the top ten countries where human development is either very high, high, medium, or low, therefore giving insight into those societies where unequal distribution of human development is likely to be greater. (See also Box 8.1.)

It is useful to explore in greater detail the disadvantages experienced by many women across the world. According to the United Nations of Public Information Department for every 100 men in the world there are 98.6 women. Nonetheless, they have not yet achieved equality compared with men in any society. Furthermore 70 per cent of the world's reputed 1.3 billion poor people are women, yet they produce in excess of 55 per cent of all food that is grown in rural areas in developing countries. It is plausible to assume that most people think soldiers are the primary victims of war today, but this is not so in reality. Civilian women and their children are the main victims of world combat, many of whom are subjected to the degradation of rape, a warfare weapon that has devastated the lives of many women leaving them feeling disrespected and violated. In twelve months of conflict from April 1994 to April 1995, it was alleged that in Rwanda, between 150,700 and 250,000 women and young girls were raped (United Nations 2011).

> Box 8.1 *Minorities in the UK and the Need for Respect*
>
> In various communities in the UK with high concentration levels of Pakistani, Black African, and Bangladeshi residents, the women were more likely than their white female counterparts to be unemployed (Innovations Report 2006). Furthermore, there has been a significant rise in the number of female graduates of working age, particularly among those of Black Afro-Caribbean, Pakistani, and Indian origins, yet their positions in the labor market fail to reflect this. This scenario could lead to feelings of discontent, discrimination, resentment, and disrespect.
>
> Recent research evidence based on findings of a study conducted over two research phases (2007–2008 and 2008–2009) suggests that respect is a common value for all, not least women. One could therefore argue that to develop a milieu of respect locally, nationally, and globally, could have a ricochet effect across businesses, yielding benefits for organizations and their employees. One might therefore ask, is this not something worth doing?
>
> The study was conducted among ethnically diverse male and female business students at Middlesex University's Business School. These students chose to share their stories of respect and disrespect as it affected them, from differing life perspectives in weekly focus group sessions. These groups comprised of four to six students of mixed gender, ethnicity, age, and cultures, from various business degree disciplines.
>
> The study revealed that for some students, respect had at least five different meanings or at most thirty-three. Respect was also a common and significant shared value for those of cultural difference and meant the same, similar, and dissimilar things to the same or culturally different students. Furthermore the study disclosed that there was an underlying assumption that everyone knew what respect meant; that is until individual students made explicit their true meaning of respect. This had a marked effect on their perceptions, attitude, and behavior towards each other, thus creating an ambience of respect among them that improved team relationships and learning outcomes. The findings also showed that respect was culturally situated and that one person's meaning of respect was in some instances another's disrespect.

Nevertheless, some progress has been made in addressing gender inequality for the betterment of women. In countries such as the USA, Canada, Norway, Finland, and Sweden, women's educational achievements and annual income tend to be higher in comparison with that of other women living and working in other parts of the world (United Nations 2011). Meanwhile, in other countries the opposite is taking place and there is a widening decline in gender equality. The Global Gender

Gap Report 2011 reports the slight decline in gender equality ranks for Spain, Sri Lanka, South Africa, New Zealand, and the United Kingdom. Nonetheless, improvements in gender equality were also evident in societies such as Tanzania, Turkey, Qatar, Ethiopia, and Brazil (Global Gender Gap Report 2011).

8.2 Male-biased Economics and Business

Feminist scholars disclose the essentially male-biased nature of modern mainstream economics. They criticize mainstream economics for presupposing an androcentric, male-biased conception of the human person. (England and Stanek Kilbourne 1990; Ferber and Nelson (eds) 1993).

Mainstream businesses value and pay for the efforts of human persons according to the narrowly defined concept of productivity. Productivity means the creation of marketable goods and services, that is, one's contribution to the money-generating capability of companies and other organizations. Mainstream businesses often neglect feminine values, such as care and compassion, and prefer to use women as sex object in marketing and advertising. (Box 8.2)

Women comprise 31 per cent of the labor force in developing countries and approximately 46.7 per cent worldwide; why then, are most women inclined to be paid less for doing the same or similar jobs as their male counterparts?

The World Development Report 2012 recognizes that closing the gender gaps is crucial as gender equality is key to smart economics. Therefore, a pledge to pursue gender equality is a quest towards the enhancement of development outcomes, harmonious working relationships, multicultural team effectiveness, and business sustainability.

> Box 8.2 *Lynx Deodorant*
>
> In November 2011 the *Guardian* reported a case involving an internet advertisement campaign for Lynx deodorant that featured model and reality TV star Lucy Pinder in a series of provocative poses.
>
> The Lynx internet advertisements that Lucy Pinder featured in provoked complaints to the Advertising Standards Authority (ASA) in the UK. The five internet advertisements, for the Lynx Dry deodorant brand, featured Pinder undertaking activities such as washing a car, jogging, and playing with a light saber.
>
> They used lines including "What will she do to make you lose control?," "Play with Lucy," and "Put premature perspiration to the test." The ASA received complaints that the campaign was offensive, degraded and objectified women, and ran on websites where it could easily be viewed by children.
>
> The majority of the complaints to the ASA were that the advertising campaign was offensive because it was sexually suggestive, indecent, provocative, glamorized casual sex, and objectified and demeaned women.
>
> Unilever said that the target market for Lynx – young men – had "come to expect, and were comfortable with the typical narrative, tone and content seen in advertising for the brand." The company added that although the model was scantily clad "she was not undressed to an extent that would be in any way unusual in that location [the beach]."
>
> (Adapted from Mark Sweney "Lynx's Lucy Pinder ads banned by ASA" *Guardian* 23 November 2011)

8.3 Feminist Ethics

Feminist ethics explores the moral experience of women. The most important contribution was made by *Carol Gilligan* her best-selling book *In a Different Voice: Psychological Theory and Women's Development* (Gilligan 1982).

Conducting empirical studies at Harvard on the moral experience of women, Gilligan found that the morality of women is strikingly different from the morality of men: "Relationships, and particularly issues of dependency, are experienced differently by women and men. (...) The quality of embeddedness in social interaction and personal relationships that characterize women's lives in contrast to men's" (Gilligan 1982, pp. 8–9).

Gilligan characterizes the morality of women as an ethic of care. "The ideal of care is thus an activity of relationship, of seeing and responding to need, taking care of the world by sustaining the web of connection so that no one is left alone." The ethic of care "is the wish not to hurt others and the hope that in morality lies a way of solving conflicts so that no one will be hurt." Women consider inflicting hurt as "selfish and immoral in its reflection of unconcern, while the expression of care is seen as fulfillment of moral responsibility" (Gilligan 1982, p. 62, p. 65, and p. 73).

Identity is defined differently by women and men. For women "identity is defined in a context of relationship and judged by a standard of responsibility and care. (...) Morality stems from attachment." For men "the tone of identity is different, clearer, more distinct and sharp-edged. (...) Thus the male 'I' is defined in separation" (Gilligan 1982, pp. 160–161).

Gilligan states that men and women represent two different moral ideologies: the ethic of rights and the ethic of care, respectively. Separation is justified by an ethic of rights while attachment is supported by an ethic of care. The morality of rights is predicated on equality and centered on the understanding of fairness, while the ethic of responsibility relies on the concept of equity, the recognition of differences in need. While the ethic of rights is a manifestation of equal respect, balancing the claims of other and the self, the ethic of responsibility rests on an understanding that gives rise to compassion and care (Gilligan 1982, p. 165).

Table 8.2 shows the contrasting features of male and female morality.

Table 8.2 *Male versus Female Morality*

	Male morality	Female morality
concept of the self	separate self	related self
problem-solving method	focusing on rights	communication
main driver	goal-rationality	caring for others

This is not an argument for the superiority of women's morality. Gilligan emphasizes the complementarity of male and female ethics. The two disparate modes of moral experience are connected in mature morality: "While an ethic of justice proceeds from the premise of equality – that everyone should be treated the same – an ethic of care rests on the premise of non-violence – that no one should be hurt. (...) [In maturity] both perspectives converge in the realization that just as inequality adversely affects both parties in an unequal relationship, so too violence is destructive for everyone involved" (Gilligan 1982, p. 174).

Inspired by feminist ethics, Machold, Ahmed and Farquhar (2008) developed a governance model which views the firm as a web of relationships rather than a nexus of contracts.

Their feminist governance model recognizes a multiplicity of actual and potential relationships with varying degrees of asymmetry of power distribution, within which there is an obligation of care. In that sense, are shareholders privileged, in caring terms, over other stakeholders? It depends on whether there is a relationship or the potential of a relationship. In addressing the issue of who counts, a feminist model prioritizes all those individuals with whom a relationship has been, or could be in future, established, regardless of whether that relationship is enshrined in legal or economic terms. Moreover, these relationships are with concrete others, taking into consideration their individuality and identity. Thus, in the feminist model, governance is not about abstract relations between anonymous and homogenous stakeholder groups in an organization, but the contextual relationships between concrete individuals belonging to one or several stakeholder groups. (Machold, Ahmed and Farquhar 2008)

From a feminist viewpoint, the universal principle underpinning the governance relationships is the obligation to care, that is for individuals to have a sense of responsibility within and outside the organization to nurture others. Individuals within governance relationships engage in a continuous process of care with the aim towards the empowerment of each other. This requires that managers learn about the background and identity of those within their immediate care, understand the individual's need for job satisfaction or a work–life balance, and empathize with it. Attending to somebody's needs often means pointing out the dangers associated with a particular course of action, with a particular form of behavior. Care does also not mean sacrificing the self in the process, the ability of individuals to care is circumscribed by their competences and the responsiveness of the cared-for. (Machold, Ahmed and Farquhar 2008)

Additionally, the organization needs to embed the values of care in internal and external systems and procedures. It also ensures that caring is not limited to a select group of individuals, such as management. Caring does not take place at the cost of replacing justice considerations, rather the obligation to care is in tandem with the duty not to harm individual stakeholders and a duty not to exploit or take advantage of unequal relationships. (Machold, Ahmed and Farquhar 2008)

The feminist model addresses some of the issues identified with a stakeholder governance perspective. It recognizes that webs of relationships exist in and around the firm, and that the nature of these relationships differs. Some relationships are prescribed by law, others are not; some are explicit, others are implicit; some are based on high power distance; others are relations between individuals of equal power. Care ethics obligates individuals to govern these relationships with respect to their particular context and specificity. Our individual identity and context lead to the creation of specific relationships that we seek to care for and in which we want to be cared about. Prioritizing stakeholders in the feminist model is about caring for those individuals close to us. (Machold, Ahmed and Farquhar 2008)

The ethic of rights and the ethic of care possibly reflect two distinct but evolutionarily stable strategies. Both strategies are viable and have their own worth. The early Chinese Yin and Yang polarity depicts both male and female principles as necessary for the health and good functioning of microcosms as well as macrocosms. An advanced concept of responsibility should integrate the reverence for rights represented by men and the nonviolence of care represented by women.

8.4 The End of Men?

In her provocative article "The End of Men," Rosin (2010) asks: "What if the modern, postindustrial economy is simply more congenial to women than to men?" She argues that the post-industrial economy is indifferent to men's size and strength. The attributes that are most valuable today – social intelligence, open communication, the ability to sit still and focus – are predominantly male. In fact, the opposite may be true. Women in poor parts of India are learning English faster than men to meet the demands of new global call centers. Women own more than 40 per cent of private businesses in China, where a red Ferrari is the new status symbol for female entrepreneurs.

In the USA men dominate just two of the fifteen job categories projected to grow the most over the next decade: janitor and computer engineer. Women have everything else: nursing, home health assistance, child care, food preparation. Many of the new jobs replace the things that women used to do in the home for free. None is especially high-paid. But the steady accumulation of these jobs adds up to an economy that, for the working class, has become more amenable to women than to men. The list of growing jobs is weighted towards nurturing professions, in which women, ironically, seem to benefit from old stereotypes and habits. Theoretically, there is no reason why men should not be qualified to do these jobs. But they have proved remarkably unable to adapt. (Rosin 2010)

According to Rosin the economic and cultural power shift from men to women would be hugely significant even if it never extended beyond working-class America. But women are also starting to dominate middle management, and a surprising number of professional careers as well. According to the Bureau of Labor Statistics, women now hold 51.4 per cent of managerial and professional jobs – up from 26.1 per cent in 1980. They make up 54 per cent of all accountants and hold about half of all banking and insurance jobs. About a third of America's physicians are now women, as are 45 per cent of associates in law firms, and both those percentages are rising fast. A white-collar economy requires communication skills and social intelligence, areas in which women have a slight edge. Perhaps most importantly it increasingly requires formal education credentials, which women are more prone to acquire, particularly early in adulthood. (Rosin 2010)

In his book, *Enlightened Power: How Women Are Transforming the Practice of Leadership*, David Gergen writes that women are knocking on the door of leadership at the very moment when their talents are especially well matched with the requirements of the day. (Gergen 2005)

The old model of command and control, with one leader holding all the decision-making power, is considered hidebound. The new model is sometimes called "post-heroic," or "transformational." The aim is to behave like a good coach, and channel your charisma to motivate others to be hardworking and creative. The model echoes literature about male–female differences.

A 2008 study attempted to quantify the effect of this more feminine management style. Researchers at Columbia Business School and the University of Maryland analyzed data on the top 1,500 US companies from 1992 to 2006 to determine the relationship between firm performance and female participation in senior management. Firms that had women in top positions performed better, and this was especially true if the firm pursued what the researchers called an "innovation intensive strategy," in which, they argued, "creativity and collaboration may be especially important." Innovative, successful firms are the ones that promote women. (Dezső and Ross 2008)

8.5 Conclusion

Gender equality and feminist ethics are not just important for their own sake. They increase the performance of businesses and economies while contributing to the quality of life of men and women alike.

The Organization for Economic Cooperation and Development (OECD) devised the Gender, Institutions and Development Database, which measures the economic and political power of women in 162 countries. With few exceptions, the greater the power of women, the greater the country's economic success. Aid agencies have started to recognize this relationship and have pushed to institute political quotas in about a hundred countries, essentially forcing women into power in an effort to improve those countries' fortunes. (OECD 2006)

Klaus Schwab, Executive Chairman of the World Economic Forum, rightly concluded that "Low gender gaps are directly correlated with high economic competitiveness. Women and girls must be treated equally if a country is to grow and prosper. We still need a gender equality revolution, not only to mobilize a major pool of talent both in terms of volume and quality, but also to create a more compassionate value system within all our institutions."

References

Dezső and Ross (2008) "Girl Power": Female Participation in Top Management and Firm Performance. University of Maryland Robert H. Smith School of Business. *Social Science working paper* RHS-06-104. Research Network Electronic Paper Collection.

England, P. and Stanek Kilbourne, B. (1990) Feminist Critiques of the Separative Model of Self, *Rationality and Society*, April, pp. 156–171.

Ferber, M. A. and Nelson, J. A. (eds) (1993) *Beyond Economic Man*. Chicago and London: University of Chicago Press.

Gender Inequality Index and Related Indicators (2011) Statistical Table 4, *Human Development Report*.

Gergen, D. (2005) Forward. In: Coughlin, L., Wingard, E. and Hollihan, K. (eds) *Enlightened Power: How Women Are Transforming the Practice of Leadership*. San Francisco: Jossey-Bass.

Gilligan, C. (1982) *In a Different Voice: Psychological Theory and Women's Development*. Cambridge, MA and London: Harvard University Press.

Global Gender Gap Report (2011) World Economic Forum.
Helsingin Sanomat International Edition Business & Finance (2011) *Companies Managed by Women more Profitable than Those Run by Men*. Analysis Focuses on Return on Capital.
Innovations Report (2006) Women Face Huge Disadvantages in their Working Lives. <http://www.innovations-report.com> accessed 2 October 2012.
Machold, S., Ahmed, P. K. and Farquhar, S. S. (2008) Corporate Governance and Ethics: A Feminist Perspective, *Journal of Business Ethics*, vol. 81, pp. 665–678.
McKinsey & Company (2007) Women Matter: Gender Diversity, a Corporate Performance Driver – Companies with a High Proportion of Women in Top Management May Perform Better. McKinsey & Company Inc.
OECD (2006) *Gender, Institutions and Development Database*. Paris.
Rogers, S. (2011) The Gender Pay Gap. *The Guardian*, 27 November. <http://www.guardian.co.uk> accessed 2 October 2012.
Rosin, H. (2010) The End of Men. *The Atlantic Magazine*, July/August, <http://www.theatlantic.com> accessed 2 October 2012.
Saadia Zahidi, S. (2011) Global Gender Gap Report World Economic Forum. <http://www.weforum.org/issues/global-gender-gap> accessed 2 October 2012.
Sweney, M. (2011) Lynx's Lucy Pinder ads banned by ASA. *The Guardian*, 23 November. <http://www.guardian.co.uk> accessed 2 October 2012.
Table News Network (2011) Fortune 500 Women CEOs. CNN Money A service of CNN Fortune and Money. Fortune 500 A Time Warner Company. <http://www.money.cnn.com> accessed 2 October 2012.
Temin, D. (2010) Leadership: Making the Business Case for Gender Equality. In: *Forbes Woman*. <http://www.forbes.com/2010/11/09/gender-gap-business-case-diversity-forbes-woman-leadership-harvard-women-public-policy.html> accessed 2 October 2012.
UNDP (1990–2011) United Nations Development Programme Human Development Reports. <http://hdr.undp.org/en/statistics/ihdi/> accessed 2 October 2012.
United Nations Department of Public Information (1997) Women at a Glance. <http://www.un.org/ecosocdev/geninfo/women/women96.htm> accessed 2 October 2012.
World Bank (2011) World Development Report 2012: Gender Equality and Development. Washington, DC: World Bank.

ZSOLT BODA
(CORVINUS UNIVERSITY OF BUDAPEST)

9 International Ethics and Globalization

9.1 The Challenge of Globalization

9.2 The Ethics of International Business
    9.2.1 The Problem of Regulation: Order and Disorder
    9.2.2 An Ethics for the Multinationals

9.3 Globalization versus Localization

9.4 The Case of the Forest and the Marine Stewardship Councils

9.5 Conclusion

Abstract

In the inherently anarchic international system the validity of moral principles is weakening. To overcome anarchy, global governance is needed. It means efficient international institutions, but also pressures from the global civil society and the self-regulation of business. Multinational firms have the duty of cooperating in governance systems. They also have the duty of reconciling in their activity the two, equally legitimate claims of universalism and cultural relativism; i.e., applying universal moral principles and respecting local moral norms. Finally, multinationals must be guided by the principle of enhanced responsibility. However, although globalizing efforts are important in overcoming international anarchy and coordinating the protection of global commons, strong arguments support the notion that economic globalization does not promote sustainable development. Some form of localization of the economy is certainly needed. The challenge is to find a way towards more global governance with less economic globalization.

Keywords: globalization, international ethics, universalism, cultural relativism, global governance, localization

9.1 The Challenge of Globalization

Ours is the age of economic globalization. Although a glimpse of globalization had already appeared at the end of the nineteenth century, current trends differ considerably from past ones. The "globalization" of the nineteenth century was marked by strong movements of capital, labor, and goods within the "world economy" of that time, which included only discreet portions of the globe. However, today's globalization is characterized by an unprecedented degree of free and fast movement of capital around the whole globe, and by the global institutions of a financial superstructure. Capital has acquired predominance over other factors of production. Economic activities are coordinated by globally integrated financial and capital markets.

In his famous essay, Karl Polanyi (1944) describes the advent of capitalism in nineteenth-century Britain as "The Great Transformation." This was the process through which the logic of the market not only transformed a multitude of economic activities, creating the "market economy," but also changed the nature of social institutions, thereby shaping a "market society." Polanyi's thesis is that a "market economy" necessitates a "market society," where social interactions and activities like labor, and even human, relations, the cultivation of land, the management of natural resources, and even the evolution of culture, are coordinated by the logic of the market. He argues that the social and environmental consequences of this process are dramatic, because a single logic rules over all others. And there is no one logic which is able to effectively coordinate all the complex and diverse interactions of the social and natural world. We need diversity and a plurality of coordination schemes: market forces must be countervailed by state regulation, the control of civil society and the self-regulation of business.

In a similar vein, we can argue that a "Great Transformation" is currently taking place on a global scale. The dominant development paradigm – preached by the International Monetary Fund, the World Bank, the World Trade Organization and global business organizations – advises countries to liberalize international trade, assist foreign investors, and privatize national assets; and to cut back government expenditures, including assistance to small farmers and spending on health, education, and environmental protection. The global economic crisis that started in 2008 first seemed to change the predominance of the market dogma, and provoked some soul searching among eminent figures of neoliberalism – like Alan Greenspan, former president of the FED, who admitted that he had to much faith in the market logic. But despite those quick reactions, in fact, paradigmatic change has not occurred in economic policies. The neoliberal arrogance has been tempered to some extent, but economic difficulties and roaring public debts brought back the well known arguments for austerity measures: less government expenditures, more private initiatives.

Thus, despite some drawbacks, the advanture of globalization continues. Economies all around the world are being reshaped under the pressure of global markets: "market economy" is being created on a global scale. And this has fundamental social and environmental consequences as well. There is evidence that national economic policies based on liberalization benefit international business, multinational companies, and global financial markets. However, their effects on people, local cultures, and the environment are more than dubious.

Where are the countervailing forces to market interests on the global level? Are the already existing institutions (such as international treaties and organizations) of global governance strong enough to create and protect the needed balance between variegated values and interests? What kind of regulation and governance do we need? This problematic, as we will see, is a reformulation of a very old one in international ethics.

However, the need for global governance raises a very fundamental ethical question about the basic values of global cooperation. The problematic of universalism versus relativism will be explored in connection with the ethics of multinational companies, because any examination of international business ethics should deal with the problems involving both the systemic and corporate levels. Besides analyzing the conditions and possibilities of global governance, the rules of the global game, we should not forget about the responsibility of individual companies when trying to resolve the ethical dilemmas of the international marketplace.

9.2 The Ethics of International Business

9.2.1. *The Problem of Regulation: Order and Disorder*

The oldest tradition of international ethics is moral scepticism. A well-known formulation of this view is given by the seventeenth-century English philosopher Thomas Hobbes. He argues in his *Leviathan* that the international system is inherently anarchic, lacking any central, order-enforcing authority, and this justifies actors (states) in defending their interests by any means they judge appropriate. That is, ethical considerations lose their validity in anarchy. According to Hobbes, the phenomenon of inter-state relations resembles the original state of nature, prior to the creation of society and the state. In the original state of nature, individuals would attack one another simply out of the natural fear that others posed a threat to their safety. They lived in constant fear and insecurity and therefore benefited greatly from contracting with a sovereign power that would enforce rights and duties. However, cooperation between states is much less compelling and fruitful than cooperation between individuals, therefore the formation of a supranational sovereignty never becomes imperative. Anarchy will remain a basic feature of international relations, even if it does not necessarily imply constant hostility between states. But even times of peace are shaped by power relations and strategic considerations.

However, is the international system really as desperately anarchic as the Hobbesian arguments suggest? Regulatory efforts are a constant presence and international law has evolved considerably in the past centuries. Thousands of international treaties and hundreds of international organizations are designed to secure the terms of international cooperation.

Nevertheless, Castells (1997) still speaks about "global disorder." He argues that while during the twentieth century states made considerable efforts to reduce anarchy through the creation of global institutions (like the United Nations) and the development of international law, the appearance, and the growing power, of international organizations in the international arena undermine their legitimacy. These international organizations, which include multinational companies, non-governmental organizations (like Amnesty International and Greenpeace), and even government-founded institutions, like the International Monetary Fund, have become a major force in the international arena. Although their performance in attracting resources and managing issues is rather remarkable, their activity puts into question the sovereignty and the intervening capabilities of states. Nowadays many interests and values are represented by many agents in the international arena. Greenpeace tries to influence governments, business, and the people in the name of environmental values; multinational companies promote their own interests, and so on. In this situation a state becomes just one kind of actor in a cast of many – and not even the most powerful one, necessarily.

In sum, although talking about anarchy in the context of international relations seems like an overstatement, the fact is that there are no political mechanisms on a global scale to channel and represent the different interests, and the legitimacy of international organizations might be problematic. In this "global disorder," the pursuit of self-interests and strategic behavior might seem to be the most rational strategy for the actors, be they states, companies, or international organizations. For instance, states are reluctant to cooperate on managing the global commons, because these issues require considerable resources with uncertain returns. This is the "tragedy of global commons" (see Box 9.1).

For international business, global disorder, or anarchy, means first and foremost an insufficient regulatory framework; and, as a consequence, good opportunities to capitalize on their own self-interest (Scherer et al. 2009). We have to admit that "the usually reliable backdrop of national law, the local legal order which tends to ensure a minimum level of compliance for domestic corporations in domestic markets, is missing in the international scene" (Donaldson 1989, p. 31). This fact sheds a different light on corporate responsibility in the global marketplace.

Domestic law is less effective in regulating the activities of multinational companies for a number of reasons. First, the empirical fact is that in developing countries regulation is less sophisticated and enforcement of the laws is less effective than in developed countries, which in turn, do not rush to impose extraterritorial regulation on their home-chartered multinational corporations (see reference to the US Foreign Corrupt Practices Act in Box 9.2, p. 174). Second, multinational companies have some latitude in offsetting domestic regulation. For instance, they can easily avoid hard taxation through the strategic use of transfer prices; or they can make use of collisions between the norms of the home and the host country. Third, multinational corporations have enormous power. Some of this power is symbolic: because they are taken to be the dynamic force of capitalism, states compete with each other in attracting foreign direct investment. And if they are unsatisfied, multinationals threaten to leave the host country. But their power is not exclusively symbolic; sometimes it is very real.

Box 9.1 *The Case of Climate Policies*

Already, for more than ten years, climate change has been an increasing concern around the world. In order to prevent its dramatic consequences, concerted global actions are urgently needed. In 1997, a number of countries, including most OECD countries, agreed on the provisions adopted by the Kyoto Protocol, which set targets for future emissions of greenhouse gases that drive climate change. But the Kyoto Protocol left many decisions to be made, and while these are still being discussed the clock ticks and the date for meeting the targets draws closer. The Kyoto targets in themselves would have done little to avert climate change but were best seen as a first step towards more ambitious worldwide action. However, even these modest potential achievements were undermined, because in 2001 US President George W. Bush announced that his administration was dropping US support for the Kyoto Protocol, although the US alone was responsible for some 25 per cent of all global greenhouse gas emissions. Bush's unilateral decision represented the interests of US oil companies, Bush's corporate backers. The decision sparked outrage around the world. The UK Deputy Prime Minister at the time, John Prescott, declared that, "The US cannot sit in glorious isolation…It must know it cannot pollute the world while free-riding on action by everyone else." Unfortunately, the US is not the only major international player acting in a rather irresponsible way in terms of climate policies. Several Western European countries have not been able either to reduce, let alone, stabilize their greenhouse gas emissions. If the EU as a whole could meet the modest Kyoto targets, it is only because the new Central and Eastern European member states have lower emissions. This fact deeply undermines the credibility of the official EU position, which is in favor of strict climate policy measures. Moreover, the 2009 negotiations in Copenhagen turned out to be a major failure partly because of a leaked European document which set as a political goal that rich countries should not make serious commitments, rather that developing countries should be persuaded to reduce their emissions. However, developing countries, including the large ones, like China, India, and Brazil, which have become important atmospheric polluters, have rejected spending more on climate protection until they see the rich countries, still the major polluters, take the lead.

> **Box 9.2 *The Case of Corruption***
>
> Corruption has been long recognized, sadly, as a typical phenomenon of international business. From the early 1970s, the OECD urged its member states to take actions against international corruption, but no binding regulation was adopted. In 1977 the United States passed its Foreign Corrupt Practices Act (in the wake of the Lockheed bribery scandal, in which Lockheed officers bribed the Japanese government for a contract), which prohibited American corporations from offering payments to officials of foreign governments. However, as no other country followed the US in adopting similar regulations, American companies began to suffer from "less ethical" competition abroad. Therefore, some years after its adoption the Foreign Corrupt Practices Act was softened somewhat. Although no one questioned that corruption in international business is a serious problem, it took several decades for the OECD member states to finally sign an international treaty in 1997 on the issue. And this is still just the first step in effectively fighting corruption. Implementation is still weak and corruption has not been significantly reduced in international business.

Comparing the annual GDP of countries and the turnover of companies, we can see that more than fifty out of the hundred biggest economies in the world are not countries, but companies (see Box 9.3). They control a large share of world markets and the overwhelming majority of patents. "Trade is defined in large measure by pricing determined internally by the multinationals, and such prices are not, properly speaking, the result of the free play of the market. The entrance of a new independent producer is complicated, given the economies of reach and scale and the preferential access to finance that the multinationals enjoy" (Ugarteche 2000, p. 108). Finally, not only are multinationals extremely powerful, but, on top of this, they are backed and assisted by international financial institutions. And evidence shows that these companies are ready to use their power when searching the world to find the cheapest human and natural resources, and the most supportive environments for their business.

Box 9.3 Selected Countries' Annual GDP and Company Revenues in 2010 (USD billions)	
Poland	468.6
Wal-Mart Stores	408.2
Austria	376.2
Argentina	368.0
Denmark	310.4
Greece	304.8
Royal Dutch/Shell Group	285.1
Exxon Mobil	284.6
BP	246.1
Finland	238.8
Egypt	218.9
Toyota Motor	204.6
AXA	175.2
China National Petroleum	165.5
Romania	161.6
General Electric	156.8
Peru	153.8
Tanzania	23.5

Source: http://www.worldbank.org and http://www.fortune.com

In sum, the regulation of the multinationals based on domestic laws is imperfect. We certainly need international regulatory framework. While many international institutions and treaties are already in place to regulate business, a number of problems still remain:

(i) regulation is only slowly evolving even in those areas which are widely recognized as problematic (corruption, money-laundering);

(ii) regulation tends to neglect some areas, or stakeholders. For instance, in international trade agreements competition is relatively well-secured, and consumer interests are also given some weight. But labor standards and environmental issues are largely disregarded;

(iii) broader ethical issues are treated almost exclusively in non-binding documents, like codes of conduct. Although their role in regulating business is more and more important and should not be neglected, it is limited in many respects. They provide rather "soft" provisions; non-compliance, by definition, is not penalized; specific codes, focusing on particular problem areas, are elaborated retrospectively – that is, after a scandal or tragedy becomes known (see Box 9.4).

When talking about the regulation of international business, George Soros stated that "the current state of affairs is unsound and unsustainable" (Soros 1998). He was, of course, talking about the regulation of financial markets, where the situation is even more dramatic, as proven by the global financial and economic crisis that started in 2008. This reality calls for a system of international regulations unthinkable before now.

But even if we leave the world of global finance behind us in order to turn back to the problem of regulating the multinationals, we can argue that Soros' statement still holds. It is widely recognized that more regulation is needed. But this time regulation should move away from the "free-trade paradigm," which means that the focus of the regulation is on securing fair competition, the enforcement of the non-discrimination principle, and the limitation of state intervention in business. The 1997 debate about the Multilateral Agreement on Investment (see Box 9.5, p. 178) and the developments under the General Agreement on Trade in Services (GATS) under the auspices of the World Trade Organization showed that even now many think that this paradigm is a relevant frame of reference for regulating not only trade, but international business in general. However, debates around the MAI and the GATS also revealed that for many people this paradigm is outdated and no longer acceptable. Not only should international business and investments not be regulated in a trade-like manner, but even trade rules should change in order to encompass broader (i.e., social and environmental) concerns. The free-trade paradigm was perhaps

Box 9.4 *Codes of Conduct for Multinationals*

One genre of codes manifests itself as specific documents, focusing on a particular problem. These codes typically emerge as a response to a scandal or tragic accident. They include intergovernmental documents (e.g., the European Economic Community's Code of Conduct for Companies with Interest in South Africa, 1977); codes elaborated under the auspices of an international organization (e.g., the World Health Organization's Code on the Marketing of Breast-milk Substitutes, 1981); and guidelines and standards developed by business organizations (e.g., the International Federation of Pharmaceutical Manufacturers Associations' code of pharmaceutical marketing practice, 1981).

Another class of codes is engendered by comprehensive charters which cover several problem areas. Some of these have been elaborated by civil and business organizations (such as the Social Accountability 8000 standard, or the charter of the GoodCorporation), and we can delineate here those intergovernmental compacts which aim at defining the basic outlines of the global corporate ethic. Their normative force is based on widely accepted moral values, norms, and the provisions of other basic international documents, like the Universal Declaration of Human Rights. The most important of such comprehensive compacts are: the OECD Guidelines for Multinational Enterprises (accepted in 1976, last amended in 2011); the International Labor Office (ILO) Tripartite Declaration of Principles Concerning Multinational Enterprises and Social Policy (1977); the United Nations Code of Conduct on Transnational Corporations (Not completed); the Ten Principles of the United Nations' Global Compact (2000 and 2004). Some of the problem areas covered in, and normative guides offered by, these compacts are (see Frederick, 1991): *Employment Practices and Policies* – multinationals should respect the right of employees to join trade unions and bargain collectively (ILO, OECD, UN Global Compact); multinationals should develop nondiscriminatory employment policies and promote equal job opportunities (ILO, OECD, UN Global Compact); multinationals should, minimally, pay basic living wages to employees (ILO); *Consumer Protection* – multinationals should safeguard the health and safety of consumers by various disclosures, safe packaging, proper labeling, and accurate advertising (UN Code); *Environmental Protection* – multinationals should disclose environmental information and minimize environmental risks and harms (OECD, UN Code); multinationals should promote the development of international environmental standards (UN Code); *Political Payments and Involvement* – multinationals should not pay bribes nor make improper payments to public officials and should avoid improper or illegal involvement or interference in the internal politics of host nations (OECD, UN).

an appropriate one in the twentieth century as a reaction to the chaotic state of trade before World War II, brought on by the Great Depression, which took the forms of high tariff barriers, extensive use of nontariff barriers to trade, widespread trade discrimination, and, as a consequence, a severely reduced volume of international trade and investment. But nowadays, under the conditions of economic globalization, the goal of the international regulation of business should move away from focusing solely on the terms of competition. It should be redesigned in order to be able to protect and promote the basic rights and the welfare of people around the world, and to preserve and sustain the natural ecosystems.

Box 9.5 *The Multilateral Agreement on Investment (MAI)*

The secret negotiations on the MAI began in 1995 under the auspices of the OECD. It was conceived as a "technical agreement," but it turned out to be more of a "constitution for the global economy." However, it was a very flawed constitution, because it laid down the rights of international business without outlining its obligations. When in 1997 the text of the MAI became public it caused worldwide indignation. The MAI was deemed unacceptable by NGOs, political organizations, and even the European Parliament. Its provisions would have prohibited discrimination of any kind against multinationals, while allowing for preferential treatment. Corporations would have had unprecedented freedom to sue governments, and in case of dispute, they would have had the possibility to "opt out" from the jurisdiction of the state in question and ask the judgment of an international dispute-settlement panel.

However, some MAI-like provisions found their ways into international treaties. The North American Free Trade Agreement (NAFTA) also allows companies to sue states if their profit is being affected by government policies, even social or environmental ones. The GATS agreement has also provoked vivid controversy, mainly on its possible effects on public services. Major European cities, including Paris, Oxford, and Florence, joined a "Stop GATS" campaign protesting against the treaty (see http://www.gatswatch.org).

Regulation does not mean solely formalization and institutionalization. In the era of "global turbulence" (Rosenau 1990) the global civil society is increasingly able and ready to contribute to the effectiveness of global governance. Informal pressures coming from NGOs, or even the media, are now part of the evolution of international regimes (governance systems). These agents voice moral claims that are difficult to neglect. International NGOs (like Amnesty International or Greenpeace), or even those formal institutions which otherwise do not have real power (e.g., the International Labour Organization), can have influence just by pointing out the problems. Thus, a "discursive multilateralism" is also part of the global regulatory setting (Weisband 2000).

Let's suppose that international regulatory efforts of all kinds will intensify in the coming years! (It is actually not a counterfactual hypothesis: in the past twenty years more than 200 international treaties were signed in the field of environmental protection alone; and many of them affect business.) Still, anarchy as a basic feature of the international system will remain for a while at least. What should multinationals do under these conditions? Some argue that under imperfect regulation, when there is no guarantee that others will follow the norms, they have only limited responsibility and should therefore primarily follow their own self-interest. In a similar spirit, "Boddewyn and Brewer (1994) have defended the view that managers should consider the host-country government on a par with other competitive factors. For his own part, Boddewyn (1986) has even argued that when companies seek competitive advantage, bribery, smuggling, and buying absolute market monopolies are not necessarily ruled out" (Donaldson and Dunfee 1999, p. 220). These recommendations are perfectly in line with Hobbesian moral scepticism.

However, acknowledging international anarchy must not lead to moral scepticism. Immanuel Kant, in his *Eternal Peace*, argues that moral law obliges us to follow ethical norms in international affairs even if nobody else is following them, and we must promote peace among nations even if it seems hopeless. But in order to secure peace and promote compliance with the norms, he proposes reducing anarchy through international cooperation and institution building. That is, while Hobbes thought that cooperation is difficult under the conditions of anarchy, Kant argues that we need cooperation, *just because of* the existing anarchy. In a similar spirit, if one thinks that it is difficult to put high moral claims on the multinationals under the conditions of imperfect regulation, we should reply that ethics is not conditional: basic duties do not vanish just because some do not follow them. Multinationals cannot justify unethical behavior with a simple reference to the circumstances. Moreover, an additional duty is incumbent upon them: that of *cooperating* somehow in global governance in order to contribute to reducing anarchy.

9.2.2 An Ethics for the Multinationals

Let's move towards the ethics of the corporation! Although the context and the quality of the regulatory framework of a behavior is very important in influencing its ethicality, we should not forget that agents always have some autonomy, and therefore some responsibility in deciding what to do. That is, as stated above, international anarchy does not discard the responsibility of the multinational to act in an ethical way. On the contrary: the enormous power of the multinational increases its responsibility in dealing with the stakeholders. In this section we will shortly overview the ethics of the multinational company.

Both international ethicists and business ethicists (e.g., Donaldson 1989, 1993, Walzer 1994, Donaldson and Dunfee 1999) argue that the main problem we face when trying to specify the universally binding obligations for multinationals is the difference in moral standards between the cultures. In very practical terms this means that the host-country standards, norms, or values might differ from the multinational's home-country standards, norms, and values. What should be done in the case of conflicting norms? This simple question has a broader relevance. The empirical fact that many moral cultures coexist in the world might cause problems for international ethics. Although we tend to believe that there are universally valid norms and values, we also cherish cultural diversity and argue that local communities should be recognized and respected. That is, at one extreme, the position of *universalism* implies that there exists a set of universally binding norms, which rules out the possibility of two conflicting ethical views in different cultures being equally valid. At the other extreme, the position of *cultural relativism* implies that "no ethical view held by one culture is better than any other view held by another culture" (Donaldson and Dunfee 1999, p. 23). Universalism is sometimes accused of implying moral imperialism and arrogant absolutism. Relativism, taken to the extreme, means that we should accept any cultural norm, no matter how inhumane or bizarre it is.

How can a balance between universalism and relativism be found? Donaldson and Dunfee argue for *pluralism* defined as follows: "There exists a broad range of ethical viewpoints that may be chosen by communities and cultures. The possibility exists that conflicting ethical positions in different cultures are equally valid. There are, however, circumstances in which the viewpoint of a particular culture will be invalid due either to a universally binding moral precept or to the priority of the view of another culture or community" (Donaldson and Dunfee 1999, p. 23). That is, pluralism is a moderate universalistic position, complemented by the value of tolerance.

In a strict philosophical sense it might be difficult to reconcile the two equally important and legitimate claims of universalism and relativism. But in practice, in the spirit of pluralism, we can and must find practical solutions to overcome the problem.

Donaldson (1989) proposes a practical tool to solve ethical dilemmas related to universalism and relativism. First, he defines the minimal moral duties of multinationals in terms of fundamental human rights following three conditions: 1) the right must protect something of very great importance; 2) the right must be subject to substantial and recurrent threats; and 3) the obligations or burdens imposed by the right must satisfy a fairness-affordability test; that is, all kinds of actors in the international scene should be able to afford the costs of respecting the right in question.

Donaldson's list of fundamental human rights generated from these conditions include: (1) the right to freedom of physical movement; (2) the right to ownership of property; (3) the right to freedom from torture; (4) the right to a fair trial; (5) the right to nondiscriminatory treatment (e.g., freedom from discrimination on the basis of such characteristics as race or sex); (6) the right to physical security; (7) the right to freedom of speech and association; (8) the right to minimal education; (9) the right to political participation; and (10) the right to subsistence (Donaldson 1989, p. 81). These rights must be honored by all actors in the international scene.

Second, he elaborates an "ethical algorithm" in order to help the decision-maker (the multinational manager) in those more subtle situations where the conflict of norms cannot be resolved with a simple reference to fundamental rights. Donaldson argues that there are two basic cases: "If the practice is morally and/or legally permitted in the host country, then either: (1) the moral reasons underlying the host country's view that the practice is permissible refer to the host country's relative level of economic development; or (2) the moral reasons underlying the host country's view that the practice is permissible are independent of the host country's relative level of economic development" (Donaldson 1989, p. 102). The first case refers to such things as labor standards, environmental regulation, and so on. Donaldson assumes that these standards evolve with economic development. The second case refers to genuine cultural norms, customs, and habits.

In the first case, the "ethical algorithm" offers the following formula: "The practice is permissible for the multinational if and only if the members of the home country would, under conditions of economic development similar to those of the host country, regard the practice as permissible" (Donaldson 1989, p. 103). The rule allows for some relativism. For instance, the multinational is not obliged to apply the home country's strict environmental protection standards, unless required by law, in an African country. Not because high standards are not desirable per se, but because the level of development requires a commensurate ordering of priorities. However, the rule certainly does not allow the release of highly toxic pollutants; that is, the rule's relativism is limited in scope.

In the second case, the decision-maker must ask the following questions: (1) Is it possible to conduct business successfully in the host country without undertaking the practice? and (2) Is the practice a clear violation of a fundamental international right? The practice would be permissible if and only if the answer to both questions is "no" (Donaldson 1989, p. 104). That is, the multinational should avoid conforming to questionable local practices, but if it is not possible, and the practice in case is a clear violation of human rights, the company should consider even disinvesting from the country, as some multinationals did in the 1980s from South Africa, because of the apartheid regime which was institutionalizing racial discrimination.

Donaldson's "ethical algorithm" is an original attempt to deal with conflicting norms and reconcile universalism and relativism. As a practical tool, it is, of course, simplifying things to a large extent. It is, for instance, legitimate to question whether we can compare the development levels of different countries, as suggested in decision rule (1). Nevertheless, the distinction between welfare norms (dependent on the level of development) and authentic cultural norms is an important one. In the case of welfare norms there is some place for "quantitative adjustments," and although we want multinationals to apply higher norms if the local ones are too permissive (for instance, in some developing countries it is allowed to pay wages under the subsistence level, and sometimes environmental regulation is highly ineffective), it would be unfair to oblige them to apply the same standards everywhere. Authentic cultural norms are more difficult to adjust: in most of the cases one should either accept or reject them. For instance, gender discrimination seems to be an integral part of the culture of many Muslim countries, and companies are forced to either follow this norm in their operations or leave the country in question.

Donaldson and Dunfee (1999) offer a different approach to deal with universalism and relativism. They abandon Donaldson's original idea about a well-defined list of rights (as minimal duties) and the "ethical algorithm." Nevertheless, their Integrated Social Contract Theory (ISCT) is still about the problem of how to put into practice the concept of pluralism. The structure of their model is similar to Donaldson's (1989), but less prescriptive. They also assume the existence of some universal principles, what they call *hypernorms*. These are key limits on the "moral free space" of the actors, and serve as ultimate points of reference in case of ethical conflicts. However, unlike Donaldson (1989), they avoid defining a limited list of hypernorms. Instead, they hold that hypernorms are constantly evolving, and in order to decide whether a principle constitutes a hypernorm, decision-makers should look for evidences: such as whether there is widespread consensus that the norm is universal, supported by the laws of many different countries, known to be consistent with the precepts of major religions and philosophies, supported by prominent NGOs or international business organizations, and so on. Hypernorms include basic ethical values (like human dignity), norms (like promise keeping), human rights, and welfare norms (like the prohibition of child labor).

However, agents have considerable moral free space as well. "Moral free space is the area bounded by hypernorms in which communities develop ethical norms representing a collective viewpoint concerning right behavior" (Donaldson and Dunfee 1999, p. 83). That is, under the umbrella of the "macrosocial contract" based on hypernorms, communities (which include local communities, professional organizations, business organizations, and so on) may generate ethical norms for their members through "microsocial" contracts.

Now, what if a multinational observes a conflict between, let's say, local norms and the provisions of the company's own code of conduct? First, norms must be screened for legitimacy under hypernorm tests. A norm is illegitimate if it clearly contradicts some hypernorms (like basic human rights), or if it is not an authentic community norm (e.g., it was forced on the community). Second, remaining legitimate norms should be screened for dominance. However, Donaldson and Dunfee do not elaborate an "ethical algorithm" to deal with this problem; they just propose some "rules of thumb" which might help. Relevant factors might include priority rules already adopted as norms between communities; potential externalities; and essentialness of the norms to the transaction environment. If a clear dominant norm emerges, ethical judgment should be based on it; if there is no clear dominant norm, ethical judgment can be based on any legitimate norm (Donaldson and Dunfee 1999, p. 206).

It is strange that neither Donaldson's (1989) nor Donaldson and Dunfee's (1999) procedures include the principle of dialogue and communication (see, e.g., Gilbert and Rasche 2007). This principle is formulated by *discourse ethics*. According to Karl-Otto Apel (1990), discourse ethics implies that only those norms that meet (or could be reasonably presumed to meet) with the approval of all concerned in a real, rational debate can claim to be valid. The debate should be as close as possible to the "ideal communication situation" which is free of domination and argumentative inequality, and in which participants do not act in a strategic way but perform a real communicative action. Whereas in strategic action one actor seeks to *influence* the behavior of another by means of threatening sanctions or offering carrots, in communicative action one actor seeks to *motivate* another *rationally* by relying on the persuasive power of the arguments (Habermas 1990, p. 63). Ideally, the validity of speech lies in its *intelligibility* (valid meaning), *truthfulness* (subjective authenticity), factual *truth* and *correctness* (normative justifiability). The principle implies that the multinational should enter into fair negotiations with the stakeholders if a conflict arises between, for instance, the home-country and the host-country norms. However, if openness to the dialogue is an undeniably important value, it is also true that cultural differences are sometimes difficult to overcome through discussion, and negotiations might become endless.

A concluding problem related to the ethics of multinationals should be mentioned. Their operations in a social, cultural, and natural environment, that frequently differs markedly from their own, can lead to unforeseen and sometimes dramatic consequences. The *Nestlé infant formula* case sadly illustrates the point: Who would have imagined that a "simple" advertising campaign might lead to human tragedies, the death of babies? Many similar cases prove that multinationals should design their policies and operations with greater prudence. Water pollution has different effects in a rich country than in the rural area of a poor country where people get their drinking water from a river; logging has different consequences in a highly sensitive tropical area than in a temperate zone forest; consumerist marketing campaigns might have brutal cultural effects in a traditionalist society; workers in a developing country might be less aware of the health and environmental risks of modern industrial technologies; and so on. All this entails *the enhanced responsibility* of doing business abroad. Unfortunately, reality often conflicts sharply with this idea).

In summary, the ethics of the multinational companies is built of the following elements:

Openness to *dialogue* and *cooperation* (in the spirit of Kantian and discourse ethics). This means both cooperating in terms of global governance and being open to the voices of different cultural communities and stakeholders.

Respecting some basic *universal values* and norms (like the norm of "Do no harm!" or human rights, or the provisions of codes of conducts). Some flexibility, however, might be unavoidable when applying the universal norms. But there are also cases when firms should disinvest from the country, particularly if basic norms are systematically violated and there is no hope that "enlightened" business can improve the situation.

Respecting the *norms* of *different communities* – even this might imply some adjustments, because the norms of different relevant communities (typically the home and the host countries) may require different approaches. A useful distinction between the norms concerns their underlying moral context: whether or not the norm in question is related to the relative level of development of the countries. A rule of thumb might be that if the local norm is independent of the level of development (i.e., if it is an authentic cultural norm) then it should be respected; but in the case of norms that are dependent on the developmental level of the host country (e.g., labor, environmental, or health standards) firms should be required to apply somewhat higher (either universal, or home country) norms, if the local ones are too permissive.

An *enhanced responsibility* of the firm abroad. In an unknown social, economic, cultural, and ecological environment, even those business practices which otherwise might be seen as "innocent" can have dramatic consequences. Firms must be particularly careful when designing their policies and actions abroad.

9.3 Globalization versus Localization

Globalization critics (Korten 1995, Hines 2000) argue that the inherent features of today's globalized economy make sustainable development impossible, both from a human and an ecological point of view.

Globalization leads to increased social inequalities. Empirical studies and historical examples show that in export-oriented economies, *ceteris paribus*, social inequalities are growing (Giraud 1996, Gowdy 1995, Rodrik 1997, Wade 2004). The revenue of those who are "internationally competitive" will depend on international markets and can have a much higher growth rate than the revenue of those who are producing for the local market. Only effective government policies can prevent growing inequalities. However, the idea of a strong government is against the ruling development paradigm, defended by the IMF and the World Bank. The fact is that social inequalities have sharply increased in the past twenty years all over the world, including the OECD countries.

Globalization means sharp competition and a "race to the bottom" in terms of social and environmental regulation. For instance, in Malaysia's and Indonesia's export processing zones even these countries' own – not too demanding – labor rights are suspended; Brazil has several times relaxed its environmental regulation during the 1990s. The erosion of wages, welfare standards, and environmental regulations reinforces the effect of trade on social inequalities, because any reduction of government welfare spending affects first and foremost the poor.

Globalization means cultural homogenization and loss of cultural identities. A "consumer monoculture" (Hines 2000, p. 4) is being imposed everywhere, which has unpleasant economic as well as ecological consequences. The former manifests itself in the growing imports of expensive consumer goods in relatively poor countries; the latter means the spread of unsustainable consumption patterns. And the cultural challenge of globalization leads to emerging identity-based social movements and cultural conflicts (see Castells 1997). The rising wave of religious fundamentalism in Islamic countries illustrates the point. Globalization means shifting power from political communities to business. This, together with identity crises and growing inequalities, leads to a fragmentation of political communities, loss of solidarity inside the society, growing apathy, decreased political activity and/or an increase in the power of radical political movements.

Globalization leads to ecological homogenization. Export-oriented agriculture is based on the extensive use of a few cash crop varieties, which means the crowding out of local varieties (Noorgard 1988). For instance, according to estimations, thousands of rice varieties have already disappeared in India during the last few decades due to agro-business trends (Johnston 1995). This has dramatic social, cultural, and ecological consequences. Shiva et al. (1991) argue that with vanishing local production local traditions are disappearing as well; that is, the ongoing homogenization in agriculture represents a double (cultural and ecological) loss.

International trade leads to the overuse of resources. This is called the growth effect of trade (Pearce 1994). If a local product becomes popular, local production might face the burden of a global demand. The growth effect of trade might have a dramatic effect on ecosystems and environmental resources. For instance, there is no way to satisfy the global demand for leopard fur; the only way to save leopards from excessive hunting is to ban fur trade all together. The global demand for shrimps caused the extension of shrimp production in South East Asia, which led to the clearing of precious mangrove forests (Ekins et al. 1994, p. 8).

And, finally, the structural features of the global economy and the huge organizations involved make impossible the application of the precautionary principle. The psychological phenomenon of discounting in space and time impedes the application of responsibility on a global scale: people are unable to make responsible decisions about remote issues. Therefore, "localizing" the economy is a necessary, though insufficient, condition of sustainable development (Gowdy 1995, Curtis 2003).

In sum, globalization implies an unjust world system and an unsound, unsustainable development concept. Some of these shortcomings might be corrected through more efficient global governance. For example, labor and environmental standards might be regulated on a global scale (Giscard d'Estaing 1995). However, some structural features of a globalizing economy seem impossible to reform. Therefore, globalization should not only be more regulated, but also restricted; we need some kind of localization instead of more globalization.

Localization has several meanings. It might mean just some "slowing down" of the global economy and a reformulation of the mission of global economic institutions (like the IMF). For instance, some form of a "Tobin tax" would slow down the flow of money in international financial markets, reducing speculative international financial movements, and, by this, the risk of financial crisis. "A 0.5 per cent tax should be collected on all spot transactions in foreign exchange, including foreign exchange deliveries pursuant to futures contracts and options" (Korten 1995, p. 321). International agreement should not promote the interests of multinationals and international finance, but they should empower local communities to control and manage local resources for local benefits. For example, preferential treatment of foreign investors would be prohibited; multinationals would be required to stay longer in a given country, to make longer-term commitments in their investment decisions. And so on.

But localization in a more radical sense means a clear-cut restructuring of the economy towards local functioning (Doughwait 1996, Robertson 1998, Hines 2000, Curtis 2003). This means localizing the capital and the money through community investment, community banking and local money creation, and localizing food security and sustainable development through local production of organic food. It also means localizing production through taxation and creating competition policies that benefit and protect local markets, shopkeepers, and small business. In such a world, the economy would not revolve around the logic of trade and international investments, but just the opposite. Trade of goods and the international movement of money would be seen as mere complements, with stress given to the rebuilding of local economies worldwide.

9.4 The Case of the Forest and the Marine Stewardship Councils

Civil society organizations (CSOs) have gained importance in public life. They increasingly influence politics, regulation of business, and the provision of social services. CSOs are increasingly turning also towards business (Boda 2010, Boda et al. 2009, den Hond and Bakker 2007). This approach is largely explained by the power shift that occurred from governments to companies, as CSOs discover that it might be easier and more fruitful to approach businesses with their criticisms and demands (Newell 2000). For instance, the traditional way for an advocacy group to change business practices is to lobby the government for a new regulation. However, it may turn out that approaching companies themselves could be a much simpler and more successful strategy). The ethical consumerism movement is a powerful representation of this approach; boycotts, media campaigns, and similar means are perceived as a real threat by companies. At the same time, other CSOs aim at developing cooperative relations with companies, partly because they need businesses' resources (money, knowledge) in order to operate effectively.

Values-driven, company-focused CSOs are also very active in the field of global business regulation. A growing literature about "private authorities", "governance structures and international regimes", "partnerships", and "global business regulation" suggests that globalization is not void of multifaceted regulatory efforts which come from different sectors. Besides international organizations, business and CSOs are also active in setting and promoting norms.

An interesting initiative is the Forest Stewardship Council (FSC). Formally, FSC is an independent, non-governmental, not-for-profit organization established to promote the responsible management of the world's forests. Originally it was initiated by the World Wide Fund for Nature (WWF), and has been created through a "bottom up" approach, and inclusion: the most important stakeholders, companies, and NGOs, have been invited to join the FSC and its activity has been based on the deliberation and cooperation of the parties. It was established in 1993 by a group of timber users, traders, and representatives of environmental and human rights organizations. This varied group of people had all had identified the need for a system that could credibly identify well-managed forests as a source of responsibly produced forest products. Since its inception many different stakeholders around the world have worked with the FSC in its equitable participatory processes in support of responsible forest management. However, also since its early days, FSC has often been criticized by conservative industries that did not believe in sharing decision-making with social and environmental stakeholders. Much like conservative industries, some environmental stakeholders believe that confrontational campaigns are a more appropriate conservation tool than equitable participatory solutions-oriented approaches. FSC believes that it is part of the solution for the conservation of natural forests and that a full set of different complementary conservation strategies are necessary to protect and maintain the world's forests. FSC now provides standard setting, trademark insurance, and accreditation services for companies and organizations interested in responsible forestry. Products carrying the FSC label are independently certified to assure consumers that they come from forests that are managed to meet the social, economic, and ecological needs of present and future generations. FSC has offices in more than forty-five countries. By August 2011 the total certified forest area attained was 140,502,262 hectares in a total of seventy-nine countries.

FSC is generally recognized as a success story, and part of the success is its inclusive nature: stakeholders were directly involved in determining key principles and organizational concepts for the FSC. An interesting comparison is with the Marine Stewardship Council, another venture of the WWF, that seeks to promote sustainable fishing practices. Both the FSC and the MSC are joint ventures of companies and NGOs promoting a market-led solution to environmental problems. Both of them involve the development by an independent council of principles and criteria for certification and eco-labeling.

Where the MSC differs from the FSC is in terms of the process of consultation to establish the Council and to determine its governance structure. In the case of the FSC, stakeholders were directly involved in determining key principles and organizational concepts for the FSC. In contrast, although the governance structure of the MSC stresses the importance of inclusivity, the origin of the MSC was the partnership between WWF and Unilever, and the structure of the MSC was proposed by the founding partners, after taking advice from the consulting firm Coopers and Lybrand. This was partly in response to the process involved in establishing the FSC, which was found to be expensive and time-consuming. There was a perceived trade-off by WWF and Unilever between undertaking lengthy consultations with all stakeholders and making a more substantial and timely impact on the industry. This contrast in the levels and processes of stakeholder participation is not restricted to the consultation process but also applies to the governance structure of the different organizations.

However, it turned out that the development of the MSC has been even slower than that of the FSC. It is probable that the limited participation was at the root of the problem that the MSC was clearly lagging behind the FSC in terms of efficacy. But this must not be the only reason. One could argue, for instance, that deforestation has been solidly established as a major environmental problem to which people are generally sensitive, while the problem of overfishing has not had so much attention in public discourse. Therefore companies in the forestry industry are more vigilant of public opinion and their image than fishing companies.

Nevertheless, statements from the representatives of the MSC suggest that they were fully aware of the need for a sense of ownership of the initiative by the stakeholders. Over the years the MSC has made considerable efforts to increase accountability and to provide balanced participation to the stakeholders.

In the past couple of years the development of the MSC speeded up. As of November 2010, there are over 1,900 seafood products available with the MSC eco-label, sold in forty countries around the world. A total of thirty-eight fisheries have been independently certified as meeting the MSC's environmental standard for sustainable fishing and over eighty are currently undergoing assessment. Over 800 companies have met the MSC Chain of Custody standard for seafood traceability.

9.5 Conclusion

Many argue that the solution to the global problems of our age – world poverty, inequalities, the destruction of the commons, and so on – is more globalization: more efficient international institutions; a global ethic, including international solidarity; and a more integrated global economy. That is, although it is undeniably part of the problem, globalization might also be part of the solution.

Nevertheless, it is obvious that globalization in its present form is not sustainable. Globalizing tendencies have long been accompanied by political, cultural, and religious fragmentation. And the functioning of the globalized economy contradicts the goal of sustainable development, because it leads to ecological homogenization, causes the overuse of resources and renders impossible the application of the precautionary principle.

Therefore localization is an important value. However, critics argue that re-localizing the economy would mean breaking the world again into small communities and we would fall back into an anarchical state of international relations. We must avoid this, because we certainly need some kind of "globalism"; that is, global governance and cooperation in order to preserve the global commons (Passet 2001). The challenge of the future is to find a way towards more globalism with less economic globalization.

References

Apel, K.-O. (1990) Is the Ethics of the Ideal Communication Community a Utopia? On the Relationship between Ethics, Utopia, and the Critique of Utopia. In: Benhabib, S. and Dallmayr, F. (eds) *The Communicative Ethics Controversy.* Cambridge, MA: MIT Press, pp. 23–59.

Bernstein, S. and Cashore, B. (2007) Can Non-state Global Governance be Legitimate? An Analytical Framework. *Regulation and Governance*, vol. 1, pp. 1–25.

Boda, Z. (2010) The Collaborative Enterprise: The Ethics of Working with Civil Society Organizations. In: Tencati, A. and Zsolnai, L. (eds) *The Collaborative Enterprise: Creating Values for a Sustainable World.* Oxford: Peter Lang, pp. 289–311.

Boda, Z., O'Higgins, E. and Schedler, K. (2009) Cooperating with Civil and Political Actors. In: Zsolnai, L. (ed.) *The Future International Manager.* Houndmills and New York: Palgrave Macmillan, pp. 130–152.

Boddewyn, J. J. (1986) International Political Strategy: A Fourth "Generic" Strategy. Paper presented at the Annual Meeting of the American Academy of Management, and at the Annual Meeting of the International Academy of Business.

Boddewyn, J. J., and Brewer, T. L. (1994) International-Business Political Behavior: New Theoretical Dimensions. *Academy of Management Review*, vol. 19, no. 1, pp. 119–143.

Castells, M. (1997) *The Information Age: Economy, Society and Culture. Vol. II: The Power of Identity.* Oxford: Blackwell.

Curtis, F. (2003) Eco-Localism and Sustainability. *Ecological Economics*, vol. 46, no. 1, pp. 83–102.

Daly, H. E. and Cobb, J. B. (1989) *For the Common Good.* Washington, DC: Island Press.

den Hond, F. and de Bakker, F. G. A. (2007) Ideologically Motivated Activism: How Activist Groups Influence Corporate Social Change Activities. *Academy of Management Review*, vol. 32, pp. 901–924.

Donaldson, T. (1989) *The Ethics of International Business.* New York and Oxford: Oxford University Press.

Donaldson, T. (1993) When in Rome, Do...What? International Business and Ethical Relativism. In: Mingus, P. M. (ed.) *The Ethics of Business in a Global Economy*. Boston and Dordrecht: Kluwer.

Donaldson, T. and Dunfee, T. W. (1999) *Ties That Bind: A Social Contracts Approach to Business Ethics*. Boston, MA: Harvard Business School Press.

Doughwait, R. (1996) *Short Circuit: Strengthening Local Economies for Security in an Unstable World*. Totnes: Green Books.

Ekins, P., Folke, C. and Constanza, R. (1994) Trade, Environment and Development: The Issues in Perspective. *Ecological Economics*, no. 9, pp. 1–12.

Fowler, P. and Heap, S. (2000) Bridging Troubled Waters: the Marine Stewardship Council. In: Bendell, J. (ed.) *Terms of Endearment: Business, NGOs and Sustainable Development*. Sheffield: Greenleaf Publishing, pp. 135–148.

Frederick, W. C. (1991) The Moral Authority of Transnational Corporate Codes. *Journal of Business Ethics*, vol. 10, pp. 165–177.

Gilbert, D. U. and Rasche, A. (2007) Discourse Ethics and Social Accountability – The Ethics of SA 8000. *Business Ethics Quarterly*, vol. 17, pp. 187–216.

Giraud, P.-N. (1996) *L'inégalité du monde*. Paris: Gallimard.

Giscard d'Estaing, O. (1996) Le défi de la mondialisation de l'économie pour les entreprises européennes. *Humanisme et Entreprise*, December, pp. 65–95.

Goulet, D. (1983) Obstacles to World Development: An Ethical Reflection. *World Development*, vol. 7, no. 11, pp. 609–624.

Gowdy, J. (1995) Trade and Environmental Sustainability: An Evolutionary Perspective. *Review of Social Economy*, Winter, pp. 493–509.

Habermas, J. (1990) Discourse Ethics: Notes on a Program of Philosophical Justification. In: Benhabib, S. and Dallmayr, F. (eds) *The Communicative Ethics Controversy*. Cambridge, MA: MIT Press, pp. 60–110.

Hines, C. (2000) *Localization: A Global Manifesto*. London and Sterling, VA: Earthscan Publications.

Johnstone, N. (1995) Trade Liberalization, Economic Specialization and the Environment. *Ecological Economics*, no. 14, pp. 19–27.

Korten, D. C. (1995) *When Corporations Rule the World*. West Hartford, CT: Kumarian Press, San Francisco: Berrett-Koehler.

Noorgard, R. (1988) The Rise of the Global Exchange Economy and the Loss of Biological Diversity. In: Wilson, E. O. (ed.) *Biodiversity*. Washington, DC: National Academy Press.

Passet, R. (2001) *Éloge du mondialisme*. Paris: Fayard.

Polanyi, K. (1944). *The Great Transformation*. New York: Farrar & Rinehart.

Robertson, J. (1998) *Transforming Economic Life*. Totnes: Green Books.

Rodrik, D. (1997) Consequences of Trade for Labor Markets and the Employment Relationship, pp. 11–27. In: *Has Globalization Gone Too Far?* Washington, DC: Institute for International Economics.

Rosenau, J. N. (1990) *Turbulence in World Politics: A Theory of Change and Continuity.* Princeton, NJ: Princeton University Press.

Scherer, A. G., Palazzo, G. and Matten, D. (2009) Globalization as a Challenge for Business Responsibilities. *Business Ethics Quarterly*, vol. 19, no. 3, pp. 327–347.

Shiva, V., Anderson, P., Schücking, H., Gray, A., Lohmann, L. and Cooper, D. (1991) *Biodiversity: Social and Ecological Perspectives.* London: Zed Books.

Soros, G. (1998): *The Crisis of Global Capitalism.* London: Little, Brown and Company.

Wade, R. H. (2004) Is Globalization Reducing Poverty and Inequality? *World Development*, vol. 32, no. 4, April, pp. 567–589.

Walzer, M. (1994) *Thick and Thin: Moral Arguments at Home and Abroad.* Notre Dame, IN: University of Notre Dame Press.

Weisband, E. (2000) Discursive Multilateralism: Global Benchmarks, Shame, and Learning in the ILO Labor. Standard Monitoring Regime. *International Studies Quarterly*, vol. 44, pp. 643–666.

ANTONIO TENCATI
(BOCCONI UNIVERSITY MILAN)

10 The Sustainability-Oriented Company

10.1 Why Sustainability?

10.2 Sustainability and Stakeholders
    10.2.1 The Concept of Sustainable Development
    10.2.2 The Sustainability-Oriented Company

10.3 Management of Corporate Social, Environmental, and Sustainability Performance

10.4 Coop in Italy and its Sustainability Policies

10.5 Conclusion

Abstract

An ethical company has to pursue the overall objective of sustainability. At the corporate level, sustainability means the capacity of an organization to continue its activities over time, taking into consideration their impact on the natural, social, and human capitals. Therefore, sustainable development is a fundamental goal that requires dealing with the different stakeholder groups in mutually reinforcing ways. In order to pursue sustainability, companies have to adopt advanced and innovative policies and tools.

Keywords: corporate performance management, intangible assets, stakeholder network, sustainable development

10.1 Why Sustainability?

Since a company's final objective is value creation (Tencati and Perrini 2006), it cannot ignore the context in which it operates. In fact, a network of relationships connects the company to a great number of stakeholders (i.e., employees and co-workers, shareholders, customers/clients, suppliers, financial partners, the state, local authorities and the public administration in general, the (national or local) community(ies) in which a company operates, and the natural environment). These relationships influence the way a company is managed and are, in turn, influenced by the company's behavior.

In the current economic, social, and institutional context the concept of sustainable development has become firmly established. It represents a multi-dimensional paradigm that, in particular, can combine economic prosperity, social cohesion, and environmental protection (Elkington 1994).

A company that pursues sustainability can protect and increase its *intangible assets* (in terms of trust, reputation, license to operate, and skills, capabilities, knowledge), which are crucial in ensuring the success of a company in the increasingly turbulent competitive arena. A *sustainability-oriented company*, therefore, is fully aware of its responsibilities and adopts methodologies and tools that allow it to improve its corporate performance in order to meet the different stakeholder expectations. In this perspective the issue of introducing more advanced managerial tools to integrate the traditional economic and financial ones in order to control the corporate performance in a really comprehensive way is of vital importance.

10.2 Sustainability and Stakeholders

10.2.1 The Concept of Sustainable Development

Sustainable development as a concept initially focused on the environment and subsequently took on a broader and more complex venue. Sustainable development is a condition in which the vector of development (quality of life) increases monotonically over time (Pearce et al. 1989). The concept of development is, therefore, much broader than mere economic growth as reflected by an increase in the GDP or real income per capita. If a community or a company achieves economic growth and consequently destroys environmental quality or social equity, it is not really developing.

In the process of development, economic and environmental elements are interrelated with social objectives: strengthening social cohesion and solidarity; equitable distribution of wealth; ensuring the right to medical care, security, welfare, food, and education; freedom to express one's cultural identity and political opinions, etc.

Thus, generally speaking, sustainable development is composed of an economic, a social, and an environmental dimension (Tencati 2002). Achieving a new model of development and pursuing sustainability, concerns not only socioeconomic systems but also the individual actors involved in the dynamics of change. For companies, the sustainability goal is in line with the ultimate objective of value creation and ensures the company's long-term survival.

10.2.2 *The Sustainability-Oriented Company*

If the final objective of the company is value creation, it can be divided into specific short- or long-term objectives. These goals are the result of strategic company choices related to the environment in which the company operates and must be coherent with its well-balanced final objective, centered on value creation. The need to constantly focus on a long-term perspective is justified by the fact that adopting mainly short-term objectives can undermine the basis of a company's survival.

As a matter of fact, if a company wants to achieve short-term economic success and begins to cut procurement and production costs without considering the effects on product quality or occupational health and safety, lays off its workers thus losing resources and skills and undermining the social consensus it enjoys, fails to invest in innovation, disregards the impact of its activities on the environment, openly violates the principles of corporate governance or "cooks the books" by adopting ethically dubious or outright fraudulent practices, it is clearly not creating value. On the contrary, it destroys the basis of its long-term success by dissipating strategic assets like the customers, market, employees, and reference community trust, knowledge and innovation capabilities, the natural capital and so on and so forth. This is true even though in the short or very short term certain company policies seem successful and lead to an increase in share prices and therefore higher capital market value.

Market value alone fails to measure the real quality of management in a firm, and to respond to the queries of the different stakeholders. It is therefore essential to understand what kind of company can ensure long-term economic success and satisfy the expectations of the various constituencies.

According to the stakeholder view of the firm (Clarkson 1995; Donaldson and Preston 1995; Post et al. 2002), a company can last over time if it is able to build and maintain sustainable and durable relationships with all the members of its stakeholder network. "These relationships are the essential assets that managers must manage, and they are the ultimate sources of organizational wealth" (Post et al. 2002, p. 8). "By placing 'stakeholder' in the center of strategic thinking, the unit of analysis is changed to a more relational view of business...Business works because the interests

The Sustainability-Oriented Company

of...stakeholders can be satisfied over time. It is the intersection of these interests which is central to effective and sustainable stakeholder management" (Freeman 2010).

Therefore, a company creates value when it adopts a managerial approach, which is *sustainability-oriented*.

In line with the definition provided by AccountAbility in 1999, *sustainability is the capability of an organization to continue its activities over time, having taken due account of their impact on natural, social, and human capitals*. Therefore, a sustainability-oriented company is able to develop over time by managing the economic, social, and environmental dimensions of its processes and performance and the underlying stakeholder needs and expectations in an integrated way. In this kind of firm, financial and competitive success, social legitimacy and efficient/effective use of natural resources are intertwined according to a synergetic and circular view of the company's goals. The value creation process aims at meeting the requests coming from not just one dominating constituency (the financiers) but multiple stakeholder groups. Thus, using broader and more comprehensive concepts like *stakeholder value* (Figge and Schaltegger 2000) is needed in order to overcome still prevailing mainstream paradigms such as maximizing profits or shareholder value that have led to unbearable behaviors and outcomes (Tencati 2007).

In this perspective, the sustainability of a firm depends on the sustainability of its stakeholder relationships: This means that the quality, that is, the sustainability, of the stakeholder relationships has to be the guiding principle for the managerial decision-making process and the pillar of innovative, advanced, aware, and inclusive corporate strategies.

Furthermore, the main value-drivers for a company are the *intangible assets*, directly affecting the quality of these stakeholder relationships. Intangibles refer to intellectual capital and include know-how, brands, trust, reputation, etc. (Castaldo 2002; Ghoshal and Bartlett 1997; Lev 2001; Pozza 1999; Vicari 1995). The intangibles can be divided into two categories (Vicari et al. 2000):

- knowledge resources that include the knowledge, capabilities, and skills available in the organization or in its stakeholder network;

- trust resources that comprise trust, reputation, image, brand-equity and the overall license to operate, i.e. the social consensus necessary for the corporate survival.

Thanks to its activities and choices a company creates and enhances (or destroys and reduces) its intangibles. By pursuing, in an integrated way, economic, social, and environmental goals a sustainability-oriented company increases its intangible assets of knowledge and trust, supporting the value creation processes. In fact, this kind of firm fosters cross-cutting innovation affecting corporate activities and the stakeholder network in which the enterprise is embedded. This allows, on the one hand, to improve management operations (through, for example, co-makership policies or waste-prevention-oriented investments) and, on the other, to make the company's value proposition much more attractive and involving for the different constituencies (e.g., through environmental, social, or carbon labeling or targeted community investing).

10.3 Management of Corporate Social, Environmental, and Sustainability Performance

Many tools, initiatives, and practices have been developed over the last decades to support firms in their efforts towards improved environmental, social, and sustainability performance. It is possible to use a framework that classifies these solutions into three broad groups (see, on this topic, Tencati, Perrini, Hofstra and Zsolnai 2009; Tencati, Pogutz and Romero 2009; Waddock 2008; World Business Council for Sustainable Development and The World Conservation Union 2007):

- *accounting and reporting/accountability tools*: methodologies and initiatives to measure, assess, control, and report corporate performance in a more comprehensive way to better support corporate decision-making and meet stakeholder information needs (see Table 10.1, pp. 204–207);

- *market-based instruments*: instruments aimed at using the market to orient producers and consumers mainly thanks to the "polluter pays principle" (see Table 10.2, p. 208);
- *certification schemes*: measures which foster proactive companies and support consumers and investors in taking informed decisions (see Table 10.3, pp. 209–210).

10.4 Coop in Italy and its Sustainability Policies

Coop is the largest Italian retail chain, with an 18.3 per cent market share in the grocery market. It is owned by 7,429,847 members and grouped in 115 territorial consumer cooperatives. The retail network consists of 1,444 points of sale, occupies 1,759,536 square meters, and employs almost 57,000 people. The 2010 turnover was 12,898 million euros (ANCC-COOP, 2011). This dominance on the market is supported and strengthened by Coop's efforts towards sustainability along its entire stakeholder network (Tencati and Pedretti 2010), therefore, sustainability becomes a stakeholder-value-creation driver.

See Table 10.4 (p. 211–212) for more details on some of the most important initiatives carried out by the Coop system.

Table 10.1 *Examples of accounting and reporting/accountability tools*

Tools	Brief description	Website(s)
Corporate Social Report	This mainly voluntary tool measures the impact of the company and its activities on the different stakeholder groups. Therefore, it is a methodology capable of supporting the management decision-making process and the corporate communication/engagement policies. The first attempts in this field were carried out, between the late 60s and early 70s, in the United States and then in Europe. Different approaches to social and ethical accounting, auditing and reporting, and accountability have been developed over time (Perrini, Pogutz and Tencati 2006).	http://www.corporateregister.com
AccountAbility 1000 Series (AA1000S)	In order to define a common set of principles to ensure the quality of the social and ethical accounting, auditing and reporting process, in 1999 AccountAbility issued the AccountAbility 1000 (AA1000) Framework. In 2002 AccountAbility launched the new AA1000 Series, consisting of the AA1000 Framework and a set of specialized modules. On 24 October 2008 the AA1000 AccountAbility Principles Standard 2008 (AA1000APS 2008) and the AA1000 Assurance Standard 2008 (AA1000AS 2008) were issued. In 2011 the second edition of the AA1000 Stakeholder Engagement Standard was published (AA1000 SES 2011).	http://www.accountability.org/standards/index.html
Corporate Environmental Report	A mainly voluntary tool a company uses to manage and control the environmental impact (in terms of consumptions and emissions) of its own activities, products, and services, and to support communication with stakeholders. The most advanced environmental reporting methodologies combine an accounting system that collects physical data with the measurement of (internal) costs and benefits related to the environmental management of processes and products. Guidelines for environmental reporting were developed by many organizations such as: CERES – Coalition for Environmentally Responsible Economies; Environment Australia; FEEM – Fondazione Eni Enrico Mattei; GEMI – Global Environmental Management Initiative; IÖW – Institut für Ökologische Wirtschaftsforschung; WBCSD – World Business Council for Sustainable Development.	http://www.corporateregister.com http://www.ceres.org/page.aspx?pid=705 http://www.enviroreporting.com/others/Australian%20PER%20Guidelines.pdf http://www.enviroreporting.com/others/feem.htm

		http://www.gemi.org/GEMIPublications.aspx
		http://www.ioew.de/english/index2.html
		http://www.wbcsd.org/home.aspx
ISO 14031:1999	Guidelines on environmental performance evaluation	http://www.iso.org/iso/iso_catalogue/catalogue_tc/catalogue_tc_browse.htm?commid=54808&published=on&includesc=true
ISO/TS 14033:2012	Guidelines and examples on quantitative environmental information	http://www.iso.org/iso/iso_catalogue/catalogue_tc/catalogue_tc_browse.htm?commid=54808&published=on&includesc=true
ISO 14040:2006 ISO 14044:2006	International standards identifying principles, framework, requirements, and guidelines for the different phases of the life cycle assessment (LCA). They include: definition of the goal and scope of the LCA, the life cycle inventory analysis (LCI) phase, the life cycle impact assessment (LCIA) phase, the life cycle interpretation phase, reporting and critical review of the LCA.	http://www.iso.org/iso/iso_catalogue/catalogue_tc/catalogue_tc_browse.htm?commid=54808&published=on&includesc=true
ISO 14051:2011	This standard provides a general framework for material flow cost accounting (MFCA).	http://www.iso.org/iso/iso_catalogue/catalogue_tc/catalogue_tc_browse.htm?commid=54808&published=on&includesc=true

Tools	Brief description	Website(s)
ISO 14063:2006	This international standard gives guidance on general principles, policy, strategy, and activities related to both internal and external environmental communication.	http://www.iso.org/iso/iso_catalogue/catalogue_tc/catalogue_tc_browse.htm?commid=54808&published=on&includesc=true
ISO 14064–1:2006 ISO 14064–2:2006 ISO 14064–3:2006	International standards for quantification, monitoring, reporting, validation, and verification of greenhouse gas emissions, reductions, removals	http://www.iso.org/iso/hot_topics/hot_topics_climate_change.htm
Carbon Disclosure Project	The Carbon Disclosure Project (CDP) is an independent not-for-profit organization which facilitates the dialogue between investors and corporations on climate change and water management and their impact on corporate policies, risk profile, value creation processes. Thanks to its state-of-the-art reporting tools CDP works also with cities and national governments to drive the change towards a low-carbon sustainable economy.	http://www.cdproject.net
Equator Principles	A banking industry framework for addressing environmental and social risks in project financing	http://www.equator-principles.com
Principles for Responsible Investment (PRI)	A UN-coordinated framework to help mainstream investors integrate environmental, social, and governance (ESG) issues in investment decisions	http://www.unpri.org
Earth Charter	The Earth Charter is a world-recognized statement on ethics, values, and principles for a sustainable way of life. Developed over a period of ten years, also thanks to the input of more than 5,000 people, the Earth Charter was formally launched in 2000. This global civil society effort has been formally endorsed by over 5,500 organizations, including enterprises and global institutions such as UNESCO and the International Union for Conservation of Nature (IUCN).	http://www.earthcharter.org http://www.earthcharterinaction.org
United Nations Global Compact	The UN Global Compact is a voluntary initiative, open to the participation of companies and to the involvement of labor, human rights, environmental, development, and academic organizations. It encompasses ten principles in the areas of human rights, labor, environment, and anti-corruption, drawn from the Universal Declaration of Human Rights, the ILO Declaration on Fundamental Principles and Rights at Work,	http://www.unglobalcompact.org/index.html

The Sustainability-Oriented Company

ISO 26000:2010	the Rio Declaration on Environment and Development, and The United Nations Convention against Corruption. The UN Global Compact has two objectives: mainstreaming the ten principles in business activities around the world; fostering actions in support of broader UN goals, including the Millennium Development Goals.	http://www.iso.org/sr
	The ISO 26000 process, started in March 2005 at the first World Meeting in Salvador (Bahia, Brazil), was completed in 2010. The international standard was issued on 1 November 2010 and provides Guidance on Social Responsibility to support not only companies, but all organizations (including public authorities and NGOs), in addressing and managing social issues. ISO 26000 is not a management system standard and is not intended for third-party certification. Accountability, transparency and stakeholder engagement are among the cross-cutting and characterizing principles of the document.	
GRI Sustainability Reporting Guidelines	The Global Reporting Initiative (GRI) is an international, long-term, multi-stakeholder project designed to develop, promote, and disseminate a set of Sustainability Reporting Guidelines as a common framework for voluntary reporting of the economic, environmental, and social performance of an organization, that is, of its activities, products, and services. The fourth generation of the Sustainability Reporting Guidelines (*G4 Guidelines*) is under discussion and is expected to be issued in 2013. This further evolution of the Guidelines will also take into account the emerging "Integrated Reporting" paradigm (Eccles and Krzus, 2010).	http://www.globalreporting.org http://database.globalreporting.org http://www.theiirc.org
Sustainability Evaluation and Reporting System (SERS)	This sustainability accounting and reporting methodology, developed by the Bocconi Center for Research on Sustainability and Value (CReSV), aims at monitoring and tracking the overall corporate performance according to a multiple bottom line perspective based on a stakeholder framework (Perrini and Tencati, 2006 and 2007).	http://www.unibocconi.eu/wps/wcm/connect/Sito Pubblico_EN/Navigation+Tree/Home/Research/Research+Centers/?lang=en

Table 10.2 *Examples of Market-based Instruments*

Instruments	Brief description	Website(s)
EU Emissions Trading System	The European Union Emissions Trading System (EU ETS) is the first international trading system for CO_2 emissions in the world. It covers some 11,000 energy-intensive installations in thirty countries, which represent almost half of the EU's emissions of CO_2 and 40 per cent of its total greenhouse gas emissions. These facilities include combustion plants, oil refineries, coke ovens, iron and steel plants, and factories making cement, glass, lime, bricks, ceramics, pulp, paper, and board.	http://ec.europa.eu/ environment/climat/ emission/index_en.htm
Carbon-offset initiatives	Voluntary initiatives, based on market mechanisms, adopted to reduce and compensate CO_2 emissions. An example is provided by the "Zero Impact" programme, developed by LifeGate, an innovative Italian company, which provides organizations and consumers with sustainability-oriented products and services.	http://www.lifegate.it

Table 10.3 Examples of Certification Schemes

Schemes	Brief description	Website(s)
Social Accountability 8000 (SA8000)	SA8000 is a comprehensive system for managing ethical workplace conditions along global supply chains. It protects workers' rights by defining a set of auditable elements for third-party verification. This international standard for ethical sourcing was issued in 1997, revised in 2001 and in 2008. SA8000 is based on the International Labour Organization (ILO) Conventions and other documents such as the Universal Declaration of Human Rights and the UN Convention on the Rights of the Child.	http://www.sa-intl.org/
OHSAS 18001	The Occupational Health and Safety Assessment Series (OHSAS) specification, OHSAS 18001, was published in April 1999. This standard, that defines the requirements for the certification of the Occupational Health and Safety Management Systems, was developed by the British Standards Institution (BSI), in association with other national standards bodies, certification bodies, and international experts. In 2007 it was replaced by BS OHSAS 18001:2007, the "Occupational health and safety management systems. Requirements" standard.	http://www.bsigroup.com/en/
EMAS	The EU Eco-Management and Audit Scheme (EMAS) is a management tool for every kind of organization to evaluate, report, and improve its environmental performance. The scheme has been available for participation by companies since 1995 and was originally restricted to firms in industrial sectors. Since 2001, thanks to a new Regulation, EMAS has been open to all economic sectors including public and private services. In 2009 the EMAS Regulation was revised and modified for the second time: The EMAS III Regulation was published on 22 December 2009 and aims at increasing the participation of companies, also by reducing the administrative burden and costs, in particular for small- and medium-sized enterprises (SMEs).	http://ec.europa.eu/environment/emas/index_en.htm http://ec.europa.eu/enterprise/environment/index_en.htm

Schemes	Brief description	Website(s)
ISO 14001: 2004	ISO 14001:1996 Environmental management systems – Specification with guidance for use was published in September 1996. It was replaced by ISO 14001:2004 Environmental management systems – Requirements with guidance for use, issued in November 2004. ISC 14001, now under review, is the only certifiable management system standard of the ISO 14000 series.	http://www.iso.org/iso/iso_catalogue/catalogue_tc/catalogue_tc_browse.htm?commid=54808&published=on&includesc=true
European Ecolabel	It is a voluntary scheme designed to encourage businesses to market goods and services that are really environmentally friendly and to signal to European consumers – including public and private purchasers – these excellence products that follow strict environmental criteria along their entire life cycle. The Ecolabeled products are available throughout the European Union as well as in Norway, Liechtenstein, and Iceland. The European Ecolabel is part of a broader strategy aimed at promoting sustainable consumption and production. The revised Ecolabel Regulation was issued on 30 January 2010 and aims to simplify the process of obtaining the Eco-Flower and broaden the product coverage.	http://ec.europa.eu/environment/ecolabel/index_en.htm
Forest Stewardship Council (FSC)	Independent, non-governmental, not-for-profit organization established to promote the responsible management of the world's forests. FSC provides forest management and a chain of custody standard setting, trademark assurance, and accreditation services for firms and organizations interested in responsible forestry. Products carrying the FSC label are independently certified to assure consumers that they come from forests that are managed according to sustainability principles, criteria and rules.	http://www.fsc.org
Marine Stewardship Council (MSC)	MSC is a global, independent, not-for-profit organization working with fisheries, seafood companies, scientists, conservation groups, and the public to promote environmentally responsible behaviour. In fact, the MSC's fishery certification program and seafood ecolabel recognize support and reward sustainable fishing.	http://www.msc.org
BS 8900	This standard provides guidance for managing sustainable development and was issued by BSI on 31 May 2006. It was based on the SIGMA Project. BS 8900 is the founding standard of the BS 8900 series.	http://www.bsigroup.com/en ttp://www.projectsigma.co.uk

The Sustainability-Oriented Company

Table 10.4 *Important Sustainability Initiatives Fostered by Coop*

Source: ANCC-COOP (2011); Compassion in Food Business (2011); E-Coop (2012); Mazzini (2012); Tencati and Pedretti (2010)

Stakeholders	Activities
Consumers/Suppliers/ Environment	Further improvement of the quality of the fresh products (meats, fruits, and vegetables) and strong attention to the promotion of local/typical products. This also means fostering short supply chains and reducing food miles.
Consumers/ Suppliers/ Environment	Extension of the "GMO-free" policy to new supply chains.
Consumers/ Suppliers/ Environment	The Coop-labeled eggs come from organic farming or are cage-free. This commitment has been recognized by the "Compassion in World Farming" organization. After receiving a "Commendation" in 2007 and a Good Egg Award for selling only cage-free eggs in their supermarkets in 2010, in 2011 Coop won a Good Chicken Award for its commitment to improve the welfare of its own-brand chickens, which aims to benefit over 2.7 million chickens every year.
Consumers/Environment	New labels for Coop-labeled products with more nutritional information and a specific section devoted to the explanation of the most proper ways for the disposal of the products on the basis of the different materials used.
Consumers/Environment	Strengthening of the supply of environmentally friendly goods through the introduction of a unique, comprehensive product category, that is, "vivi verde" (i.e., Live Green). The "vivi verde" category includes Ecolabeled goods (according to the European scheme) and organic products (certified according to the European requirements).
Consumers/Environment	Since 2010 promotion of the campaign "Acqua di casa mia" (i.e., Home Water) to foster the consumption of tap water.
Consumers/Suppliers/ Environment/Local Communities	Further promotion of the Fair Trade production through the organization of a devoted week called 'Io faccio la spesa giusta' (i.e., I Shop Right). Furthermore, in order to support the flourishing of local communities in developing countries, in 2008–2010 Coop carried out the project "Stop World Poverty", which involved local communities and producers, NGOs, suppliers, Banca Etica, Fairtrade Italia, and academics. Eleven projects out of more than sixty proposed were selected. The nations affected by these projects were Brazil, Ecuador, Nicaragua, Uganda, Burkina Faso, Senegal, Palestine, Sri Lanka, and Nepal. The Coop category of Fair Trade products is called 'Solidal' and also includes a collection of clothes.

Stakeholders	Activities
Workers/Suppliers	Development and enforcement of specific projects in the most critical supply chains (e.g., tomato collection) aimed at protecting workers' rights, especially in the occupational health and safety area. Moreover, the leading commitment in the supply chain management for the Coop-labeled products thanks to the adoption of SA8000 since 1998 is further confirmed and maintained.
Environment/Consumers/Suppliers	Innovation for prevention in order to design and adopt new packaging systems to reduce/minimize the production of waste.
Environment/Consumers/Suppliers	In 2011 launch of the Project "Woods and Forests" to fight deforestation and to foster sustainable productions and sustainable forest management, for example by using raw materials certified according to the FSC scheme.
Environment/Future Generations	In 2010 completion of the construction of sixty-two photovoltaic power plants with an overall peak power of more than 10,300 KWp, which serve points of sale and warehouses. Moreover, the Coop system bought around 34 GWh generated from renewable (hydro) sources.
Environment/Future Generations	Feasibility study for the energy certification of some malls, introduction of stringent procedures for energy auditing in the points of sale, and development, where possible, of local projects to foster material and energy flows/relationships according to the industrial ecology perspective.
Environment/Future Generations/Suppliers	Further implementation of the "Coop for Kyoto" project through which Coop provides its contribution to the achievement of the 20/20/20 goal fixed by the European Union. In particular, the plan endorsed by the European heads of state calls for a 20 per cent increase in energy efficiency, 20 per cent reduction in greenhouse gas (GHG) emissions and 20 per cent share of renewables in overall EU energy consumption by 2020. Coop is committed to provide its contribution by involving its main suppliers.
Environment/Future Generations/Consumers/Suppliers	Introduction of carbon footprinting projects to minimize/offset the CO_2 emissions during the entire life cycle of Coop-labeled products.

10.5 Conclusion

Because of the negative effects of the current economic growth processes (Tencati and Pogutz 2012; Tencati and Zsolnai 2012), the concept of sustainable development was proposed. According to the definition advanced by the World Commission on Environment and Development (1987), sustainable development meets the needs of the present without compromising the ability of future generations to meet their own needs. Thus, in the long term, economic growth, social cohesion, and environmental protection must go hand in hand (Commission of the European Communities 2001, p. 2).

For a company this innovative pattern of development means that in creating value it should look beyond mere economic performance and include environmental and social considerations and the underlying stakeholder expectations. Sustainability, which means the capacity to continue operating over a long period of time, is the result of an integrated approach. Therefore, this calls for new systems to manage the corporate performance according to a multiple bottom line perspective (Tencati and Zsolnai 2009).

The final objective is to guarantee the long-term success of a company through a strong commitment to sustainability along its entire *stakeholder network*. This is possible only by making a deep change in the corporate strategic perspective beyond the conventional paradigms and by significantly expanding the set of managerial tools.

References

Accountability (1999) *AccountAbility 1000 (AA1000) Framework. Standard, Guidelines and Professional Qualification*. London: Accountability.
ANCC-COOP (National Association of Consumer Cooperatives) (2011) *Settimo Rapporto Sociale Nazionale 2010 della Cooperazione di Consumatori*. <http://www.e-coop.it> accessed 2 October 2012.
Castaldo, S. (2002) *Fiducia e relazioni di mercato*. Bologna: il Mulino.

Clarkson, M. B. E. (1995) A Stakeholder Framework for Analyzing and Evaluating Corporate Social Performance. *Academy of Management Review*, vol. 20, no. 1, pp. 92–117.

Commission of the European Communities (2001) *A Sustainable Europe for a Better World: A European Union Strategy for Sustainable Development*. Brussels, COM (2001) 264 final.

Compassion in Food Business (2011) <http://www.compassioninfoodbusiness.com/winner/co-op-italia> accessed 7 March 2012.

Donaldson, T. and Preston, L. E. (1995) The Stakeholder Theory of the Corporation: Concepts, Evidence, and Implications. *Academy of Management Review*, vol. 20, no. 1, pp. 65–91.

Eccles, R. G. and Krzus, M. P. (2010) *One Report: Integrated Reporting for a Sustainable Strategy*. Hoboken, NJ: John Wiley & Sons.

E-Coop (2012) <http://www.e-coop.it/portalWeb/portale/index.jsp> accessed 7 March 2012.

Elkington, J. (1994) Towards the Sustainable Corporation: Win-Win-Win Business Strategies for Sustainable Development. *California Management Review*, vol. 36, no. 2, pp. 90–100.

Figge, F., and Schaltegger, S. (2000) *What Is "Stakeholder value"? Developing a Catchphrase into a Benchmarking Tool*. Lüneburg: Universität Lüneburg, Pictet & Cie: UNEP.

Freeman, R. E. (2010) Preface to the 2010 Reissue. In: Freeman, R. E., *Strategic Management: A Stakeholder Approach*. Cambridge: Cambridge University Press (first published under the Pitman Publishing imprint, Boston, in 1984).

Ghoshal, S., Bartlett, C. A. (1997) *The Individualized Corporation: A Fundamentally New Approach to Management*. New York: HarperBusiness.

Lev, B. (2001) *Intangibles: Management, Measurement, and Reporting*. Washington, DC: Brookings Institution Press.

Mazzini, C. (2012) Coop, accordo sul carbon footprinting. *Consumatori*, vol. 1, January/February, p. 4.

Pearce, D., Markandya, A. and Barbier, E. B. (1989) *Blueprint for a Green Economy*. London and Sterling, VA: Earthscan Publications.

Perrini, F., Pogutz, S. and Tencati, A. (2006) *Developing Corporate Social Responsibility. A European Perspective*. Cheltenham: Edward Elgar Publishing.

Perrini, F. and Tencati, A. (2006) Sustainability and Stakeholder Management: The Need for New Corporate Performance Evaluation and Reporting Systems. *Business Strategy and the Environment*, vol. 15, no. 5, pp. 296–308.

Perrini, F. and Tencati, A. (2007) Stakeholder Management and Sustainability Evaluation and Reporting System (SERS): A New Corporate Performance Management

Framework. In: Sharma, S., Starik, M. and Husted, B. (eds) *Organizations and the Sustainability Mosaic: Crafting Long-Term Ecological and Societal Solutions*, vol. 4 in Edward Elgar Series "New Perspectives in Research on Corporate Sustainability". Cheltenham: Edward Elgar Publishing, pp. 168–192.

Post, J. E., Preston, L. E. and Sachs, S. (2002) Managing the Extended Enterprise: The New Stakeholder View. *California Management Review*, vol. 45, no. 1, pp. 6–28.

Pozza, L. (1999): *Le risorse immateriali. Profili di rilievo nelle determinazioni quantitative d'azienda*. Milan: Egea.

Tencati, A. (2002) *Sostenibilità, impresa e performance. Un nuovo modello di evaluation and reporting*. Milan: Egea.

Tencati, A. (2007) Il Male nella sfera economica. In: Spreafico, S. and Carrattieri, M. (eds) *Problema, tentazione, mistero. La cultura occidentale e la domanda sul male*, Reggio Emilia: Edizioni San Lorenzo, pp. 42–57.

Tencati, A. and Pedretti, U. (2010) Coop in Italy. In: Tencati, A. and Zsolnai, L. (eds) *The Collaborative Enterprise: Creating Values for a Sustainable World*. Oxford and Bern: Peter Lang, pp. 117–136.

Tencati, A. and Perrini, F. (2006) The Sustainability Perspective: A New Governance Model. In: Kakabadse A. and Morsing M. (eds) *Corporate Social Responsibility: Reconciling Aspiration with Application*. Houndmills and New York: Palgrave Macmillan, pp. 94–111.

Tencati, A., Perrini, F., Hofstra, N. and Zsolnai, L. (2009) Engaging in Progressive Entrepreneurship. In Zsolnai, L. and Tencati, A. (eds) *The Future International Manager: A Vision of the Roles and Duties of Management*. Houndmills and New York: Palgrave Macmillan, pp. 153–171.

Tencati, A. and Pogutz, S. (eds) (2012) *Prevenzione e innovazione per una economia della sostenibilità*. Milan: Egea.

Tencati, A., Pogutz, S. and Romero, C. (2009) Achieving Environmental Sustainability. In: Zsolnai, L. and Tencati, A. (eds) *The Future International Manager: A Vision of the Roles and Duties of Management*. Houndmills and New York: Palgrave Macmillan, pp. 23–48.

Tencati, A. and Zsolnai, L. (2009) The Collaborative Enterprise. *Journal of Business Ethics*, vol. 85, no. 3, pp. 367–376.

Tencati, A. and Zsolnai, L. (2012) Collaborative Enterprise and Sustainability: The Case of Slow Food, *Journal of Business Ethics*, vol. 88 <http://www.springerlink.com/content/d7wl48jl510661kx> accessed 7 March 2012.

Vicari, S. (ed.) (1995) *Brand Equity. Il potenziale generativo della fiducia*. Milan: Egea.

Vicari, S., Bertoli, G. and Busacca, B. (2000) Il valore delle relazioni di mercato. Nuove prospettive nell'analisi delle performance aziendali. *Finanza Marketing e Produzione*, vol. 3, pp. 7–54.

Waddock, S. (2008) Building a New Institutional Infrastructure for Corporate Responsibility. *Academy of Management Perspectives*, vol. 22, no. 3, pp. 87–108.

World Business Council for Sustainable Development (WBCSD) and The World Conservation Union (IUCN) (2007) *Business and Ecosystems. Markets for Ecosystem Services – New Challenges and Opportunities for Business and the Environment. A Perspective*, WBCSD and IUCN, Geneva and Gland, <http://www.wbcsd.org/Pages/EDocument/EDocumentDetails.aspx?ID=27&NoSearchContextKey=true> accessed 7 March 2012.

World Commission on Environment and Development (1987) *Our Common Future*. Oxford: Oxford University Press.

KNUT J. IMS
(NHH NORWEGIAN SCHOOL OF ECONOMICS)

11 From Welfare to Well-Being and Happiness[1]

11.1 The Tragic Search for Happiness

11.2 Traditional Approaches to Happiness
    11.2.1 The Welfare Approach
    11.2.2 Philosophy of Happiness

11.3 Positive Psychology, Deep Ecology and Buddhist Strategies
    11.3.1 Positive Psychology
    11.3.2 Deep Ecology
    11.3.3 Buddhist Strategy towards Happiness

11.4 Real-world Examples
    11.4.1 Bhutan
    11.4.2 Norway

11.5 Conclusion

---

[1] The author is indebted to Laszlo Zsolnai for encouraging to write this chapter and for providing invaluable comments on an earlier draft.

Abstract

A tragic fallacy in the Western world is the belief that higher income leads to greater happiness. Empirical evidence shows that it's not money that makes us happy, but people. The more-the-better strategy is a destructive track. Happiness is activity-based and strongly related to self-realization and orientation towards others.

The GDP-based welfare approach is a materialistic, economic description of human wellness. There is a need to complement this approach with "well-being" as a holistic, multidimensional concept. Happiness research and positive psychology may contribute to the development of more fruitful measurements. Deep Ecology assumes a world-view that looks at organisms as knots in a field of intrinsic relations. Its fundamental theorem is the self-realization of all beings – not only of humans. Self-realization for humans cannot be obtained unless they take into consideration the self-realization of other sentient beings.

The Buddhist Kingdom of Bhutan demonstrates a comprehensive approach to human well-being by employing the measure of Gross National Happiness. In contrast, Norway is a rich country that faces the problems of a welfare disease called "affluenza."

Keywords: material welfare, GDP, the happiness paradox, well-being, good life

11.1 The Tragic Search for Happiness

His Holiness the Dalai Lama writes: "no matter what is our situation, whether we are rich or poor, educated or not, of one race, gender, religion or another, we all desire to be happy and to avoid suffering. Our every intended action, in a sense our whole life, how we chose to live it within the context of the limitations imposed by our circumstances – can be seen as our answer to the great question which confronts us all: 'How am I to be happy?'" (Dalai Lama 2005, pp. 5–6).

There is a popular belief in Western society that happiness can be achieved through the modern market which presumes that the good life is highly dependent upon a bundle of material goods. The more I can buy, own, and consume the better. The logic is simple; more is better than less, and material commodities are essential for achieving happiness. This idea is part of the consumer culture that has dominated the Western world since the 1960s, a culture that created an ever-growing demand for goods. Many people consider shopping to be the most important activity in their life. During the last 100 years we have seen a radical shift from a spiritually oriented culture of frugality to a materialistic culture of hedonism supported by the modern media such as television, movies, videos, and magazines. The commercials and advertising in these media homogenize perspectives, tastes, and desires. In 2011 the corporate spending for advertisement was more than 500 billion US dollars globally. Happiness pills have created a new industry called "happyology." In Norway, from 1967 to 2010, the use of anti-depressants has grown from 0.4 to 6 per cent of the population. This means that about 300,000 people in a country of 5 million use "happiness pills" daily. And this is happening in one of the richest countries in the world.

The ecological consequences of happyology are clear. The overuse of natural resources, including ecosystem services, is common in every Western country. In addition, important psychological problems are linked with the high level material consumption. Several writers have diagnosed the problem as *affluenza*. In using the influenza analogy, this term draws attention to the damage that material welfare causes to our health, families, communities, and the natural environment. At the core of affluenza lies an obsessive quest for material gains in an endless effort to keep up with one's neighbors. Family-conflicts, higher rates of divorce, longer working hours, anxiety for children, rising debt, loneliness, and rampant commercialism are the symptoms of the welfare disease. (James 2008, Hamilton and Denniss 2005, De Graaf et al. 2005).

In his book *Living It Up: Our Love Affair with Luxury*, Twitchell writes that luxury spending in the USA has been growing four times faster than overall spending. The consumption of unnecessary goods and services is occurring at different levels of society except the lowest level. This phenomenon can be considered as a democratization of luxury. Twitchell contends that it has been the single most important marketing phenomenon of our time, and this love affair has united the USA and the globe in a way that no war, movement, or ideology ever has (Twitchell 2002).

The extravagant, wasteful, and conspicuous consumption is not a new phenomenon. It was described in Thorstein Veblen's theory of the Leisure Class in the late nineteenth century (Veblen 1994/1899). Hamilton and Denniss (2005) argue that the obsession with material acquisition erodes the more desirable values of a fairer society, because the individualistic self-absorbed capitalism is replacing cooperation with competition. In spite of this malady there is hope. Counter-cultures such as "slow food" and "downshifting" are good examples of people's voluntary search for a simpler life.

GDP (Gross Domestic Product) is the conventional indicator used to measure a nation's economic performance and its achieved material welfare. Such a one-dimensional materialistic approach to welfare leads to catastrophic consequences for the natural environment. It leads to the depletion of limited natural resources, and at the same time creates enormous mountains of waste, and more pollution in the ground and the atmosphere, which ultimately leads to more illness and to climate change.

An indication of the tragic search for happiness is illustrated in Figure 11.1, which compares growth of income with the percentage of very happy people in the USA over the last five decades.

From Welfare to Well-Being and Happiness 221

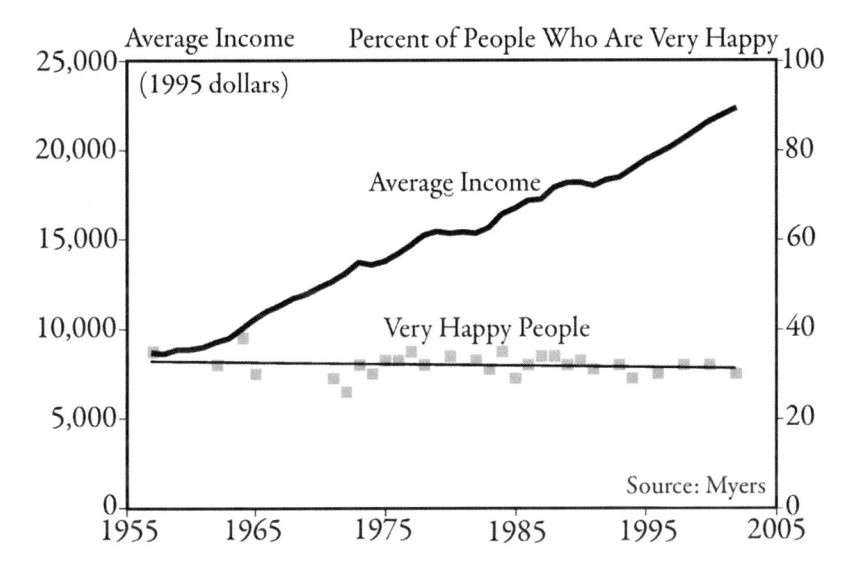

Figure 11.1 *Average Income and Happiness in the United States 1957–2002*
Source: *State of the World*, 2004

Figure 11.1 shows that while the average income has more than doubled in the USA in the last fifty years, the percentage of very happy people has not changed despite this enormous economic growth. The phenomenon is known as the *Easterlin paradox* (or the happiness–income paradox), described by American economist Richard Easterlin (Easterlin 1974, 1995, 2001; Easterlin and Angelescu 2009). The phenomenon is not only found in the USA, but also in other affluent countries, including Japan (Frey 2008, p. 39). As a tentative conclusion we can state that the relation between income and happiness is "far more complex than income-oriented theorists have tended to presume" (Sen 2009, p. 273).

11.2 Traditional Approaches to Happiness

11.2.1 *The Welfare Approach*

From the 1930s onwards one particular method of capturing people's "welfare" has been widely used. Its key focus has been economic growth measured by GDP (Gross Domestic Product). As a consequence, economic policy became concentrated almost exclusively on the growth of income and the creation of wealth. The growth of income was regarded as "economic progress." In 1948 the United Nations adopted an underlying System of National Accounts, which made the standards of living and the level of development of different economies comparable worldwide.

The results of the welfare focus produced surprising effects on human happiness. While income increased above a certain level, happiness did not. In the short term a certain increase in income may increase the level of welfare, i.e., at a given point in time happiness varies directly with income, but over time happiness does not increase when a country's income increases. In the short term, when there are fluctuations in macroeconomic conditions, happiness and income are positively related. Easterlin's explanation is that in the long term the aspiration level will increase and people will adapt to the new income. This increase in the level of aspiration occurs when there is long term growth. However, when the income is not increasing, but decreasing, Easterlin does not find that the aspiration level adapts by being reduced. This means that people who suffer from a reduced income will suffer a loss in their welfare. Accordingly, there is no symmetry between an increase and a decrease in income (Easterlin 1974, 1995, 2001; Easterlin and Angelescu 2009).

When comparing rich countries with poor countries, rich countries are usually happier on average. The evidence indicates that extra income matters only when we do not have a lot of it. Thus we have a phenomenon showing diminishing marginal returns.

In general economists are well aware of the shortcomings of the GDP approach. British economist Richard Layard (2005) criticizes GDP as a reductionist view on happiness. Frey & Stutzer (2002) points to the "destruction of utility" which is partly measured as output and in fact raises national product. The Norwegian philosopher Arne Næss makes fun of GDP and writes that the acronym means "Gross Domestic *Pollution*."

Clearly GDP is an unsatisfactory measure of happiness because:

(i) everybody's dollar counts equally;
(ii) GDP measures the average buying power in the market. It does not take income inequality into consideration, even if it is well known that relative income does matter for well-being;
(iii) it is based upon a behaviorist view of humans which assumes that we can never know what people are feeling – we can only watch how people behave;
(iv) it is based upon the exchanges in the market where externalities are not accounted for. However, in real social life externalities are pervasive. When a colleague is given a wage rise, it affects the other colleagues' perception of the fairness of their own salary;
(v) it also assumes that preferences do not change over time. This implies that "more is better;"
(vi) if there is a growth in GDP, it is assumed that the gainers can compensate the losers. One person's income will compensate for another's fall;
(vii) the national product considers only market goods and services. Therefore it "excludes a large part – if not the major part – of social activities." Services that are done in private households, as well as all other interpersonal relationships not based on money are not measured (Frey & Stutzer 2002, p. 37).

According to Layard the challenges are: how to take inequality into consideration; how to account for external effects; and how to take into consideration changes in values when we know that personal norms and values change in response to external influences, and that loss aversion is worse than a proportional gain (Layard 2005, p. 135). In an address about the gross national product Robert F. Kennedy said: "The gross national product does not allow for the health of our children, the quality of their education, or the joy of their play. It does not include the beauty of our poetry or the strength of our marriages; the intelligence of our public debate or the integrity of our public officials. It measures neither our wit nor our courage, neither our wisdom nor our learning; neither our compassion, nor our devotion to our country; it measures everything, in short, except that which makes life worthwhile" (cited in Gable and Haidt 2005, p. 103).

We need to develop richer measures of human well-being. Veenhoven developed an interesting classification of different perspectives on the terms "happiness" and "welfare", and distinguishes between different qualities of life (Veenhoven 2000). On the one hand she makes a distinction between chances and results, and on the other hand between outer and inner qualities. The outcome is the following matrix (Table 11.1).

Table 11.1 *Different Qualities of Life*

	Outer Qualities	Inner Qualities
Life Chances	livability of environment	life-ability of the person
Life Results	utility of life	appreciation of life

The meaning of "livability of environment" is relatively close to the term "welfare", as used by mainstream economists. However, it includes not only material conditions, but also the habitability of the environment. Ecologists describe livability in the natural environment in terms of pollution, global warming, and degradation of the ecosystem. The term "life-ability of the person" refers to personal capacities, and how well a person is equipped to grapple with the problems of life. This quality of life aspect is termed "capability" by Sen (2002, 2009). "Utility of life" refers to how a good life must be good for something beyond the individual person. It presumes some higher transcendental values like the "meaning of life." The term "appreciation of life" is used to denote the inner outcomes of life – the quality "in the eye of the beholder" (Veenhoven 2000, p. 7). This is a conscious and subjective appreciation and is often referred to by terms like "happiness," "life-satisfaction," and "subjective well-being." It may include both an intense and enduring enjoyment of life.

A good life involves all four qualities identified by Veenhoven. The matrix expresses that a life can be useful but not happy, or happy but not useful. However, we believe that these qualities often go together.

A deeper understanding of the idea of the good life and the way to reach a good or happy life is to be found in our philosophical traditions. We will look at some of the most famous philosophers who have stamped their mark in the history of thought.

11.2.2 Philosophy of Happiness

A conventional distinction is made between "hedonic" and "eudemonic" theories of happiness. Epicurus is attributed to the hedonic position and Aristotle to the eudemonic position. Epicurus may be considered as a forerunner of social reformer Jeremy Bentham (1748–1832), known for his utility calculus, which has served as a model for modern cost–benefit analysis. The utility calculus presumes that all pleasure is good and all pain is bad. Since pleasure is always good, we should maximize the pleasure in society. In this way, happiness is reduced to pleasure.

On the other hand, Aristotle's conception defines happiness as the realization of one's best abilities. Aristotle considered hedonic happiness to be a vulgar ideal, and claimed that deep happiness is linked to expression of virtue – it is not a feeling or a mental mode. Thus happiness is connected to activities, and to be happy is to have success with one's projects. It is not enough to win a lottery, because happiness has to be based on one's own efforts. The eudemonic theories tell us that human beings are happiest when they are able to live as they really are – that is as *authentic* individuals that have a *telos*, a worthwhile goal.

Box 11.1 summarizes different conceptions of happiness in the history of Ancient and Medieval Thought:

Box 11.1 *Happiness in the History of Ancient and Medieval Thought*

When we take a look at the inspirational teachers in the history of thought, we see that the most famous philosophers did not believe that radical materialism is a key to happiness.

The good life as knowledge and self-examination

Socrates (470–422 BC) claimed that having the right knowledge is a good route to happiness. When Socrates had the choice between compromising his convictions or drinking a cup of poison, he decided to take the poison and die. It is better to suffer from injustice than to commit a bad act, he stated. To take care of his soul was much more important for him than caring for his body. Socrates had a conception of happiness as living a virtuous life. The point of departure for him was the need for wisdom formulated as "Know Thyself! The unexamined life is not worth living." A man should engage in critical thinking and not live a life based upon illusions. We should think about what kind of life we are living and what kind of goals we should be pursuing. As human beings have the capacity for rational thinking, we should understand that virtue alone is the road to happiness. In fact, virtue is necessary as well as sufficient for happiness. So the central question is: What is virtue and how can virtue be developed?

For Socrates virtue was something that should be pursued, and in order to know that we are pursuing the right thing, we need wisdom. And wisdom could be learned through philosophical investigation and discussions with other rational beings. The acquisition and cultivation of knowledge are central to gaining wisdom. The good life is where a man lives in harmony with the cardinal virtues: being courageous, self-controlled, just, and wise. Such a life will obtain respect and honor. Summing up, the Socratic notion of happiness presupposed theoretical wisdom, a kind of critical knowledge of how to excel in the virtues and to live a good life. We may conclude that self-knowledge and integrity were primary values for Socrates.

The self-mastery model of happiness

The most famous student of Socrates, Plato (427–347 BC), developed a model that can be called the self-mastery model of happiness. Plato's moral doctrine was that we are good when we are following reason and bad when we are dominated by our desire. The good man is stronger than himself (Taylor 1989, p. 115), and he lets the higher parts of the soul rule over the lower parts of the soul. The good soul enjoys order, concord, harmony, and calmness, while the bad soul lives in constant agitation and distress. Those who are dominated by their desire are suffering from perpetual conflicts. The emphasis of this model is the insatiable character of human desire, and the fruits of the mastery of self are "unity with oneself, calm, and collected self-possession." The fear of passions is very strong, but reason can master all temptations. (Taylor 1989, p. 116)

Happiness as eudemonia

Aristotle (384–322 BC) – a prominent student of Plato – stated that Socrates' view of the importance of pure knowledge as the road to virtue and happiness, was grossly exaggerated. Aristotle claimed that to develop virtue, practice is essential (Aristotle 1925/1980). Practice is learning by doing, and learning by looking at how older, wise men are grappling with concrete cases in specific contexts. You learn by examples and role models; you learn to judge well by looking at wise men who are judging well. Aristotle developed and elaborated on the Socratic concept of happiness. A man's happiness is measured according to his entire life. Happiness consists of practicing virtues, which leads to the formation of the virtuous character. Such a character is living in a well-balanced way, avoids extreme behavior, and flourishes by cultivating his or her virtues. In Aristotle's view of happiness, the development of one's capabilities from the actual to their fullest potential means self-realization. This self-realization can only take part in the "polis" – a community in which the virtuous man's abilities can excel. Flourishing is the ultimate purpose of life.

Happiness in the Aristotelian sense involves having enough external goods. Too little material wealth may lead to unnecessary suffering, and too much wealth may lead to a preoccupation with the means, and thus draw the focus away from the most important goals, like participating in the life of the community and cultivating friendship. Aristotle also emphasized the importance of contemplation on the cosmic order and the divine. According to Aristotle every human being has a potential to function in certain ways, and when we realize this potential, we are living a good life. The good man experiences delight when he does the right thing and thus completes the good action. The highest good is to do activities that have no purpose outside of them. Happiness is activity based, and not a feeling or a state of mind.

Happiness as pleasure

Epicurus (342/1–272 BC) is known for creating the hedonic school of happiness. However, his philosophy was much more complex, because he stressed more the negative sides of pleasure, focusing on the feelings of calm and tranquility. (Copleston Epicurus (342/1–272 BC) is known for creating the hedonic school of happiness.

However, his philosophy was much more complex, because he stressed more the negative sides of pleasure, focusing on the feelings of calm and tranquility. (Copleston 1946/93) Epicurus's teaching is hedonistic in the sense that he conceives of happiness as enjoyment. When the body is in harmony, we have no pain. We should try to obtain harmony and tranquility before getting more extreme pleasures. (Russell 1995, p. 252) Epicurus writes that calm and tranquil contemplation is highly valuable and that that friendship gives us the safest of social delights. The absence of pain and the avoidance of fear and mental unrest are Epicurus's main principles. Neither virtue nor excesses are at the center of Epicurus's conception of the good life. And it is important to distinguish between desire and enjoyment, because desire is the main source of mental pain and inconvenience. Desire for fame, power, and wealth will not contribute to peaceful experiences. Epicurean hedonism would not result in excess, because "The wise man will not multiply his needs, since that is to multiply sources of pain: he will rather reduce his needs to a minimum." (Copleston 1946/93; see also Bouckaert 2008) Epicurus insisted that maximum enjoyment consists of the least possible disturbance.

Accordingly, the Epicurean position on happiness is that the ultimate good is the quality of the pleasure, and the highest evil is the pain. And pleasure is everything in which one takes delight, and pain is everything that distresses one. Epicurus made a hierarchical distinction between different kinds of pleasures, giving more weight to those which were longer lasting and less accompanied by pain and trouble. "The highest form of pleasure is ataraxia – or imperturbability – a state in which the soul is as the sea when the wind has calmed." (Bouckaert 2008, p. 5)

The Epicurean ethic leads to a moderate asceticism, self-control, and independence. He laid a great stress on frugality and held that frugality and enjoyment go hand in hand (Bouckaert 2008).

Happiness as controlling the will

As an early Christian thinker, Augustine (354–430) problematized the will in relation to happiness. While Socrates and Plato believed that a good character was able to master those bodily appetites and inclinations that might lead him astray from doing the right thing, Augustine complicates this view by focusing on the nature of the human will. We do not always act for the good we see. This is the problem of the weakness of the will – "akrasia." Augustine used St. Paul's Epistle to the Romans (7:19–25): "For the good that I would I do not: but the evil which I would not, that I do." Augustine showed us that "the perversity in the will can never be sufficiently explained by our lack of insight into the good: on the contrary, it makes us act below

From Welfare to Well-Being and Happiness

> and against our insight." (Taylor 1989, p. 138) In its turn it leads to a kind of slavery, in which we are "captured by our own obsession and fascination with the sensible." (Taylor 1989, p. 139)
>
> Thomas Aquinas (1225–1274) interpreted and synthesized the thoughts of Aristotle and was the main philosopher of the Catholic Church up to our times. One important notion of Aquinas was that external goods have a natural limit. Material wealth is needed to a certain extent but should be used only as an instrument. The highest good is of a spiritual character. Appetite for external goods is vicious because one ends up as a slave, rather than a master of wealth. Thus, it is not wealth in itself that is evil, but the individual's attachment to wealth that is the problem (Langholm 1992, p. 209). This view corresponds with Aristotle's recommendation of the golden mean, which condemns all kinds of excess.

Bentham developed what he called "felicific calculus." Bentham was convinced that his calculus would solve the problems of the measurement of happiness once and for all. His idea was that the calculus could measure happiness with mathematical precision, and thereby also provide a system to guide all moral choice and public policy. The basis of the system was psychological hedonism, a theory according to which human beings seek to attain pleasure and avoid pain.

The overriding moral principle was to create *"the greatest happiness of the greatest number"*, a central principle in the utilitarian tradition. Bentham redefined the concept of happiness to mean happiness as *utility*: "that property in any object, whereby it tends to produce benefit, advantage, pleasure, good, or happiness (all this in the present case comes to the same thing) or (…) to prevent the happening of mischief, pain, evil, or unhappiness to the party whose interest is considered" (cited in Bok, S. 2010, p. 85).

For Bentham the measurement of happiness was reduced to a simple matter of calculation. The task was to compute the value of each "prospective pleasure or pain for an individual by measuring its intensity, its duration, the certainty or uncertainty" of its likelihood, its remoteness, its likelihood of producing further pleasure or pain and the chance of not being followed by sensations of the opposite kind, i.e. its purity (Bok, S. 2010, p. 85.).

It may be fair to say that Bentham's moral vision was too limited in assuming that humans are incapable of developing excellence as moral virtue. But by promoting a utilitarian view on political reform, Bentham has played an undeniable historical role. His view of the *common good*, that the happiness of the majority of the member of any state should be the standard by which all the affairs of the state should be judged, was radical and has played an influential role in economic thinking until now.

One strong opponent of the utilitarian view is the British philosopher Bernard Williams who argues that the utilitarian view violates personal integrity in favor of advantages for the common good. Williams states strongly that the character, identity, and virtue of a person should not be ignored. Williams's argument is that according to utilitarian moral thinking, it is morally right to kill a person in order to save nineteen lives (Williams 1989, pp. 190–191). From a common good perspective it may be acceptable, but it is not so clear for the agent who kills or for the person who would be killed. Looking only at the *consequences* of lives saved is just part of the story. Williams argues that we as moral subjects are responsible for what we *do*, rather than for what we do not do, or what other people might do. Williams states that utilitarianism shows simple-mindedness in having too few thoughts and feelings to match the concrete experienced complexity of actual moral situations.

Another objection to utilitarian reasoning is that the theory cannot account for justice and freedom, and in some instances even runs against it (Sen 2002). In his analysis of justice Sen (2009) relates happiness to the agent's capabilities to do things he or she has reason to value. A person's advantage in terms of opportunities is more important than concentrating on individual happiness or pleasure. Evidently, human objectives can be quite different from seeking personal happiness. Contrasting human agency and well-being, Sen argues that happiness should not have such an imperialist role in society as given by welfarism.

There are many examples of how the pursuit of personal goals might be for reasons other than personal well-being. The agent's freedom to advance his or her personal goals might be more important than his or her own well-being. When Gandhi acted to liberate India from the British Empire, he fasted for long periods for political reasons. It is clear that Gandhi gave priority to agency over his own well-being (Sen 2009, p. 290). In this sense we may say that a person's freedom to act for the benefit of other persons may be more valuable for him or her than concentrating only on his or her own well-being.

Summing up, the principle of *"the greatest happiness of the greatest number"* may violate individual rights in favor of the common good. Utilitarian reasoning is an amalgam of three axioms: consequentialism, welfarism, and sum-ranking with no attention to inequalities. Utilitarian thinking does not see actions as good or bad in themselves, because the moral value of actions is based upon their consequences and nothing else. Actions are simply means that lead to certain consequences.

11.3 Positive Psychology, Deep Ecology and Buddhist Strategies

11.3.1 Positive Psychology

American psychologists Seligman and Csikszentmihalyi state that the study and cure of pathology have almost been the exclusive focus of the discipline of psychology. The result has been a model of the human being as lacking hope, wisdom, creativity, courage, spirituality, responsibility, and future mindedness. They maintain that psychology should also be the study of strength and virtue: "Treatment is not just fixing what is broken; it is nurturing what is best." To amplify strength rather than repair the weaknesses is a quite different approach. Furthermore, they suggest that psychology should also be concerned with important domains in a person's life, such as work, education, love, growth, and play (Seligman and Csikszentmihalyi 2000, p. 7). Some of the assumptions in positive psychology tell us that human strengths and virtues can act as buffers against mental illness.

Happiness as a research field was introduced in 2000 in a dedicated international journal, the *Journal of Happiness Studies*. The new science of happiness tries to measure feelings of happiness. Most happiness studies ask people questions like: "Taking all things together, would you say you are very happy, quite happy, or not very happy?" The central element is *subjective well-being* (SWB), and whichever mood one experiences as prevailing (cf. Hellevik 2008, pp. 11–13). Some researchers have been concerned with whether engagement and meaning in life is one aspect of happiness (see

Vittersø 2005). Other researchers like Veenhoven (2000), take the whole life into consideration and define happiness as "the degree to which an individual judges the overall quality of his life-as-a-whole favorably." This conception of happiness is similar to the eudemonic view put forward by Aristotle. It means that well-being may be distinct from happiness per se, because not all desires – not all outcomes that a person values – would promote well-being when achieved. Even if some outcomes generate pleasure, they "are not good for people and would not promote wellness" (Ryan and Deci 2001, p. 146).

Hungarian-born American psychologist Mihaly Csikszentmihalyi studied artists and other people who enjoyed what they were doing but were not rewarded for it by fame or money. They were motivated by the quality of experience they felt when they were immersed in the specific activity. These strong motivational feelings did not come to them when they were taking drugs or alcohol, or consuming the expensive privileges of wealth, or when they were relaxing. In contrast their projects often involved difficult and painful activities that stretched the person's capacity and involved elements of discovery and novelty. This optimal experience was called *flow* (Csikszentmihalyi 1975, 1990). The flow activity is enjoyable, as opposed to being simply pleasurable. The flow activity is a kind of "autotelic" reward – which has its own reward in the present. The persons are not searching for pleasure but perform an activity due to intrinsic motivation. To obtain flow is a very healthy state with many positive outcomes like increased self-esteem. (Csikszentmihalyi 1990, p. 196).

The flow model has two central concepts – skills and challenges – and flow is obtained when there is a *balancing of skills and challenges* (Csikszentmihalyi 1990, p. 74). There are different levels of skills and challenges and to avoid being bored one has to steadily increase the challenges. This demands greater skills from the doer. When the challenges are higher than the skills, the doer will feel a state of anxiety. Thus the doer will strive to be in the *flow channel* thereby get beyond anxiety and boredom and enjoy more complex experiences. It is a dynamic feature of the model that the enjoyment motivation will lead to behavior at an ever higher level of complexity. Every flow activity provides a sense of discovery, a creative feeling of transporting the person into a new reality, pushing the person to a higher level of performance.

According to Seligman (2002, 2006) psychology should not only concentrate on repairing what is wrong. It should also be about identifying and nurturing what is good. Positive psychology are based upon three pillars: (i) positive emotions; (ii) positive properties – first and foremost the strengths and the virtues; (iii) the positive institutional contexts, such as democracy, family, etc.

Seligman has given virtues a new focus and a new place within psychology, emphasizing the possibilities any person has to be happy by finding and cultivating his or her signature strengths. Researchers collected character strengths and virtues that were common in different cultures, philosophies, and religions. These virtues are: (1) wisdom and knowledge; (2) courage; (3) love and humanity; (4) justice; (5) moderation; (6) spirituality and transcendence. The latter virtues included strengths like gratitude and optimism. Gratitude is a kind of thanks that is very effective as self-therapy ("counting your blessings"), but it is always other directed, and thus it may start a positive self-enforcing circle of thanksgiving.

According to positive psychology there are three routes to happiness: 1) the pleasant life; (2) the good life; and (3) the meaningful life. If all are satisfied it is described as the full life.

"A pleasant life is a life that successfully pursues the positive emotions…". Positive emotions can be divided into pleasures and gratifications. While pleasures are feelings, gratifications are activities that absorb and engage us fully. Gratifications block felt emotion, except in retrospect (Seligman 2002, p. 262).

In the "good life" your signature strengths are used to obtain "abundant gratification in the main realm of your life" (Seligman 2002, p. 262). It means that you apply your virtues and your signature strengths in work, family life, and in your leisure time. Happiness is realized via many routes and might be connected to an individual who does not feel any positive emotions and gratifications. However, flow is a very important activity that characterizes the good life.

The "meaningful life" includes the good life, but assumes that you use your signature strengths and virtues in the service of something larger than yourself (Seligman 2002, p. 263). The "full life" then includes the pleasant life, the good life, and using these strengths beyond oneself in order to obtain meaning.

In the tradition of positive psychology, Jonathan Haidt (2006) has put forward the following equation to sum up the degree of happiness an individual may have (Box 11.2).

Box 11.2 *The Happiness Hypothesis*

$H = S + C + V + VE$

- H is happiness.
- S is a biological set point that is genetically determined. The assumption is that S counts for about 50 per cent and is constant. Whether you feel you are happy or not, depends considerably upon your genetic heritage.
- C is conditions that in principle are changeable in the long run. But in the short run there are conditions, like commuting distance, neighborhood noise, and the people you relate to, that affect your happiness. C assumes that people are ultra-social creatures and need friends, strong connections, and dependable relationships, and that love and work are to people what water and sunshine are to plants.
- V is voluntary activities which, first and foremost, are your capacity and the possibilities to be absorbed in flow activities that have an intrinsic motivation.
- VE is vital engagement, which is the extent of fittingness of what you are doing, not the least your work and how it is rewarded in your environment. If you have a job you are proud of, you may be rewarded by the activities themselves. You may also be rewarded by a receiving a fair salary and respect from people in society. Vital engagement is a relationship with the world, characterized by experiences of flow and meaning with a strongly felt connection between self and external objects.

Some of the insights from the formula are that happiness comes from "between." You cannot reach happiness directly; it only comes as a byproduct (Haidt 2006).

Haidt also argues that happiness is related to two central principles:
1) *The progress principle*, which states that it is not the destination, but the journey – the pursuit of the goal – that leads to happiness. The psychology terms for this are two types of positive affect: (i) the "pre-goal attainment positive affect," which is a feeling of pleasure that arises when you progress towards a goal; (ii) the "post-goal positive affect," which arises when you have obtained the goal and is usually of very short duration. Shakespeare framed this in one sentence: "Things won are done; joy's soul lies in the doing."

> 2) *The adaption principle*, which states that you will judge your situation based upon what you have been accustomed to. If you have become used to a certain income level then that particular level will not cause positive feelings. It is change, not steady states, that nerve cells respond to. As Haidt writes, "we don't just habituate, we recalibrate. We create for ourselves a world of targets, and each time we hit one we replace it with another. After a string of successes we aim higher, after a massive setback (...) we aim lower. Instead of following Buddhist and Stoic advice to surrender attachments and let events happen, we surround ourselves with goals, hopes, and expectations, and then feel pleasure and pain in relation to our progress" (Haidt 2006, p. 86).

In his book *Authentic Happiness* (2002), Martin Seligman, focuses on the cultivation of character. When an individual's well-being stems from engaging his or her own virtues and strength, the person's life is imbued with authenticity. Virtues are the positive characteristics that create the good feelings and gratification. "Positive emotions alienated from the exercise of character lead to emptiness, to inauthenticity, to depression, and, as we age, to the gnawing realization that we are fidgeting until we die." (Seligman 2002, p. 8). Seligman's message is that as long as we are not entitled to the positive feelings we have, we have a problem. For sure we have a lot of shortcuts to feeling good such as television, chocolate, shopping, and drugs, but Seligman insists that happiness comes from an exercise of kindness more readily that it does from having fun (Seligman 2002, p. 9). The reason is that "the exercise of kindness is a gratification, in contrast to a pleasure." (Seligman 2002, p. 9). Seligman stresses that well-being needs to be anchored in strengths and virtues, which in turn must be seen from a wider perspective. Just as the good life is something beyond the pleasant life, the meaningful life is beyond the good life" (Seligman 2002, p. 14).

The American economist Robert Frank writes about the happiness traps and the misguided pursuit of happiness (Frank 1999). His findings include:

- Conspicuous consumption (values come from the statement the goods make about the owner's status) is not a valid way to happiness. It does not lead to good and close social relationships. In contrast, it may awaken envy and distrust since the goal is often to show off. Another

problem is that this kind of consumption is analogous to an arms race. Inconspicuous consumption, which is goods and activities that are valued in themselves, and are usually consumed privately, have a better social potential.
- Doing versus having. The pursuit of luxury goods is a happiness trap. The key difference is between simply doing activities with other people instead of being trapped by the motivation to impress others. Activities connect us (to others), while objects separate people.
- The paradox of choice. Too much choice does not give people the expected greater happiness, because it takes a lot of time to make a reasonable choice, and after the choice has been made, you cannot be sure you have taken the right decision. There is evidence that it might be an advantage to have constraints and limit the number of alternatives. According to Schwartz (2004) you can use your time more wisely by getting to know better your lovers, children, parents, and friends.

Swiss economist Bruno Frey finds a correlation, although a very weak one, between income and happiness (Frey 2008). One of his findings is that additional income does not increase happiness ad infinitum. It is not a linear relationship between income and happiness because there is diminishing marginal utility with absolute income. One of Frey's conclusions is that there are many factors other than higher income that are decisive for happiness. One personality factor that might be relevant is how a person values material goods. Those that "prize material goods more highly than other values in life tend to be substantially less happy;" people "with intrinsic goals (...) tend to be happier than those with extrinsic goals" such as financial success or social approval (Frey 2008, p. 29).

11.3.2 Deep Ecology

Most approaches to happiness assume an anthropocentric worldview in which the human being is free to utilize other sentient beings for his or her purposes. Deep ecology is an alternative philosophy that presupposes an ecocentric worldview where animals and other sentient beings have intrinsic values. Norwegian philosopher Arne Næss (1912–2009) is acknowledged as a pioneer of deep ecology, which in contrast to shallow ecology, can be seen as a reformist and technocratic approach to environmental problems.

The highest norm in deep ecology is *self-realization* for *all beings* (Næss and Rothenberg 1989). The meaning of self-realization within deep ecology extends the usual concept of self-realization. In Western society self-realization is typically regarded as an ego trip, an individual's effort to satisfy his or her own wishes. Deep ecology redefines the Western concept of self, and opens up the possibility that all sentient beings are ecological selves. Self-realization in this wider sense assumes that human beings have the ability to identify with other sentient beings and to develop a transpersonal Self. This thinking has a consequence in that if we damage nature, we hurt our Selves. The unit of survival is not the organism alone, but organism and its environment together.

Deep ecology is not only an abstract philosophy, but also a practical platform for action that can be summed up in eight points. Only the main points are presented here (for a broader description see Ims 2011):

- The well-being and flourishing of human and nonhuman life on Earth have value in themselves, independent of their usefulness for human purposes.
- The ideological change needed is mainly that of appreciating life quality (dwelling in situations of inherent value) rather than adhering to an increasingly higher standard of living. There is a profound difference between big and great.
- Those who support these points have an obligation to directly or indirectly attempt to implement the necessary changes in a non-violent way.

In the context of happiness we may see the need for an ideological change in the direction of non-material consumption. Appreciating life quality by using time on activities outside of the market can lead us to sustainable well-being. Happiness as *hilaritas* is a notion inspired by Spinoza who noted that the perfection of one's abilities may lead to deep and intense enjoyment. We may sum up the essence of deep-ecology thinking with the motto of Næss: "Live a rich life with simple means."

11.3.3 Buddhist Strategy towards Happiness

Buddhism has a well-developed philosophy that presents a radical challenge for mainstream Western economic thinking (Zsolnai 2008, 2011). While Western economics is characterized as an "egonomic framework" centered on self-interest understood as satisfaction of the wishes of one's ego, Buddhism has a radically different conception that is "no-self" or "anatta." What is typically thought of as the Western "self" is an aggregated mix of constantly changing physical and mental constituents, "which give rise to unhappiness if clung to as though this temporary assemblage represented permanence" (Zsolnai 2008, p. 280). Aided by wisdom, moral living, and meditation, Buddhist practitioners detach themselves from this clinging to the illusion of a self.

Core to Buddhist wisdom is the simplifying of desire in order to want less, and to be liberated from all suffering. By want negation and purification of the human character one may be able to reach Nirvana as an end state. The British economist E. F. Schumacher states in his book, *Small is beautiful*, that the central values of Buddhist economics are simplicity and non-violence (Schumacher 1973). Mindful living, practicing the Middle Way, and knowing how much is enough or "just right" will result in substantial benefits for the person, community, and nature. One important consequence of this approach is that non-consumption can also contribute to well-being.

Thai economist Apichai Puntasen connects the Buddhist conception of happiness with Aristotle's concept of human flourishing. Puntasen differentiates between necessities needed for survival and the higher values known as "the good life." In the Buddhist tradition "sukha," or wellness, from acquisition represents a lower level and has similarities with hedonism. Sukha from non-acquisition, from giving, from meditation, or from helping others to be relieved from pain are examples of a higher level of wellness. (Puntasen 2007)

If we are summing up some of the insight from the Buddhist tradition, the degree of wellness might be written as the following formula:

Wellness = Wealth/Desire

Buddhism may therefore be seen as a sustainable and very rational strategy for the future of the humanity in general. By reducing our desires we may increase our happiness by the same level of material properties and level of consumption. People in the West may be liberated from the hedonic treadmill by a reorientation of their values, by changing the consumption mix in favor of low environment-intensity goods. It means to change from fossil fuels and meat consumption toward "services" and human activities which includes enjoyment of music, entertainment, and cultural experiences, education, crafts, skills, charity, physical exercises, and apprehension of art and nature (Daniels 2011, p. 46).

11.4 Real-World Examples

11.4.1 Bhutan

Bhutan is a small Buddhist kingdom in the Himalayas between India and China. The land is characterized by high mountains, deep forests, and glacier-fed rivers, which are not easily accessible to foreigners. In 1972 the King of Bhutan declared that "Gross National Happiness" rather than Gross National Product would be the nation's measure for progress. Since then, Bhutan's new economic and social policy followed "Four Pillars" of Gross National Happiness. The pillars are as follows:

1) Good governance and democratizations. The assumption is that democracy offers the surest guarantee of happiness in the long run. The king gradually moved the ruling institutions towards democracy based upon an elected assembly, and executive council of ministers chosen by the assembly, and a separate system of courts.
2) Stable and equitable socioeconomic development. This means to refrain from maximizing immediate growth and to maintain a slower, steadier expansion in the long run. The gains from this development should be shared equitably.

3) Environmental protection.
4) Preservation of culture. This means retaining certain elements of Bhutan's traditional culture while also promoting values such as voluntarism and service to others, tolerance, cooperation, and a harmonious balance between family, work, and leisure.

The Government of Bhutan has produced seventy-two indicators for measuring progress along these pillars, and a remarkable progress has been reported. Gross per capita income exceeds that of India, infant mortality has fallen from 163 deaths per 100,000 births to forty. The average life expectancy has risen from forty-three years in 1982 to sixty-six years in 2010. The World Bank Survey writes that the quality of governance has improved steadily and Bhutan now ranks well above India, China, and Nepal (Bok, D. 2010).

Bhutan's Gross National Happiness (GNH) index is a holistic measure while GDP is a one-dimensional measure. GNH has become a multidimensional measure of true well-being. GDP on the other hand is measuring welfare from a materialistic viewpoint. GNH is much more complex, associated with the multiple dimensions of life, and includes a plurality of values of which many are not easily measurable.

11.4.2 Norway

Norway is one of the richest countries in the world. It became affluent with increases in prosperity after discovering oil in the 1970s. On examining the period 1985–2001, it appears that Norway fits well into the patterns reported in Figure 11.1.

Why has the level of happiness not risen as would be expected by welfarism? Hellevik (2003, 2008) analyzes the development of happiness in Norway. One interesting finding is the *change in value orientation*, that is a change in the materialism–idealism dimension. From 1985 to 1987 the development was in an idealism direction, but from 1987 the trend changed towards materialism in a shift that was particularly strong from 1989 to 1995. From 1999 to 2001, we then find a minor shift towards idealism. But as a whole the Norwegians are on average more materialistic than ever before, which has a negative effect on their happiness.

There has been a growing inequality in Norwegian society and results from Norway show that economic inequality in society reduces happiness (Hellevik 2008, p. 261). Financial incentives and performance based salaries, and sometimes exorbitant executive compensation, could be seen as a kind of "social pollution." Such compensation schemes are provoking a sense of fairness in Norwegian society.

There are strong forces that draw Norwegians into a materialistic value orientation. Signs at the airports, such as "Shopping is good for you," and at the large number of shopping malls, are hardly subtle in their efforts to increase sales. The aim is to make people dissatisfied with themselves, and to then present shopping as a solution to their problem. A number of TV channels, some of them directed at children, present movies and advertising with exciting clothes and tempting toys. This materialistic pushing will probably influence the value orientation in the long run.

In Table 11.2 different values and their scores relating to happiness are presented (based on Hellevik 2008, p. 245). All the value-items contribute to happiness, but to different degrees.

Table 11.2 *Value Scores Pertaining to Happiness*

Proximity (a wish to have a close relationship to other people)	25
Anti-materialistic	24
Self-realization	18
Law respect	18
Altruism	14
Private solutions	10
Religion	10
Reason before feelings	9
Hedonism (pleasures of life)	9
Tolerance	8

The Norwegian data indicates that women are happier than men. Why? Women are on average more idealistic than men, and prioritize different goals to men. This value orientation compensates for some of the negative consequences that women suffer in several domains of life because they are in a worse position to men in terms of resources and pay. (Hellevik 2008, p. 246) While the objective economic differences are relatively small, the subjective differences are substantial. The materialistic oriented persons express that they need more money to be able to live a satisfactory life. It seems as if materialists typically have a gnawing feeling that they lack things and very strong wishes to acquire these, but they lack enough money to buy what they feel they need to live a good life. With materialistic values people suffer from economic worries and frustrations, which in the last resort decrease happiness. For a given income an idealist will experience his or her economic situation as relatively better than a materialist does. We might then speak of the "the curse of materialism."

The Norwegian example shows that economic growth generates a problem if it stimulates materialistic value orientation. As Hellevik reports (2008), this kind of development made Norwegians not only less happy, but also less willing to share their affluence with others or care for the environment.

11.5 Conclusion

The concept of happiness is a rich concept. Philosophers like Epicurus and Aristippus who have been regarded as hedonists, valued a moderation in life in order not to be enslaved by external goods. Valuing friendship and cultivating social relationships were an important aspect of a good life. In Aristotle we find a eudemonic holistic view considering a person's whole life span, which is now prevalent in the thinking of today's positive psychologists.

Socrates's claim for self-examination can be useful to reflect on how we are living and how our life affects society, nature, and future generations. Clearly Socrates challenged a hollow happiness concept and demanded that meaning, integrity, and life-projects should be part of a good life. A meaningful activity for an economist could be to care for the existential conditions of the stakeholders of "economic" decisions, and not least start to count the individual and organizational "ecological footprints."

We may also see Socrates's quest for self-reflection as a requirement of human dignity. A human being's dignity should not depend on producing material value. The philosopher Immanuel Kant stated that any human being has moral worth by being a person, which presumes some degree of freedom of choice. Sen's (2002, 2009) capability approach supports the view that human freedom might be more important than human well-being.

The importance of the phenomenon of flow is multifold. Optimal experiences are not based upon pleasure, but gratification, which means that they demand that the doer is an active and creative being. Flow activities do not need extrinsic rewards. The hidden cost of extrinsic rewards is well explained by Frey (1997) and should be taken into account also in instrumental organizations. Extrinsic rewards are either scarce or expensive in terms of human economy. Material possessions and money require the exploitation of natural resources and labor. The obvious danger is to drain the planet from its natural resources. Another type of extrinsic motivation concerns power, fame, and esteem, which are based upon comparisons between persons. However, status and conspicuous consumption are following a zero-sum pattern. There are always winners and losers and the latter pay with decreased self-esteem (Frank 1999). In contrast, autotelic rewards of flow activities put less pressure on ecosystems, and lead to increased self-esteem.

In organizational theorizing and practice we find many elements of a "positive" neo-humanistic turn, which focus on how positivity might be developed. With reference to Socrates's quest for self-examination, and organizational whistle-blowing when organizations are not practicing what they should, it is important to take a critical look at some of the "tools" used within HRM (Human Resource Management) programs of empowerment and fun at work (Fineman 2006). One recent strand in organizational thinking is to find ways of "unlocking capacities for (...)

meaning creating, relationship transformation, positive emotion, cultivation and high-quality connections" (Cameron et al. 2003, p. 10). Such organizational efforts should not be overused, because they can easily be misused and have a conservative and stifling effect on the ethical reflection of the members of the organization. From the perspective of positive psychology we know that depressive people are more accurate observers of themselves and the actions of their organization. If happiness is reduced to pleasurable feelings, it is certainly dysfunctional.

Peter Singer (2009) claims that Western people has not yet understood the profound happiness that can be gained by giving, not acquiring, and so had not realized a sense of meaning, fulfillment, or even "kick" in what would otherwise be less-rewarding lives (Singer 2009, p. 78). The most important task in establishing a new culture of giving is to challenge the norm of self-interest. There is empirical evidence that an idealistic value orientation offers the highest probability of increased happiness (Hellevik 2008). Since these are the values that are compatible, too, with permanent and genuine life on Earth, we do not have to choose between our own well-being and the well-being of others. The American psychologist Tim Kasser summarizes the problem of materialistic value orientation eloquently: "research shows that the more that people focus on materialistic goals, the less they tend to care about spiritual goals. Further, while most spiritual traditions aim to reduce personal suffering and to encourage compassionate behaviors, numerous studies document that the more people prioritize materialistic goals, the lower their personal well-being and the more likely they are to engage in manipulative, competitive, and ecologically degrading behaviors." (Kasser 2011, p. 204)

References

Aristotle (1925, 1980) *The Nicomachean Ethics*. (Translated with an introduction D. Ross) Oxford: Oxford University Press.
Bok, D. (2010) *The Politics of Happiness: What Government Can Learn from the New Research on Well-Being.* Princeton, NJ: Princeton University Press.

Bok, S. (2010) *Exploring Happiness: From Aristotle to Brain Science*. New Haven, CT: Yale University Press.
Bouckaert, L. (2008) Rational versus Spiritual Concepts of Frugality. In: Bouckaert, L. Opdebeeck, H. and Zsolnai, L. (eds): *Frugality: Rebalancing Material and Spiritual Values in Economic Life*. Oxford: Peter Lang.
Cameron, K. S., Dutton, J. E., and Quinn, R. E. (2003) Foundations of positive organizational scholarship. In: Cameron, K. S., Dutton, J. E. and Quinn R. E. (eds) *Positive Organizational Scholarship: Foundations of a New Discipline*: 3–13. San Francisco: Berrett-Koehler.
Copleston, F. (1946/93) *A History of Philosophy*, vol. I: Greece and Rome History. New York: Image Books, Doubleday.
Copleston, F. (1966/94) *A History of Philosophy*, vol. VIII: Modern Philosophy. New York: Image Books, Doubleday.
Csikszentmihalyi, M. (1975) *Beyond Boredom and Anxiety*. San Francisco: Jossey Bass.
Csikszentmihalyi, M. (1990) *Flow: The Psychology of Optimal Experience*. New York: Harper and Row.
Dalai Lama (2005) *The Essential Dalai Lama*. London: Hodder Mobius.
Daniels, P. (2011) Buddhism and Sustainable Consumption. In: Zsolnai, L. (ed.) *Ethical Principles and Economic Transformation – A Buddhist Approach*. Berlin: Springer.
De Graaf, J. D., Naylor, T. H. and Wann, D. (2005) *Affluenza: The All-Consuming Epidemic*. San Francisco: Berrett-Koehler.
Easterlin, R. A. (1974) Does Economic Growth Improve the Human Lot? In: David, Paul, A. and Reder, M. W. (eds) *Nations and Households in Economic Growth: Essays in Honor of Moses Abramovitz*. New York: Academic Press.
Easterlin, R. A. (1995) Will Raising the Incomes of All Increase the Happiness of All? *Journal of Economic Behavior and Organization*, vol. 27, no. 1, pp. 35–48.
Easterlin, R. A. (2001) Income and Happiness: Towards a Unified Theory. *The Economic Journal*, vol. 111, no. 473, pp. 465–484.
Easterlin, R. A. and Angelescu, L. (2009) Happiness and Growth the World Over: Time Series Evidence on the Happiness–Income Paradox. *Discussion Paper* no. 4060 IZA. Bonn: The Institute for the Study of Labor.
Fineman, S. (2006) On Being Positive: Concerns and Counterpoints. *Academy of Management Review*, vol. 31, no. 2, pp. 270–291.
Frank, R. (1999) *Luxury Fever: Why Money Fails to Satisfy In An Era of Excess*. New York: Free Press.
Frey, B. S. (1997) *Not Just for the Money: An Economic Theory of Personal Motivation*. Cheltenham: Edward Elgar Publishing.
Frey, B. S. (2008) *Happiness: A Revolution in Economics*. Cambridge, MA: MIT Press.
Frey, B. S. and Stutzer, A. (2002) *Happiness & Economics: How the Economy and Institutions Affect Human Well-Being*. Princeton, NJ: Princeton University Press.

Gable, S. L. and Haidt, J. (2005) What (and Why) Is Positive Psychology? *Review of General Psychology*, vol. 9, no. 2, pp. 103–110.

Haidt, J. (2006) *The Happiness Hypothesis: Putting Ancient Wisdom and Philosophy to the Test of Modern Science*. London: Arrow Books.

Hamilton, C. and Denniss, R. (2005) *Affluenza: When Too much is Never Enough*. Sydney: Allen & Unwin.

Hellevik, O. (2003) Economy, Values and Happiness in Norway. *Journal of Happiness Studies*, vol. 4, pp. 243–283.

Hellevik, O. (2008) *Jakten på den norske lykken. Norsk Monitor 1985–2007*. Oslo: Universitetsforlaget.

Huxley, A. (1977/1932) *Brave New World*. London: Grafton Books.

Ims, K. J. & Jakobsen, O. (2008) Consumerism and Frugality: Contradictory Principles in Economics? In: Bouckaert, L., Opdebeeck, H. and Zsolnai, L. (eds) *Frugality: Rebalancing Material and Spiritual Values in Economic Life*. Oxford: Peter Lang.

Ims, K. J. and Zsolnai, L. (2010) Self-realization in Business: Ibsen's Peer Gynt. In: Ghesquire, R. and Ims, K. J. (eds) *Heroes and Anti-heroes European Literature and the Ethics of Leadership*. Antwerpen-Apeldoom: Garant.

Ims, K. J. (2011) Deep Ecology. In: Bouckaert, L. and Zsolnai, L. (eds) *The Palgrave Handbook of Spirituality and Business*. Houndmills and New York: Palgrave Macmillan.

James, O. (2008) *The Selfish Capitalist: Origins of Affluenza*. London: Vermilion.

Jonas, H. (1984) *The Imperative of Responsibility*. Chicago: Chicago University Press.

Kasser, T. (2011) Materialistic Value Orientation. In: Bouckaert, L. and Zsolnai, L. (eds) *The Palgrave Handbook of Spirituality and Business*. Houndmills and New York: Palgrave Macmillan.

Langholm, O. (1992) *Economics in the Medieval Schools: Wealth, Exchange, Value, Money and Usury According to the Paris Theological Tradition, 1200–1350*. Leiden: E. J. Brill.

Layard, R. (2005) *Happiness. Lessons from a New Science*. London: Penguin Books.

Næss, A. and Rothenberg, D. (1989) *Ecology, Community and Lifestyle*. Cambridge: Cambridge University Press.

Puntasen, A. (2007) Buddhist Economics as a New Paradigm towards Happiness. *Society and Economy*, vol. 29, no. 2, August, pp. 181–200.

Russell, B. (1995) *History of Western Philosophy*. New York: Routledge.

Ryan, R. M. and Deci, E. L. (2001) On Happiness and Human Potentials: A Review of Research on Hedonic and Eudaimonic Well-Being. *Annual Review of Psychology*, vol. 52, pp. 121–166.

Schumacher, E. F. (1973) *Small is Beautiful*. London: Abacus.

Schwartz, B. (2004) *The Paradox of Choice. Why More is Less*. New York: Harper Perennial.

Seligman, M. E. P. (2002) *Authentic Happiness. Using the New Positive Psychology to Realize your Potential for Lasting Fulfillment.* New York: Free Press, a division of Simon & Schuster, Inc.

Seligman, M. E. P. (2006) *Learned Optimism. How to Change Your Mind and Your Life*, New York: Vintage Books.

Seligman, M. and Csikszentmihalyi, M. (2000) Positive Psychology: An Introduction. *American Psychologist*, vol. 55, no. 1, pp. 5–14.

Sen, A. (2002) *Rationality and Freedom.* Cambridge, MA: Harvard University Press.

Sen, A. (2009) *The Idea of Justice.* London: Penguin Books.

Singer, P. (2009) *The Life You Can Save.* New York: Random House.

Taylor, C. (1989) *Sources of the Self: The Making of the Modern Identity.* Cambridge: Cambridge University Press.

Tideman, S. G. (2011) Gross National Happiness. In: Zsolnai, L. (ed.): *Ethical Principles and Economic Transformation – A Buddhist Approach.* Berlin: Springer.

Twitchell, J. B. (2002) *Living It Up: Our Love Affair with Luxury.* New York: Columbia University Press.

Veblen, T. (1994/1899) *The Theory of the Leisure Class.* New York: Penguin Books.

Veenhoven, R. (2000) The Four Qualities of Life: Ordering Concepts and Measures of the Good Life. *Journal of Happiness Studies*, vol. 1, no. 1, 1–39.

Vitterso, J. (2005) Lykken er mangfoldig. *Tidsskriftet for norsk psykologforening*, October, pp. 913–916.

Williams, B. (1989) Against Utilitarianism. In: Pojman, L. P. (ed.) *Ethical Theory: Classical and Contemporary Readings.* Belmont, CA: Wadsworth Publishing Company.

Zsolnai, L. (2008) Buddhist Economic Strategy. In: Bouckaert, L., Opdebeeck, H. and Zsolnai, L. (eds) *Frugality: Rebalancing Material and Spiritual Values in Economic Life.* Oxford: Peter Lang.

Zsolnai, L. (2011) Why Buddhist Economics? In: Zsolnai, L. (ed.) *Ethical Principles and Economic Transformation – A Buddhist Approach.* Berlin: Springer.

LASZLO ZSOLNAI
(CORVINUS UNIVERSITY OF BUDAPEST)

12 Future of Capitalism

12.1 The Legitimacy of Capitalism

12.2 Competitiveness and its Failures

12.3 Collaborative Business

12.4 World Religions and Their Economic Teachings
    12.4.1 Jewish Economic Man
    12.4.2 Catholic Social Teaching
    12.4.3 Buddhist Economics
    12.4.4 The Taoist Economy

12.5 Conclusion

Abstract

The moral foundation of capitalism should be reconsidered. Modern capitalism is disembedded from the social and cultural norms of society, and produced a deep financial, ecological and social crisis. Competitiveness is the prevailing ideology of today's business and economic policy. Companies, regions, and national economies seek to improve their productivity and gain competitive advantage. But these efforts often produce negative effects on various stakeholders at home and abroad. Competitiveness involves self-interest and aggressivity, and produces monetary results at the expense of nature, society, and future generations.

The collaborative enterprise framework promotes a view in which economic agents care about others and themselves and aim to create values for all the participants in their business ecosystems. Their criterion of success is mutually satisfying relationships with the stakeholders. New results of positive psychology and the Homo reciprocans model of behavioral sciences support this approach.

The economic teachings of world religions challenge the way capitalism is functioning, and their corresponding perspectives are worthy of consideration. They represent life-serving modes of economizing which can assure the livelihood of human communities and the sustainability of natural ecosystems.

Ethics and the future of capitalism are strongly connected. If we want to sustain capitalism for a long time we have to create a less violent, more caring form of it.

Keywords: market fundamentalism, competitiveness ideology, collaborative business, world religions, ecology, future generations and society

12.1 The Legitimacy of Capitalism

The financial, ecological, social crisis of the first decade of the twenty-firstst century clearly shows that the legitimacy of capitalism is in many respects questionable. The *moral foundations* of *capitalism* should be reconsidered.

The economic crisis of 2008–2010 produced financial losses of billions of USD in the form of poisoned debts, decline of stock prices, and value depreciation of properties. Formerly successful economies such as Ireland, Spain, Singapore, and Taiwan experienced 5–10 per cent decline in their GDP. The fundamental cause of the crisis is the avarice of consumers, fueled by greedy financial institutions. The prospect of future economic growth is supposed to be the guarantor of the indebtedness of households, companies, and economies. Yet today we are experiencing a considerable reduction in economic activity.

Current data shows that *climate change* is more drastic in speed and magnitude than predicted. The increase in global temperature and the rise in sea level could speed up as a result of biosphere degradation. The accumulated CO_2 in the atmosphere will cause devastating effects even if we would stop CO_2 emission completely today. According to James Lovelock, even by 2020 climate change will have tragic effects on humankind but by 2100 the majority of humankind – even 5–6 billion people – could perish because of changing climates and melting ice (Lovelock 2009).

According to the Millennium Ecosystem Assessment (2005), fifteen out of twenty-four of the *ecosystem services* have been *degraded* or used unsustainably, including fresh water, capture fisheries, air and water purification, and the regulation of regional and local climate, natural hazards, and pests. These services are fundamental for the well-being of current and future human generations, and other living species. In many cases, ecosystem services have been depleted because of interventions aimed at increasing the supply of other services, such as food.

The latest data available, provided by the Living Planet Report 2008, indicates that humanity's *ecological footprint* – our impact on the Earth – has more than doubled since 1961. In more detail, since the late 1980s, mankind has been operating in overshoot. As of 2005, the Ecological Footprint has exceeded the world's biocapacity by about 30 per cent. This means that the planet's resources are being used faster than they can be renewed. In parallel, the Living Planet Index shows a related and continuing loss of biodiversity: between 1970 and 2005, populations of 1,686 vertebrate species declined by nearly 30 per cent (WWF International 2008).

In 2009, worldwide, 1.02 billion people were classified as *undernourished*. This represents the greatest number of hungry people since 1970 and a worsening of the unbearable trends that had emerged even before the economic crisis. In 2006–2008 a food crisis, which especially affected populations in developing countries, was created by a strong increase in international food commodity prices resulting also from international financial speculation. Because of this, at the end of 2008, domestic staple food prices remained, on average, 17 per cent higher in real terms than two years earlier (FAO, 2009).

Most (if not all) of the *Millennium Development Goals* (MDGs) will not be achieved by 2015. Adopted by the world leaders on 8 September 2000, thanks to the approval of the Millennium Declaration by the General Assembly of the United Nations, the MDGs concern social justice; improvements in the living conditions of children and women, particularly in developing countries; the protection of the environment; and the strengthening of international collaboration (United Nations 2009).

According to the last *Happy Planet Index* (HPI) report, no country in the world is able to achieve, all at once, the three goals of high-life satisfaction, high-life expectancy, and one-planet living. In addition, the elaborated estimates show that between 1961 and 2005 developed nations became substantially less efficient in supporting well-being. In fact, in that period the average HPI calculated for nineteen of the twenty original OECD members dropped by more than 17 per cent (NEF 2009, pp. 36–37).

One of the most successful capitalists of our age, George Soros calls the underlying ideology of global capitalism "*market fundamentalism*." According to market fundamentalism, all kinds of values can be reduced to market values, and the free market is the only efficient mechanism that can provide for a rational allocation of resources. (Soros 1998)

The market as an evaluation mechanism has inherent deficiencies. First of all, there are *stakeholders* that are simply *non-represented* in determining market values. *Natural beings* and *future generations* do not have the opportunity to vote on the marketplace. Secondly, the preferences of human individuals count rather unequally; that is, in proportion to their purchasing power, the interests of the *poor* and disadvantaged are necessarily *underrepresented* in free market settings. Thirdly, the actual preferences of the *market players* are rather *myopic*; that is, the economic agents' own interests are often *misrepresented*.

These inherent deficiencies imply that free markets cannot produce socially optimal outcomes. In many cases *market evaluation* is misleading from either a social or environmental point of view. This means that market is *not a sufficient form* of evaluating economic activities.

In its present form, capitalism does need counter-veiling forces. Both *politics* and *civil society* should play important roles in correcting the deficiencies of market fundamentalism. The instabilities and inequalities of the global capitalist system could feed into nationalistic, ethnic, and religious fundamentalism. In order to prevent a return to that kind of fundamentalism, we should *correct* the excesses of *laissez faire capitalism*.

12.2 Competitiveness and its Failures

Competitiveness is the prevailing ideology of today's business and economic policy. Companies, regions, and national economies seek to improve their productivity and gain competitive advantage. But these efforts often produce negative effects on various stakeholders at home and abroad. Competitiveness involves self-interest and aggressivity and produces monetary results at the expense of nature, society, and future generations. (Tencati and Zsolnai 2009)

The late *Sumantra Ghoshal* of the London Business School heavily criticized the current management ideology, including competitive strategy. He argues: "If companies exist only because of market imperfections, then it stands to reason that they would prosper by making markets as imperfect as possible. This is precisely the foundation of Porter's theory of strategy that focuses on how companies can build market power, i.e., imperfections, by developing power over their customers and suppliers, by creating barriers to entry and substitution, and by managing the interactions with their competitors. It is market power that allows a company to appropriate value for itself and prevent others from doing so. The purpose of strategy is to enhance this value-appropriating power of a company..." (Ghoshal 2005, p. 15).

Economic efficiency has become the greatest source of social legitimacy for business today. The focus on efficiency allows economics to neatly sidestep the moral questions on what goals and whose interests any particular efficiency serves. Ghoshal refers to Nobel Laureate institutional economist *Douglas North*, who demonstrated that there is no absolute definition of efficiency. What is efficient depends on the initial distribution of rights and obligations. If that distribution changes then a different efficient solution emerges. As long as the transaction costs are positive and large, there is no way to define an efficient solution with any real meaning. And the transaction costs are not only positive and large but they are growing in our economically advanced societies (Ghoshal 2005, p. 24).

Competition cannot tackle the following challenges, generated by an unleashed globalization enabled by privatization, deregulation, and liberalization:

- the growing poverty and socioeconomic inequalities within and between nations;
- the delinking process between the richest and the poorest people/countries;
- the rise of an international criminal economy;
- the declining role of the state as a founding political institution, and the absence of a real and effective political democracy at the global level;
- the increasing pressure on and the misuse/overexploitation and pollution of global environmental commons such as water, air, and land;
- the depletion of biodiversity and natural resources;

- the loss of human values, such as peace, justice, dignity, solidarity, and respect, in our societies. (Worldwatch Institute 2006)

Competition could be a very useful tool if it supported and fostered broad and shared innovation and emulation processes. But when the only purpose of our socioeconomic systems is to engage in a Darwinian "struggle for life" on a global scale, it results in a disruptive global war among companies, affecting also the overall well-being of regions, nations, and cities.

12.3 Collaborative Business

If we want to get closer to a sustainable world we need to generate *virtuous circles* in economic life where good dispositions, good behavior, and good expectations reinforce each other. The collaborative enterprise framework promotes a view in which economic agents care about others and themselves and aim to create values for all the participants in their business ecosystems. Their criterion of success is mutually satisfying relationships with the stakeholders. (Zsolnai and Tencati 2010)

The contrasting characteristics of the competitive and collaborative models are summarized in Table 12.1.

Table 12.1 *Competitiveness versus Collaboration*

	The Competitive Model	The Collaborative Model
Basic motive	self-interest	care about others and oneself
Main goal	maximizing profit or shareholder value	creating values for all the participants in the network
Criterion of success	growth in money terms	mutually beneficial relationships with the stakeholders

The skeptics, including most of the economists, may believe that the premises of the collaborative model are naive. Recent discoveries in social sciences suggest that this is not the case.

What we need in business and economics is a commitment to helping individuals and organizations identify their strengths and use them to increase and sustain the well-being of others and themselves. The discovery of the *Homo reciprocans* phenomenon in behavioral sciences supports this claim.

Samuel Bowles and Herbert Gintis summarize the model of Homo reciprocans as follows. Homo reciprocans comes to new social situations with a propensity to cooperate and share, responds to cooperative behavior by maintaining or increasing his or her level of cooperation, and responds to selfish, free-riding behavior by retaliating against the offenders, even at a cost to himself/herself, and even when he or she could not reasonably expect future personal gains from such retaliation (Bowles and Gintis 2011). This is certainly in line with empirical observations: people do produce public goods, they do observe normative restraints on the pursuit of self-interest (even when there is nobody watching), and they will put themselves to a lot of trouble to hurt rule breakers.

Robert Frank's research shows that socially responsible firms can survive in competitive environments because social responsibility brings substantial benefits for firms. Frank identifies five distinct types of cases where socially responsible organizations are rewarded for the higher cost of caring: (i) opportunistic behavior can be avoided between owners and managers; (ii) moral satisfaction induces employees to work more for lower salaries; (iii) high quality new employees can be recruited; (iv) customers' loyalty can be gained; and (v) the trust of subcontractors can be established. In this way, caring organizations are rewarded for the higher costs of their socially responsible behavior by their ability to form commitments among owners, managers, and employees and to establish trust relationships with customers and subcontractors (Frank 2004).

These behavioral findings give us the hope that noble efforts of economic agents are acknowledged and reciprocated even in highly competitive markets. Institutions and individual behavior co-evolve in social interactions and shape the evolution of individual preferences; in turn, these preferences shape the overall evolution, and may lead to the emergence of new economic organizations (Shalizi 1999).

12.4 World Religions and Their Economic Teachings

World religions have alternative views on economic activities, which have great relevance for the renewal of capitalism. The economic teachings of *Judaism, Catholicism, Buddhism*, and *Taoism* will be presented. Each of them challenges the way capitalism functions today. Other world religions (e.g. Hinduism, Islam, and Protestantism) have developed their own alternative economic views which are also worthy of study (Bouckaert and Zsolnai 2011).

12.4.1 Jewish Economic Man

Meir Tamari has reconstructed the principles of Jewish economic ethics and the main features of the "Jewish Economic Man" (Tamari 1987, 1988).

Judaism considers the role of the *entrepreneur* as legitimate and desirable. Entrepreneurs are morally entitled to a profit in return for fulfilling their function in society. The real problem is the challenge of *wealth*. How should the Jewish Economic Man use his or her accumulated wealth? What are his or her obligations to the other members of the community, especially to the poor and disabled?

It is an axiom of Judaism that stronger and more successful members of the community have a duty to provide for those who do not share their prosperity. The Hebrew word for charity (Tzedakah) has the same root as the word for "justice."

Jewish Economic Man should give 10–20 per cent of his or her profit for *charity* to aid weaker and less successful members of the community.

The central point of the Jewish economic ethics is the insistence that one should *not cause damage* – directly, indirectly, or even accidentally. As the rabbinic dictum says, "One has a benefit and other does not suffer a loss." This principle poses hard ecological and human constraints for economic activities. Jewish Economic Man needs to choose second- or third-best alternatives, which do not harm anybody.

In Judaism man is the pinnacle of God's creation so that everything exists for the benefit of humans. However, this imposes an obligation on men and women to hand over the world to *future generations* in a state that provides *equally well* for them.

In sum, we can say that Jewish Economic Man has two fundamental obligations. First, he or she can make profit if and only if his or her enterprise does not harm anybody. Second, he or she should give a portion of the generated profit for charity. (See also Pava 2011.)

12.4.2 Catholic Social Teaching

The Catholic vision of economic life is based on the *Social Teaching* of the *Church* (U.S. Bishops 1986, Mele 2011).

According to Christianity, the *human person* is sacred because he or she is the clearest reflection of God on Earth. Human dignity comes from God, not from nationality, race, sex, economic status, or any human accomplishment. Thus every economic decision and institution must be judged in light of whether it protects or undermines the *dignity* of human persons.

Catholic social teaching generates an interconnected web of duties, rights, and priorities. First, *duties* are defined as love and justice. Corresponding to these duties are the *human rights* of every person. Finally, duties and rights entail several *priorities* that should guide the economic choices of individuals, communities, and the nation as a whole.

Love is at the heart of Christian morality: "*Love thy neighbor as thyself.*" In the framework of contemporary decision theory this commandment can be formulated in such a way that actors should give the same weight to others' payoffs as their own.

Justice has three meanings in Catholic social teaching. Commutative justice calls for fairness in all agreements and exchanges between individuals and social groups. Distributive justice requires the allocation of income, wealth, and power to aid persons whose basic needs are unmet. Finally, social justice implies the participation of all persons in economic and social life.

In Catholic social teaching human rights play a fundamental role. Not only are the well-known civil and political rights emphasized but also those concerning human welfare at large. Among these *"economic rights"* are the rights to life, food, shelter, rest, medical care, and basic education, because all of these are indispensable to the protection of human dignity.

The main priorities for the economy include the following:

(i) the fulfillment of the basic needs of the poor;
(ii) increased participation of excluded and vulnerable people in economic life;
(iii) the direction of investments toward the benefit of those who are poor or economically insecure;
(iv) economic and social policies to protect the strength and stability of families.

All persons are called on to contribute to the common good by seeking *excellence* in production and service. The freedom of business is protected but *accountability* of *business* to the common good and justice must be assured. Government has an essential moral function: *protecting human rights* and *securing justice* for all members of society.

In sum, we can say that Catholic social teaching favors serving the dignity of human persons. Economic activities are subordinated to this goal.

12.4.3 Buddhist Economics

Buddhist economics is based on the Buddhist way of life. The main goal of a Buddhist life is *liberation* from all suffering. *Nirvana* is the final state, which can be approached by want negation and purification of human character.

Schumacher describes Buddhist economics in his best-selling book, *Small is Beautiful* (Schumacher 1973).

Central values of Buddhist economics are *simplicity* and *non-violence*. From a Buddhist point of view the optimal pattern of consumption is to reach a high level of human satisfaction by means of a low rate of material consumption. This allows people to live without pressure and strain and to fulfill the primary injunction of Buddhism: "Cease to do evil; try to do good." As natural resources are limited everywhere, people living simple lifestyles are obviously less likely to be at each other's throats than those overly dependent on scarce natural resources.

According to Buddhist economics, production using local resources for local needs is the most rational way of organizing economic life. Dependence on imports from afar and the consequent need for export production is uneconomic and justifiable only in exceptional cases.

For Buddhists there is an essential difference between renewable and non-renewable resources. *Non-renewable resources* must be used only if they are absolutely indispensable, and then only with the greatest care and concern for conservation. To use non-renewable resources heedlessly or extravagantly is an act of violence. Economizing should be based on *renewable resources* as much as possible.

Buddhism does not accept the assumption of man's superiority to other species. Its motto could be, "*noblesse oblige*"; that is, man must observe kindness and compassion towards natural creatures and be good to them in every way.

In sum, we can say that Buddhist economics represents a middle way between modern growth economy and traditional stagnation. It seeks the most appropriate path of development, the *Right Livelihood* for people (See also Zsolnai 2011b).

12.4.4 The Taoist Economy

Taoism (and Confucianism) greatly influences the economies of Far Eastern countries. Studying the economic system of Taiwan, *Li-teh Sun* describes the main features of the Taoist Economy (Li-teh Sun 1986).

"*Tao*" is the fundamental concept, which represents the way of *equilibrium* and *harmony* among myriad things of the universe. Taoists believe that in the universe two basic forces exist: yin and yang. *Yin* is the feminine principle; the yielding, co-operative force. *Yang* is the masculine principle; the active, competitive force. Yin and yang are complementary to each other. Humans need to find a balance between yin and yang forces in their own selves as well as in their societies. This results in the fulfillment of Tao.

Future of Capitalism

In the Taoist economy two basic values play decisive roles, the *inner equilibrium* of individuals and *social harmony*. The former is necessary in resolving microeconomic problems, while the latter is fundamental in handling macroeconomic issues.

At the *microeconomic* level the following yin and yang pairs are balanced in the Taoist economy:

(i) public interest versus self-interest;
(ii) morality versus profit;
(iii) want negation versus want satisfaction;
(iv) cooperation versus competition;
(v) leisure versus work.

In the Taoist economy, economic activities are directed not only by self-interest. Entrepreneurs should promote the supply of public goods, and services too. Profit cannot be the sole incentive of work and investment. Since profit comes from society, a portion of it should be returned to society in the form of social responsibility. The Taoist consumer is a want regulator even without income constraints. Want negation is valued. The maximization of wants is unwise and has detrimental effects on the community and the natural environment. In production the cooperative and competitive instincts are balanced. Competition without cooperation would create chaos, but cooperation without competition would generate poverty. For people, leisure and work have equal importance. Work produces wealth while leisure is necessary for moral development.

At the *macroeconomic level* the following yin and yang pairs are balanced in the Taoist economy:

(i) the poor versus the rich;
(ii) labor versus capital;
(iii) public sector versus private sector;
(iv) planning system versus market system;
(v) stagnation versus growth;
(vi) full employment versus price stability.

Balance between the poor and the rich requires equitable distribution of income and wealth. Taoist social policy aims at the elimination of artificial inequalities among people but does not try to eliminate natural inequalities altogether. Balance between labor and capital has two faces: one is the right proportion between labor production and machine production, and the other is the right proportion between labor ownership and capital ownership. Balance between the public sector and the private sector is necessary because the public sector provides public goods and services while the private sector assures economic efficiency. Balance between the planning system and the market system is also important, for similar reasons. Balance between stagnation and growth requires some reduction of the natural growth rate of the economy. In the Taoist economy there is no trade-off between unemployment and inflation. Since yin and yang forces rule the economy, a balance between employment and price stability is feasible.

In sum, we can say that the Taoist economy is based on the balance of yin and yang forces and tries to actualize the inner equilibrium of individuals as well as social harmony. (See also Allinson 2011.)

Table 12.2 summarizes the different responses of the studied world religions to the economic problematic. Like other world religions, Judaism, Catholicism, Buddhism, and Taoism represent *life-serving modes* of *economizing*, which assure the livelihood of human communities and the sustainability of natural ecosystems.

Table 12.2 *World Religions and the Economic Problematic*

	Basic Values	Economic Means
Judaism	causing no harm, solidarity	constraints on profit making, charity
Catholicism	love, justice	personal excellence, responsible enterprises, duties of the government
Buddhism	simplicity, non-violence	reduced consumption, using local resources, ecological conservation
Taoism	inner equilibrium of the individual, social harmony	yin and yang forces at micro-economic and macro-economic levels

12.5 Conclusion

Ethics and the future of capitalism are strongly connected. If we want to sustain capitalism for a long time we have to create a less violent, more caring form of it.

Economic activities should pass the test of *ecology, future generations,* and *society* to get legitimacy in today's society.

(α) Economic activities may not harm nature or allow others to come to harm.
(β) Economic activities must respect the freedom of future generations.
(γ) Economic activities must serve the well-being of society. (Zsolnai 2011a)

Ecology, respect for future generations, and serving the well-being of society call for a *radical transformation* of *business*. The future of capitalism is highly dependent on its ability to adapt to contemporary ecological and social reality.

References

Allinson, R. (2011) Confucianism and Taoism. In: Bouckaert, L. and Zsolnai, L. (eds) *The Palgrave Handbook of Spirituality and Business*. Houndmills and New York: Palgrave Macmillan, pp. 95–102.

Bouckaert, L. and Zsolnai, L. (eds) *The Palgrave Handbook of Spirituality and Business*. Houndmills and New York: Palgrave Macmillan.

Bowles, S. and Gintis, H. (2011) *A Cooperative Species. Human Reciprocity and Its Evolution*. Princeton, NJ and Oxford: Princeton University Press.

FAO (2009) *The State of Food Insecurity in the World 2009. Economic Crises – Impacts and Lessons*.

Frank, R. (2004) *What Price the Moral High Ground? Ethical Dilemmas in Competitive Environments*. Princeton, NJ and Oxford: Princeton University Press.

Ghoshal, S. (2005) *Sumantra Ghoshal on Management: A Force for Good*. Harlow: Prentice Hall.

Li-teh Sun (1986) Confucianism and the Economic Order of Taiwan. *International Journal of Social Economics*, no. 6.

Lovelock, J. (2007) The Prophet of Climate Change: James Lovelock. *Rolling Stone Magazine*, 17 October.

Mele, D. (2011) Catholic Social Teaching. In: Bouckaert, L. and Zsolnai, L. (eds) *The Palgrave Handbook of Spirituality and Business*. Houndmills and New York: Palgrave Macmillan, pp. 118–128.

Millennium Ecosystem Assessment (2005) *Ecosystems and Human Well-being: Synthesis*. Washington, DC: Island Press.

NEF (2009) *The Happy Planet Index 2.0. Why Good Lives Don't Have to Cost the Earth*. London: The New Economics Foundation.

Pava, M. (2011) Jewish Economic Perspective on Income and Wealth Distribution. In: Bouckaert, L. and Zsolnai, L. (eds) *The Palgrave Handbook of Spirituality and Business*. Houndmills and New York: Palgrave Macmillan, pp. 111–117.

Schumacher, E. F. (1973) *Small is Beautiful*. London: Abacus.

Shalizi, C. R. (1999) Homo reciprocans. Political Economy and Cultural Evolution. *Santa Fe Institute Bulletin*, vol. 14, no. 2, Fall, pp. 16–20.

Soros, G. (1988) *The Crisis of Global Capitalism*. London: Little, Brown and Company.

Tamari, M. (1987) *With All Your Possessions: Jewish Ethics and Economic Life*. New York: The Free Press.

Tamari, M. (1988) *The Social Responsibility of the Corporation: A Jewish Perspective*. Bank of Israel.

Tencati, A. and Zsolnai, L. (2009) The Collaborative Enterprise. *Journal of Business Ethics*, vol. 85, no. 3, pp. 367–376.

United Nations (2009) *The Millennium Development Goals Report 2009*. New York: United Nations Department of Economic and Social Affairs.

U.S. Bishops (1986) Economic Justice for All. *Origins*, no. 24.

Worldwatch Institute (2006) *State of the World 2006: The Challenge of Global Sustainability*. London and Sterling, VA: Earthscan Publications.

WWF International (2008) *Living Planet Report 2008*.

Zsolnai, L. (2011a) Redefining Economic Reason. In: Opdebeeck, H. and Zsolnai, L. (eds) *Spiritual Humanism and Economic Wisdom*. Antwerpen-Apeldoom: Garant, pp. 187–200.

Zsolnai, L. (ed.) (2011b) *Ethical Principles and Economic Transformation: A Buddhist Approach*. Berlin: Springer.

Zsolnai, L. and Tencati, A. (2010) Beyond Competitiveness. In: Tencati, A. and Zsolnai, L. (eds) *The Collaborative Enterprise: Creating Values for a Sustainable World*. Oxford: Peter Lang, pp. 375–388.

Notes on Contributors

THOMAS BESCHORNER is Chair in Business Ethics and Director of the Institute for Business Ethics at the University of St. Gallen, Switzerland. He studied economics at the University of Kassel in Germany and at the National University of Ireland. In 2001 he received his PhD from the Max-Weber-Kolleg für kultur- und sozialwissenschaftliche Studien, University of Erfurt in Germany. In 2002–2007 he served as project leader of the research group "Societal learning and sustainability" at the University of Oldenburg. In 2004–2006 he was member of the junior researchers' network at the Center for Interdisciplinary Research at the University of Bielefeld. In 2005–2006 he was Visiting Professor at McGill University in Montreal, Canada. In 2007–2009 he served as DAAD Professor at the Université de Montréal where he is still *professeur associé*.

ZSOLT BODA was born in 1969 in Budapest, Hungary. He holds an MA in economics and a PhD in political science. He is senior research fellow at the Institute of Political Science, Hungarian Academy of Sciences, and Associate Professor at the Business Ethics Center, Corvinus University of Budapest. He is also active in the Hungarian green movement and has worked as an expert for environmental NGOs. He has co-edited and written books in Hungarian on corporate ethics, political theory, and environmental politics and policy. He has published several papers in academic journals and books on international ethics involving the fair trade problematic, trade and environmental issues, and the politics of global environmentalism.

KNUT J. IMS is Professor of Business Ethics at the NHH Norwegian School of Economics in Bergen, Norway. He received his PhD from the School of Economics and Legal Sciences, University of Gothenburg, Sweden. He has taught courses such as "Ethical Action – Individual, Organization and Society" and "Business Strategy and Business Ethics" for more than a decade at NHH. He has also taught PhD courses in system development and information and management. He is chairman of the board of the Centre of Ethics and Economics at NHH.

JOSEP M. LOZANO is Full Professor in the Department of Social Sciences and Senior Researcher in CSR at the Institute for Social Innovation at ESADE Business School in Barcelona, Spain. His academic and professional activity encompasses the fields of applied ethics, corporate social responsibility, and values, leadership and spirituality. Josep Lozano's books to date include *The Relational Company* (Oxford 2010); *Governments and Corporate Social Responsibility* (Basingstoke 2008; also translated into Chinese); and *Ethics and Organizations: Understanding Business Ethics as a Learning Process* (Dordrecht 2008). His personal website is <http://www.josepmlozano.cat>.

LARS JACOB PEDERSEN is Assistant Professor at NHH Norwegian School of Economics in Bergen, Norway where he is affiliated with the Department of Accounting, Auditing and Law. He also coordinates the research project on Smart and Sustainable Business Models and Corporate Social Responsibility at the Centre for Service Innovation at NHH. He teaches business ethics, accounting ethics and corporate social responsibility at bachelor, master and executive level at his school.

CHRISTOPH SCHANK is Senior Research Fellow at the Institute for Business Ethics at the University of St. Gallen, Switzerland. He holds degrees in sociology and business administration from the University of Trier, Germany as well as a European Master's Degree in Labour Studies from Warwick Business School, UK. In 2010 he received his doctoral degree in economics from the University of Flensburg, Germany.

From 2006–09, he worked as a project lead at the Institut für werteorientierte Unternehmensführung (Berlin) and as Studienleiter der Evangelischen Akademie der Pfalz. Christoph Schank teaches at the University of Lüneburg and Goethe University Frankfurt. Moreover, he works as a corporate and political consultant.

Notes on Contributors

ALOY SOPPE is Associate Professor at the Erasmus University in Rotterdam, The Netherlands. He was a stock analyst for the Amsterdam Stock Exchange at ABN/AMRO Bank, and later worked as director of Soppe Currency Consultants and advisor for the implementation of option strategies in managing currency risk. Since 1987, he has worked at the Department of Finance and Investments at Erasmus University in Rotterdam. In 1993, he moved into sustainability research and started teaching financial ethics. In 2001, he joined the Erasmus University Law Faculty to teach financial ethics. He completed his PhD with a thesis entitled "Finance as an Instrument to a Sustainable Company" and published articles in national and international journals and books.

ANTONIO TENCATI is Assistant Professor of Management and Corporate Social Responsibility at the Institute of Technology and Innovation Management, Department of Management, Bocconi University Milan, Italy. He is a senior researcher at SPACE, the European Research Centre of Bocconi University on Risk, Security, Occupational Health and Safety, Environment and Crisis Management, and a member of the CSR Unit, Department of Management, Bocconi University. Antonio Tencati's research areas comprise business management, management of sustainability, corporate social responsibility, environmental management, innovation and operations management. His recent publications include *Developing Corporate Social Responsibility. A European Perspective* (Cheltenham 2006; co-authors: F. Perrini and S. Pogutz) and *The Future International Manager. A Vision of the Roles and Duties of Management* (Houndmills and New York 2009; co-edited with L. Zsolnai).

PETER ULRICH has been Full Professor and founding director of the Institute for Business Ethics at the University of St Gallen, Switzerland, from 1987 to 2009. Before, he has worked as a management consultant in Zurich and been a Full Professor for Business Administration at the University of Wuppertal, Germany. He is editor of the book series *St. Galler Beiträge zur Wirtschaftsethik* at Haupt publishers in Bern. Today, he chairs the ethics committee of the Prime Values funds for ethically responsible investment and is vice-president of "Kontrapunkt – Swiss council on economic and social policies".

Among his thirty books are *Transformation der ökonomischen Vernunft* (Bern 1986; 3rd edn 1993), *Integrative Wirtschaftsethik* (Bern 1997; 4th edn 2008), *Integrative Economic Ethics: Foundations of a Civilized Market Economy* (Cambridge 2008; paperback 2010), *Zivilisierte Marktwirtschaft* (Freiburg i. Br. 2005; 4th edn Bern 2010), *Integre Unternehmensführung* (Stuttgart 2007; with Th. Maak), *Standards guter Unternehmensführung* (Bern 2009; with U. Thielemann) and *60 Jahre Soziale Marktwirtschaft: Illusionen und Reinterpretationen einer ordnungspolitischen Integrationsformel* (Bern 2009; ed. with M. S. Aßländer).

DOIREAN WILSON is Senior Lecturer at Middlesex University Business School in London, UK. She leads two professional practice post-graduate programmes in HR and leadership and is a Fellow of the Chartered Institute of Personnel Development (CIPD). Her research area includes leadership and management, gender disparity, culture, and identity.

Her recent publications include (with L. Martins) *Effective Management of Organization Consulting* (New York 2010), *The Effective Development of Personal and Professional Competencies* and *Managing Personal Effectiveness* (New York 2010) and "Critical Issues in Equality and Diversity (2): Defining and Challenging Institutional Racism": In: Roper, I., Prouska, R. and Chatrakul Na Ayudhya, U. (2010) *Critical Issues in HRM* CIPD.

LASZLO ZSOLNAI is Professor and Director of the Business Ethics Center at the Corvinus University of Budapest. He is chairman of the Business Ethics Faculty Group of the CEMS – The Global Alliance in Management Education. He serves as editor of the *Frontiers of Business Ethics* book series at Peter Lang publishers in Oxford. With Luk Bouckaert he founded the European SPES Forum in Leuven, Belgium.

Laszlo Zsolnai's most recent books include *Spirituality as a Public Good* (Antwerp and Apeldoorn 2007), *Frugality: Rebalancing Material and Spiritual Values in Economic Life* (Oxford 2008), *Europe–Asia Dialogue on Business Spirituality* (Antwerp and Apeldoorn 2008), *Responsible Decision Making* (New Brunswick and London 2008), *The Future International Manager: A Vision of the Roles and Duties of Management* (Houndmills and New York 2009) and *The Collaborative Enterprise: Creating Values for a Sustainable World* (Oxford 2010). His website is <http://laszlo-zsolnai.net>.

Index

accountability 129
accounting and reporting/accountability tools 202, 204–207
affluenza 219–220
Ames, Ruth 39
Amnesty International 170, 179
Anderson, Ray 121
Apel, Karl-Otto 184
Apple Inc. 97–98
Aquinas, Thomas 229
Arendt, Hannah 139
Aristotle 11, 57, 67, 89, 225, 227, 229, 238, 242
Augustine 228–229

behavioral finance 72–73
Bentham, Jeremy 225, 229–230
Berlin, Isaiah 88
Beschorner, Thomas viii, 265
Bhutan 6, 218, 239–240
Boatright, John 62–63
Boda, Zsolt viii, 265
bounded rationality 40–41, 72
"bourgeois" versus "citoyen" 88–90
Bowles, Samuel 256
Buchanan, James 21–22
Buddhism 6, 238–239, 257, 262
Buddhist economics 259–260
business ethics 1, 2, 8, 9–11, 30, 31

capitalism 6, 250, 251–253
Carasso, Isaac 119
Carroll, Archie B. 87–88
Catholic Social Teaching 258–259

CEMS – The Global Alliance in Management Education viii
certification schemes 203, 209–210
Christianity 6, 258, 262
civic ethics 26
civil society organizations (CSOs) 189–192
"civilized" market economy 30
climate change 251
climate policy 173
Coase, Ronald 60
co-determination model 48–49
collaborative enterprise 250, 255–256
common morality 135, 136
companies' responsibilities 63–64
competitiveness 250, 253–255
conflicting loyalties 137
contractual theory 62
contribution to the public good 39
Coop 203, 211–212
corporate "bourgeois" 86, 91, 93
corporate citizenship (CC) 3, 86, 87–88, 90, 91, 92, 93, 94, 98
corporate "citoyen" 86, 90–96
corporate ethics 28–29
corporate social responsibility (CSR) 3, 64, 73, 74–75, 86, 87–88, 89, 96, 97, 98
corporate values 114, 115–117
correspondence rationality 43
corruption 174
corruption ranking of countries 50–51
Corvinus University of Budapest xi
Csikszentmihalyi, Mihaly 231, 232

Dahrendorf, Ralf 24
Dalai Lama, His Holiness 219
Danone 119–121
Deep Ecology 218, 236–237
deontological ethics 68–69, 71
discourse ethics 184–185
Donaldson, Thomas 181–183, 184
Dunfee, Thomas 183–184
duty, self-interest, and love 47–48

Easterlin, Richard 221, 222
ecological footprint 251–252
ecology, future generations, and society 6, 263
economic behavior 2, 36, 49–50
economic determinism 20–21
economic efficiency 254
economic rationality 2, 17, 19, 40–48
economic reason 2, 8, 15
economic reductionism 2, 21–22
economics 9–11, 12
economism 2, 8, 20
efficiency 16
Elster, Jon 45–46
"End of Men" 163–164
Epicurus 225, 227–228
ethical action versus unethical action 131–132, 148
ethical algorithm 181–183
ethical finance 3, 56
ethical reason 19
ethics 1
ethics of care 152, 162
ethic of rights 162
Etzioni, Amitai 36, 48–49
"exit," "voice," and "loyalty" 4, 128, 140, 148
experienced utility 41

feminist ethics 5, 152, 159–161, 164
feminist governance model 161–162

firm as a nexus of stakeholders 76, 161–162
flow 232, 243
Forest Stewardship Council (FSC) 190–191
Frank, Robert H. 38, 44–45, 235, 256
Frey, Bruno 235

Gandhi 230
GDP (Gross Domestic Product) 6, 174–175, 218, 220, 222, 223, 240
gender equality 4–5, 152, 164
gender gap 4, 152, 157–158, 165
Gender Inequality Index 154–155, 156
General Agreement on Trade in Services (GATS) 176
Ghoshal, Sumantra 253–254
Gilligan, Carol 5, 152, 159–161
Gintis, Herbert 256
Glaeser, Edward 39
global commons 193
globalization 5, 168–170, 186–188, 192–193
Grameen Bank 120
"great transformation" 2, 8, 13, 169
Greenpeace 141, 142, 149, 170, 179
Greenspan, Alan 169
Gross National Happiness 6, 218, 239–240

Haidt, Jonathan 234
happiness 6, 218, 219–221, 225–231, 242
happiness hypothesis 234–235
happiness–income paradox 221
Happy Planet Index 252
Hirschman, A. O. 4, 140, 142, 146, 147, 148
Hobbes, Thomas 88, 170–171
Homann, Karl 15
Homo Oeconomicus 2, 10, 18, 36–37, 39, 40

Index

Homo reciprocans 250, 256
Human Development Report 153
human resource management 243
hypernorms 183–184

"I & We" paradigm 36, 48–49
Ims, Knut J. viii, 135, 136, 137, 265–266
intangible assets 201
Integrated Social Contract
 Theory 183–184
integrative business ethics 2, 8, 15, 16,
 18–24, 31
Interface 121–122
international system 170–172
International Labour Organization
 (ILO) 179
International Monetary Fund (IMF) 169,
 171

Jewish Economic Man 257–258
Jonas, Hans 129, 132, 149
Judaism 6, 257, 262

Kahneman, Daniel 41–43
Kant, Imanuel 68–69, 89, 179, 243
Kasser, Tim 244
Kennedy, Robert F. 223

Layard, Richard 222–223
legitimacy 16, 105–106
liberal conception of the self 46–47
liberalism 3–4
liberty 88
Living Planet Report 251–252
localization 5, 188–189, 192–193
Locke, John 88
"lost-letter" experiment 38
Lozano, Josep viii, 266
Löhr, Albert 89
Lynx Deodorant 159

MacIntyre, Alasdair 47
mainstream businesses 158
mainstream economics 4, 12, 158
male-biased conception of the human
 person 158
male-biased economics 158–159
male versus female morality 160
Mansbridge, Jane 47–48
Marine Stewardship Council
 (MSC) 191–192
market economy 170
market evaluation 253
market fundamentalism 252
market metaphysics 14–17
market-based instruments 203, 208
Marwell, Gerald 39
materialistic management vii
Mill, John Stuart 12
Millennium Development Goals 252
Millennium Ecosystem Assessment 251
minorities in the UK 157
modular brain theory 44–45
Monsen, Per-Yngve 128, 142–146, 149
Moral Economic Man 2, 36, 52
moral whispering 146–148
Multilateral Agreement on Investment 176, 178
multinational companies 5, 172–176, 177,
 180–186
myopic and deficient choices 41–43

Næss, Arne 236, 237
Nestlé infant formula 185
North, Douglas 254
Norway 6, 218, 240–242
Norwegian Defence 142–146

*Organization for Economic Cooperation
 and Development* (OECD) 165,
 174

organizational citizenship 123, 124–125
organizational ethics 4, 104, 106, 107, 108, 109, 110, 111–113, 115, 116, 117, 119, 123–124
organizational learning 118

Pareto efficiency 21
Pedersen, Lars Jacob viii, 266
personal responsibility 4, 134–138, 148
Plato 226–227, 228
pluralism 181
Polanyi, Karl 2, 8, 12, 169
politico-economic ethics 26–27
Positive Psychology 233–236
post-materialistic management vii
predicted utility 41–42
prisoner's dilemma game 37–38
professional ethics 137–138
property rights model 60–61
prospective responsibility 95
Puntasen, Apichai 238

quality of life 224

rational choice 40
rational fools 43–44
real-time utility 42
republican liberalism 26, 30
republicanism 3–4
responsibility 94–95, 128, 129–130, 132–133
responsible decision making 133–134, 138
retrospective utility 42
Riboud, Antoine 119, 120
role-mediated responsibility 135, 136
Rousseau, Jean-Jacques 89

Sartre, Jean-Paul 139
Schank, Christoph viii, 266
Schumacher, E. F. 238, 259
securitization process 58

Seligman, Martin 231–232, 233–234, 235
Sen, Amartya 43–44, 230, 242
shared responsibility 138–140
shared value horizon 110
shareholder activism 146, 147
shareholder paradigm 3, 56
Siemens 142–146
Simon, Herbert A. 40–41
Singer, Peter 244
Smith, Adam 11
Smith School of Enterprise and the Environment, University of Oxford xi
social norms 45–46
socio-economic rationality 15, 16, 22–24, 31
socio-economic responsibility 25–29
Socrates 226, 228, 243
Soppe, Aloy viii, 267
Soros, George 176, 252
stakeholder network 213
stakeholder value 201, 203
stakeholder view of the firm 200–201
Statoil 140–142, 149
Steinmann, Horst 89
Storebrand 146–148
strategic role of emotions 44–45
subjective well-being 231
Sun, Li-teh 260
sustainability 5–6, 198–199, 213
sustainability-oriented company 199, 200–202
sustainable development 199, 213

Tamari, Meir 257
Taoism 6, 257, 262
Taoist economy 260–262
Taylor, Charles 46
teleological ethics 69–70, 71
Tencati, Antonio viii, 267
theory of the firm 59–66, 80
transformation of business 263

Index

Transparency International 50
trust game 39

Ulrich, Peter viii, 89, 90, 267–268
ultimatum bargaining game 37
Unilever 191
United Nations Development
 Programme 153
universalism versus cultural
 relativism 180–181
USA 220–221

Veblen, Thorstein 220
virtue ethics 67–68, 71, 77–78
"Vitalpolitik" 27, 28

Wallage, Inge 128, 140–142, 149
wealth creation 65
Weber, Max 13, 30, 94

welfare 222–225
Wieland, Josep 76–77
Williams, Bernard 230
Wilson, Doirean viii, 268
women-oriented company 164
World Bank 169
World Development Report 153, 159
World Economic Forum 165
World Trade Organization (WTO) 169,
 176
World Wide Fund for Nature
 (WWF) 190, 191

Yezer, Anthony M. 38
yin and yang 162, 260

Zsolnai, Laszlo viii, 91, 129, 131, 133–134,
 138, 148, 217, 268